PROMOTING RACIAL, ETHNIC, AND RELIGIOUS

Understanding

AND

Reconciliation

Edited by

Robert L. Hampton and

Thomas P. Gullotta

Research Assistants

Jessica M. Ramos and Jennifer C. Messina

Child Welfare League of America
Washington, DC

CWLA Press is an imprint of the Child Welfare League of America. The Child Welfare League of America is the nation's oldest and largest membership-based child welfare organization. We are committed to engaging people everywhere in promoting the well-being of children, youth, and their families, and protecting every child from harm.

CHILD WELFARE LEAGUE OF AMERICA, INC.
HEADQUARTERS
440 First Street, NW, Third Floor, Washington, DC 20001-2085
E-mail: books@cwla.org

CURRENT PRINTING (last digit)
10 9 8 7 6 5 4 3 2 1

Cover and text design by Jennifer R. Geanakos
Edited by Julie Gwin

Printed in the United States of America

ISBN # 0–87868–872–2

Library of Congress Cataloging-in-Publication Data
Promoting racial, ethnic, and religious understanding and reconciliation
in the 21st century / edited by Robert L. Hampton and Thomas P. Gullotta.
    p. cm.
Includes bibliographical references.
    ISBN 0-87868-872-2 (alk. paper)
    1. Multiculturalism--United States. 2. Pluralism (Social sciences)--United
        States. 3. United States--Race relations. 4. United States--Ethnic
        relations. 5. Religious tolerance--United States. I. Hampton, Robert L.
        II. Gullotta, Thomas, 1948- III. Title.
HM1271.P78 2004
305.8'00973--dc22   2003023278

Contents

List of Tables and Figures

Acknowledgments

Many people contributed to this volume. The authors of the eight outstanding chapters are the key contributors. These individuals include academicians, mental health professionals, and other practitioners, and they all share a commitment to research and practice in the area of multiculturalism, diversity, and cultural competence. This book would not have been possible without them.

I would like to thank Lucia Magarian, Alicia Rutt, and Jamie Marghi, who worked closely with me as we explored conceptual and applied issues associated with this project. They were invaluable as we worked through many drafts, discussed the changing nature of intergroup relations, and dealt with the painstaking details associated with an edited volume. Thanks to Victoria Albright, Melanie Burgess, Jenelle (Ferry) Coates, Diane Gaboury, Tawanna Gaines, Nina Harris, Janet Kearns, Nicole Menton, Stephanie Settanni, Marie Tomarelli, and Jennifer Wolbransky for their assistance with this project. I also thank my colleagues in the Department of Family Studies and in the Division of Undergraduate Studies at the University of Maryland, College Park, who understand the role of the scholar/teacher/dean in higher education. Finally, special thanks to my colleague Cordell Black, Associate Provost for Equity and Diversity, who continues to be an inspiration to those who remain committed to access, equity, and justice in higher education.

—Robert L. Hampton
University of Maryland, College Park

Preface

As the United States begins the new millennium, one of the great issues facing the nation is how the needs and expectations of the new majority will be addressed. In particular, will we become a country more divided along the lines of race, religion, and ethnicity, or will we become a country that embraces diversity in a manner that builds a more inclusive society? We should focus on this issue for two reasons: First, compelling evidence exists that there is a need to promote understanding across social categories, and societal consensus about how to do this is lacking. Terms such as *cultural sensitivity, cultural competence,* and *diversity* are often used and frequently ill defined. Similarly, terms such as *affirmative action* and *hate crimes* are often lightening rods and can enhance perceptions of ethnic hostility or conflicts. Second, as the United States becomes more diverse, we must live with and learn from people who think, believe, eat, and behave differently than we do.

Even prior to the catastrophic events of September 11, 2001, many Americans acknowledged that we live in a nation that is changing. Others would say we live in a country that is forever changing. Issues associated with group identity and group differences frequently enter our lives on a personal level as either a direct, lived experience or indirectly through the media. These issues matter to us on many levels and have real consequences.

The ideal we want to accomplish is recognition of every person as someone who deserves an equal chance to not only live, but to live and prosper. Although we want to see this happen, we know that because of neighborhood segregation, discrimination, and unequal opportunities, we live in an America where there remains unequal access to life, liberty, and the pursuit of happiness.

This volume is a testimony to the belief that as a nation, we have more work to do if we are to reach our full potential as a culturally heterogeneous society. We also acknowledge that we must find better ways to embrace the cultural diversity that is the world today.

In Chapter 1, Robert L. Hampton, Lucia A. Magarian, and Thomas P. Gullotta suggest that we need to rethink racial, ethnic, and religious understanding in America, and look beyond the narrow concepts of cultural sensitivity to social equity and social justice. Where are we going, what are our goals, and how are we going to get there? Chapters 2 through 8 of the book answer how are we going to get to racial, ethnic, and religious understanding in America.

Chapters 2 and 3 provide a theoretical foundation for the development of racial and ethnic understanding, as well as racial prejudice, and suggest ways to use multicultural education to facilitate intergroup cooperation and understanding. In Chapter 2, Stephen Quintana and Patricia Aleman detail children's psychological experiences of race and ethnicity in four developmental stages: the preschool years, early childhood, middle through late childhood, and adolescence. Quintana and Aleman draw on the voices of Mexican American children, African American children, transracially adopted Korean American children, and Latin American children to illustrate their theory. Quintana and Aleman relate that youth want to talk about race and ethnicity in frank, honest, engaging discussions. Quintana and Aleman detail multicultural education applications to promote interracial and interethnic cooperation for each developmental stage.

In Chapter 3, Christine Clark explores the implications of white antiracist identity development for multicultural education. The chapter begins by tracing the progression of thinking regarding white antiracist identity development in the United States from the 1400s to the present. Clark discusses white student resistance to multicultural education. Finally, she suggests ways multicultural education can encourage students to develop antiracist thought and engage in antiracist action.

In Chapter 4, Jeffrey F. Milem, Paul D. Umbach, and Marie P. Ting argue that American colleges and universities are in a unique position to give students exposure to diverse races, ethnic groups, and cultures. At universities, frank discussions, facilitated by multicultural education, can take place. They cite research that exposure to diversity in college can help students develop skills to participate in an increasingly global community.

In Chapter 5, Matthew Mock defines *cultural competence* as a set of skills, behaviors, attitudes, and policies that ensure culturally sensitive assessment, diagnosis, and intervention. Mock's goal for mental health professionals is to connect with their own stories of culture to make the practice of cultural competence more authentic.

Michael L. Benjamin and Marva P. Benjamin discuss principles for cultural competence and the role of executive leadership in furthering the American ideal of social justice. They suggest that strong leadership has the power to advance and promote racial and ethnic equity.

Chapter 7 describes the Coming Together Project, a community-level approach to promote racial and ethnic understanding that originated in Akron, Ohio. Fannie L. Brown invites readers to look at the grassroots application of eradicating prejudice, one heart at a time. Former President Bill Clinton honored the Coming Together Project in his Initiative on Race in December 1997.

Finally, Everett L. Worthington Jr. and Jack W. Berry enjoin the reader to look at the virtue of forgiveness with fresh eyes. Worthington and Berry state that systematic attention has not been given to the overall potential societal effects that could come from forgiveness. Worthington and Berry begin a dialogue on forgiveness and reconciliation using a societal benefit model.

Readers should consider this volume a place to begin a fresh dialogue about the challenge of racial, ethnic, and religious differences that can divide our nation and potentially our global community. As Americans, let us not rest with priding ourselves on our nationalism and independence, but let us take pride when our great nation is a recognized as a world leader in promoting unity among its diverse people. What may begin as a discussion about intergroup relations in the United States will ultimately be a discussion that may speak to the possibilities of racial, ethnic, and religious reconciliation globally.

We close this preface by acknowledging the Gimbel Foundation, which has underwritten these learning communities over the past decade. We express our thanks to the board of the Children and Family Agency of Southeastern Connecticut, which has embraced the belief that scholarship must be translated into practice. Their support over these many years has made that belief a reality.

—*Robert L. Hampton and Thomas P. Gullotta*

CHAPTER 1

BEYOND CULTURAL SENSITIVITY
Rethinking Racial, Ethnic, and Religious Understanding in America

ROBERT L. HAMPTON, LUCIA MAGARIAN, AND THOMAS P. GULLOTTA

To ponder the state of America at the dawn of the third millennium is to stand on a bridge between two worlds: a past full of noble aspirations, shameful humiliations, and awkward solutions, and a future unforeseen, where honorable intentions quiver in the shadow of our chaotic history, as history awaits the emergence of a new age that fulfills the destiny of a nation founded on the principles of equality and freedom.

The chapters that follow are about examining segments of that bridge, analyzing the different parts of its basic infrastructure, investigating and testing its design so that, like good civil engineers, we can leave the basic structure in place as we attempt a modern expansion that handle the increased flow of human traffic across its span. To begin this scrutiny, we need to be aware of the complexity of the bridge. We need to understand the materials of its composition and the chasm that the bridge originally tried to cross. For the sad truth is that although the United States was founded on the notion of religious freedom and cultural pluralism, it was also mired in racial division and ethnic hatred. How else can we reconcile the notion of equality with slavery? How can we reconcile religious tolerance with puritanical persecutions or ethnic sensitivity with reservations and internment camps?

Eric Erikson (1950), a half century ago, wrote of this contradiction in the American identity:

> Thus the functioning American, as the heir of a history of extreme contrasts
> and abrupt changes, bases his final ego identity on some tentative combina-
> tion of dynamic polarities....To leave his choices open, the American, on the
> whole, lives with two sets of truths: a set of religious principles or reli-
> giously pronounced political principles of a highly puritan quality, and a set
> of shifting slogans, which indicate what, at a given time, one may get away
> with on the basis of not more than a hunch, a mood, or a notion. (p. 286)

Thus it is today. The modern slogan, "cultural diversity," is widely embraced by
most Americans, as if its mere utterance is enough to ensure its implementation.
No one is against cultural diversity, just as no one, today, would be against equal
rights, civil liberties, or religious tolerance. Yet, each week, news broadcasts ne-
gate this view, not just on an individual basis, but at a deeper, more systemic
level. Witness the public spectacle at Bob Jones University, Greenville, South Carolina, on the issue of interracial dating. For days, the American people watched as
the college administration tried to extinguish the flames that threatened to burn
them as racist and bigoted, until they morphed into their own version of a fire-
eater, publicly swallowing their own positions, denying they were against biracial
dating as long as there was, on record, a note from the students' parents. Some of
us might dismiss this as an example of political, right-wing hypocrisy. But the
truth is that hate spans all races, all party affiliations, all genders, all religious
groups, and all ethnicities, and its progeny—poverty, discrimination, and violence—
threaten to hold future generations hostage unless we can begin to repair the
moral, spiritual, and ethical foundations of our society, not just the latest decay.
Like any concrete bridge, if we look closely, we can see cracks. Mere resurfacing
will not hold up over time; we need to examine the underlying issues.

How important is race and ethnicity, and how does it affect the pluralism of
America? What are the implications for children growing up in America today? What
kinds of programs will promote racial, religious, and ethnic understanding? How do
we encourage cultural competence in our institutions, our youth, and our media?
Who is forgotten? And how do we promote forgiveness, reconciliation, and healing?

Many of the problems we face as a nation—domestic abuse, substance abuse,
violence in the workplace, violence among our youth, poverty, and racism—are, in
part, due to unresolved issues regarding the role of institutions and role of individuals in a diverse democracy. In 1776, a few months before this country was to go to
war for freedom, Thomas Paine (1995/1776) published a powerful pamphlet entitled Common Sense, in which he drew a distinction that is worth remembering:

> Some writers have so confounded society with government, as to leave little or
> no distinction between them; whereas they are not only different, but have

different origins. Society is produced by our wants, and government by our wickedness; the former promotes our happiness positively by uniting our affections, the latter negatively by restraining our vices. The one encourages intercourse; the other creates distinctions. The first is a patron, the last is a punisher....For were the impulses of conscience clear, uniform and irresistibly obeyed, man would need no other lawgiver; but that not being the case he finds it necessary to surrender up a part of his property to furnish means for the protection of the rest; and this he is induced to do by the same prudence which in every other case advises him out of two evils to choose the least. Wherefore, security being the true design and end of government, it unanswerably follows that whatever from thereof appears most likely to ensure it to us, with the least expence [*sic*] and greatest benefit, is preferable to all others. (p. 1)

Over the past 50 years, the institutions that comprise the girders of society, marriage, family, church, and school, began to lose their footing. The result is that our children are in trouble and our nation suffers. Consider a report, published by the Department of Justice (Snyder & Sickmund, 1999), that showed that between 1985 and 1997, the number of youth sentenced to adult state prisons doubled, and the majority were incarcerated for a violent offense. These children, especially children of the poor and of ethnic minorities, are spending more time in prison. When we interpret these data in light of examples of violence, like the murder of James Byrd in Jasper, Texas, or the ethnic conflict in the Crown Heights section of New York City in the early 1990s, following an automobile accident that killed a 7-year-old black child, the need to change our national ethos about safety against behaviors and attitudes about race, religion, ethnicity, and gender should be evident.

We sometimes see that the very agencies that have a responsibility to maintain our freedom and security have engaged in activities that tend to undermine our goals for a better functioning and healthier society.

For instance, under the guise of a drug interdiction program, Illinois police routinely stop Hispanic and African American drivers simply on the basis of race or ethnicity. In one district, although Hispanics composed less than 1% of the driving-age population, they represented 29% of those stopped by police for speeding less than 5 miles above the speed limit. "While Hispanics comprise less than eight percent of the total state population...they comprise 27 percent of the searches....While African Americans comprise less than 15 percent of the Illinois population...they comprise 23 percent of the searches" (Harris, 1999, p. 17).

The scandal in Los Angeles known as the Rampart scandal, after the division of the city police department mired in allegations and convictions of misconduct and widespread corruption, confirms what many economically disadvantaged people have known all along: Justice is not evenly distributed, and for many, the system is corrupt. The American dream for success may be more hype than hope if one is poor and a minority living in an inner city. When evidence is planted, when police officers lie, when false reports are filed, how is the presumption of innocence, which is essential to this country's legal integrity, preserved (Martin, 2000, B3)?

Biskupic (1998) described the uneasy reality of life in the inner city for many minorities. She captured the voices of those caught in the race trap of urban life:

> As an African American woman who had seen black men tormented by police, Jamesetta Harris was suspicious when she first heard about proposals to allow police to stop gang members from gathering on street corners. But that was before she moved to Chicago's South Side.
>
> There were 20 or 30 people hanging out on the corner....Gangs that sold drugs owned the block. There was shooting 24 hours a day. You did not raise your shades or open your blinds. You crawled around in the house.
>
> But American Civil Liberties Union lawyer Harvey Grossman, protesting the city's policy on behalf of some of the people who were arrested said most of those picked up were African Americans or Hispanics who were innocently milling about.
>
> People need to understand that young Latinos and young black males are just like everyone else, said Gutierrez, who was 23 and visiting his parents near their South Side neighborhood when he was picked up by police. They just want to talk, get together, ask how's the family? How is school going? (p. A4)

Gutierrez says it precisely—People do need to understand. America is great at shaping ideals, articulating the noble, defining principles. We want to believe that, as a nation, we are magnanimous in spirit, charitable in our actions, fair to everyone, and kind to all. We teach this to our children in the patriotic songs that they learn, but the reality is that the collective identity of America is liberal in ideals, conservative in values, and paradoxical in behavior. It appears as if the DNA of every American citizen has coded into it a predisposition for genetic dysfunction inherited from one of our greatest founding fathers, Thomas Jefferson (1776). For how else can we describe the irrationality of such a humanist who could so eloquently write, "We hold these truths to be self-evident, that all men are created equal, that they are endowed by their Creator with certain unalienable Rights, that among these are Life, Liberty and the pursuit of Happiness," even while he capitulated to the notion of slavery? How can we explain a man who fell in love with, and yet denied the freedom of, his black mistress, Sally Hemmings?

This ability to disassociate actions from attitudes, behaviors from beliefs, and consequences from self-culpability is at the root of our current dilemma. In fact, this has been a slow, evolutionary, downward spiral. We began as a nation with false social conceits, moved through the last century with philosophical and political inconsistencies, and now, at the beginning of a new millennium, are frantically trying to stop the widening psychosis developing in our national identity that has children killing each other in school.

This is what Bateson, Jackson, Haley, and Weakland (1956) described as the double bind, a no-win situation. Double binds are communicative and behavioral paradoxes wherein two or more levels of communication conflict and society has an injunction against commenting on the conflict (Guillaume, 1991). We live in a society that routinely communicates in double binds. We hold on to the ideal of color blindness as we defend affirmative action. We hold onto the belief that all children need loving homes as we debate the issue of biracial or gay adoption. The point of this observation is not that one position is right and the other wrong, the point is to note the disparity between ideals and actions. These conflicting messages can have a profound effect on society's behavior, just as they do with individuals. If we are to promote a healthy society, we have to acknowledge that those discrepancies exist without the fear of being labeled an extremist, bigot, or racist.

Hacker (1992) documented the discrepancy between the ideal of social equality and the reality of white racism in American society:

> To the minds of most Americans, the mere presence of black people is associated with a high incidence of crime, residential deterioration, and lower educational attainment. Of course, most whites are willing to acknowledge that these strictures do not apply to all blacks. At the same time, they do not want to have to worry about trying to distinguish blacks who would make good neighbors from those who would not....Even when not in white company, you know that you are forever in their conversations. Ralph Ellison once said that to whites, you are an invisible man. You know what he meant. You see yourself reduced to data in research, statistics in reports. Each year, the nation asks how many of our teenagers have become pregnant, how many of your young men are in prison. Not only are you continually on view; you are always on trial. (p. 38–39)

In our struggle to shape and change behavior, we have resorted to legal and social sanctions. In some instances, we may be dangerously close to defining acts, words, or ideas as being suspect, and thus lumping segments of our population together in disturbing ways. Whereas we used to have a wide spectrum that had, at one end, social blunders; in the middle, distasteful jokes; and at the other end, political incorrectness, the standard has since been extended to hate speech—a label that not only carries social stigmatization but potential criminal sanctions. The problem is that the distance between political incorrectness and hate is more difficult to discern. Who articulates the difference? Who sits in judgment? How do we distinguish the inappropriate from the criminal?

For example, at a time when the nation was attempting to unite to fight against the common enemy "international terrorism," many were shocked by two racially offensive events at two southern universities. In one instance, members of an all-white fraternity were shown wearing Ku Klux Klan robes while one member was pretending to hang another member in blackface. In another instance, one white student wearing blackface and a straw hat was photographed picking cotton while another student dressed as a police officer and held a gun to his head (Lords, 2001). As a result of their actions, several students were suspended indefinitely and could face expulsion. People generally agree that these acts were racially offensive, however, considerable debate remains regarding the appropriate level of institutional response.

If we are to genuinely become more culturally sensitive, we have to risk losing the comfort of labels. We have to be willing to acknowledge that no one has the moral high ground, regardless of how noble the intentions, what the skin color, or to what church, synagogue, or temple one belongs. This recognition is not easy. Andrew Sullivan (1999) wrote of this dilemma in a New York Times essay on hate. He described having

> conservative friends who oppose almost every measure for homosexual equality; yet genuinely delight in the company of their gay friends. It would be easier for me to think of them as haters, and on paper, perhaps, there is a good case that they are. But in real life, I know they are not. (p. 54)

Real life—that is the problem. There *are* people who hate. There *are* people who are bigoted. There *are* people who are racists. They may be indistinguishable from the average person who is just trying to go along to get along—who has the occasional bad day, who may have had a fight with his teenage son that morning, who may be ticked off for having been the victim of someone else's road rage that afternoon, and in a moment of irrationality lets fly an inflammatory statement, a crude remark, or a bad joke. How do we distinguish him from the closet bigot, homophobe, or even ourselves? Perhaps an example of our moral distaste for people with these attitudes is former Atlanta Braves' pitcher John Rocker, who unleashed a barrage of inflammatory remarks to a *Sports Illustrated* reporter. Taylor's (2000) analysis was typical of the tortured, intellectual perplexity that permeated the subsequent press coverage:

Many of us have heard worse examples of bigotry. But this was no mere lapse into political incorrectness. It was quite loathsome and very public....The tricky question is what should be done beyond denunciation and disavowal?...No criminal penalty could be imposed in this country, at least not as long as the First Amendment guarantees "freedom for the thought that we hate" (in the words of Justice Oliver Wendell Holmes, Jr.) from that heavy hand of government coercion. (p. 140)

So, what do we do with the uneasy feelings that a John Rocker instigates? Perhaps even more important, are we, as a society, willing to look in the mirror and realize that perhaps there is a little of John Rocker in each of us? As former Mayor Andrew Young (2000) observed, "Yes, he was irrational and explosive and when that happens, all of your deep-seated prejudices and insecurities come to the surface. And let's not kid ourselves, we all have them" (p. A11).

Of course there is a difference between a John Rocker and, say, John William King, who along with two white supremacists tied James Byrd to the back of his pickup truck and dragged him to his death simply because he was black. Or Russell Henderson, who joined another man in kidnapping and brutally beating (to his eventual death) Matt Shepherd because he was a homosexual. Yet, sadly, unless we can begin to un-self-consciously hold a conversation on religion, race, cultural differences, and the stereotypes that have infiltrated the mass collective unconscious, how are we to discern the merely misguided from the seriously ill? How are we to discriminate between those who are acting out of fear, economic insecurity, or loneliness and those who take delight in the destruction of anyone who represents difference?

This dilemma is a serious threat for if we, out of anxiety, fear, or ignorance, generalize the Rockers and Kings into an amorphous *them* and lump them all together from a moral position of righteousness; if we subtly deal with all of them in disdain, we will be infusing not only anger into their psyche, but rage. Is not this what we saw in Oklahoma City and Jasper, Texas? Or even in the acts of terror in New York's Twin Towers or on the streets of Jerusalem?

As America struggles to redefine the relationships between rights and respect, responsibility and self-interest, and violence and power, the behavior and rhetoric of these interactions both in our national debate and our international stance is vaguely familiar. It is the language of the unsupervised playground, might equals right. In some ways, this might be called the "bullying of America." In America's playground, there seem to be two dominant minorities: the bullies and the monitors. The problem is that for the majority of the population, these two roles are blurring together. The bullies want everyone to look alike, speak alike, dress alike, and think alike. Cultural differences are tolerated like cheap costume jewelry—It is okay as an accessory, but everyone must otherwise be a uniform American. She must speak English, he must be computer literate, they must both lack passion and courage so as not to seem too challenging and confrontational. Hardy (1993) wrote of this duality:

> To avoid being seen by whites as troublemakers, we suppress the part of ourselves that feels hurt and outraged by the racism around us. Instead developing an "institutional self"—an accommodating facade of calm professionalism calculated to be non-threatening to whites....Familiar only with our institutional selves, white people don't appreciate the sense of immediate connection and unspoken loyalty that binds black people together....We are united by being raised with the same messages most black families pass on to their children: You were born into one of the most despised groups in the world. You can't trust white people. You are somebody. Be proud, and never for one minute think that white people are better than you. (p. 52–54)

The majority of white culture does not see the white privilege they inherit. It is not that they are in denial, for that implies that they know it to deny it. It is that they shall never experience the hundreds of slights, gestures, remarks, and slurs that those who are of color must endure as a part of their daily lives. Instead, white America tends to see groups of African Americans sitting in the lunchroom as self-segregation, instead of self-empowerment—that which many from the 60s coined *black power.*

On the other hand, the monitors only want security and peace. To them, the schoolyard masses are only a breeding ground for potential bullies. No one is beyond suspicion, and everyone wears a label. If one is white, one could potentially be a closet racist or homophobic. If one is black, one could potentially be a criminal or drug dealer. If one is Hispanic, one must be an illegal alien. If one is from the Middle East or is a Muslim, one is a potential terrorist. The monitors defend themselves against accusations of their own bigotry by saying they do not see everyone in such extreme terms, and that they like people of all races and nationalities. Rather, they are merely protecting the greater good of society. Racial profiling is a prime example of this type of justification. Under the guise of fighting the drug war, civil liberties are routinely violated, people are harassed, and the innocent are assumed to be guilty. Do this enough, and eventually the expectation will produce the result. And why?

Because people are scared. They arm themselves both as protection from others and to protect others. They do not know any other tactic to survive. We have a generation of children and adolescents who are standing atop a slide, daring us to coax them back down the ladder into a warm embrace, to show that we care. If we do not meet that challenge, they will slide down into the mud and will then rise up, covered in the grime of our own neglect, ready to wreak havoc. Why should they stop? They have no stake in society because society has no stake in them. The new common denominator is rage mixed with hate. Class will not matter, poverty will not matter, and ethnicity will not matter. Family ties will not matter. Rage will mask it all.

If we are to protect our children, if we are to protect society, and if we are to move beyond cultural sensitivity, we must rethink our notions of race, religion, and ethnicity. We must honor the differences between us. We must see those differences as part of the mosaic that creates a resilient child, family, and community. Fostering resilience gives people a way to survive their environment and a chance for the future. A large part of fostering that resilience is to honor the spiritual and religious needs of individuals, to honor their language and customs, their history, and race.

We worry about Balkanizing America. But those who promote this fear do not understand the histories of the Balkans or America. What makes this country unique, what protects us from creating a Bosnia in downtown Boston, is our very heritage. Lady Liberty welcoming the immigrants—"Give me your tired, your poor, your huddled masses yearning to breathe free."

As Americans, we do not have thousands of years of religious tension, past war crimes, or cultural servitude to overcome. True, if one is an African American or Native American, one has to struggle with the injustice of slavery and cultural dominance and the ongoing legacy of discrimination. We fought the Civil War, we amended the Constitution, and we are seeking parity. It is our very self-awareness as a country, our remorse and longing to develop policy, programs, and a public discourse to correct the historic wrongs, that speaks best about who we are and our ideals. Yet these ideals are in danger of being undermined if we do not or can not realign our thinking.

Unfortunately, we are reaping the rewards of our misplaced assumptions that promoted assimilation as the supreme good and placed the individual over the family. The issue of acculturation and ethnic identity is a critical factor in any society that promotes diversity and open immigration policies. In the past, social scientists assumed that acculturation was synonymous with assimilation and that successful acculturation had occurred when an individual or group shed its old skin of cultural or ethnic values and replaced it with a new one that reflected the dominant culture. Laroche, Kim, and Tomiuk (1998) summarized this world view:

> The most widely adopted has been a linear bipolar model. It postulates that as one acquires aspects of a host culture one is also bound to lose aspects of one's

culture of origin. Use of this model indicates a tendency to confound ethnic identity with acculturation and to assume an assimilationist stance. (p. 126)

This idea promulgates the concept that ethnic identity is an either/or proposition. It sees identity as a fixed spotlight that engulfs an individual's life; one can insert filters to change the color that envelops one, but one cannot be simultaneously bathed in both blue light and red light. Rumbaut (1997) explained it:

The master concept of assimilation, whether as noun or verb, outcome or process, confounds elements that are both descriptive and prescriptive, empirical and ideological, ethnographic and ethnocentric. The trouble has come from their confounding. On the one hand it seems like a simple enough proposition: an outcome of adaptation to new environments, a process of "learning the ropes" and "fitting in" through which "they" become like "we," a convergence hypothesis, a sort of regression to the mean. (p. 483)

This model of viewing acculturation as the proverbial American melting pot, in which all identities would eventually blend, resulting in the quintessential American, worked fine as long as the immigrants entering this country reflected the same basic mores that the early founders had. America, at the turn of the last century, needed a steady immigration of new workers to fuel the industrial revolution. The work was in large part rote and manual. It allowed one to provide security for one's family while trying to grab for the brass ring of American success:

To begin with, the people of the last great immigration, from the 1890s to the 1920s, shared a common European heritage with the then dominant WASPs, blunting discrimination's edge. The old factory-based economy also allowed for a multi-generational move up the totem pole. (Perlmann & Waldinger, 1998, p. 74)

Suro (1999) observed, "The predictable transition was complete by the time the newcomers' grandchildren grew up—speaking just a few words in the mother tongue and practicing an ethnic identity attached to holidays rather than everyday life" (p. 30).

Given this situation, the idea that acculturation must result in a complete replacement of one's old ethnic views and behaviors with the host country's values and lifestyle is understandable, albeit misguided. The obvious flaw in this line of reasoning is what happens when immigrants come from a different culture and cannot blend into the landscape?

Racial prejudice is an avoidable reality, in America that needs to be understood in an acculturation context. Perlmann and Waldinger (1998) stated:

Yet today we are told that the earlier immigrants were able to move ahead because they were white, and that the immigrants of today will have trouble doing so because they are not white. At best, this view drastically needs to be fleshed out with historical detail; at worst, it mistakes cause and effect. (p. 83)

Add to this the fact that, today, new immigrants do not have easy access to jobs that provide security, upward mobility, and a chance to blend invisibly, and the result is that the process of understanding acculturation and ethnic identity must be re-examined. Legislators, responding to frustrated citizens, want to adhere to the old model. This is reflected in the debates on affirmative action, an English-only educational policy, and the various propositions that surface in California's referendums—a test market of whether an idea can be sold to the greater American electorate. Stephen (1996) called this phenomenon a form of "ethnic cleansing, U.S. style" (p. 17).

Some social scientists, however, respond from a different perspective, redefining and expanding the definition of acculturation. Berry (1997) identified several categories of acculturation that focus both on a group's desire to maintain its cultural identity and the extent to which it interacts with other groups.

In Berry's (1997) framework, assimilation is no longer the highest and best goal of an immigration policy. In fact, assimilation would be akin to an ethnic self-loathing, and thus undesirable for a healthy, pluralistic society. Here, integration and cultural sensitivity form the new paradigm. This view posits that one can retain a multiethnic identity. In other words, two spotlights can shine on the individual, and the individual can make a choice, depending on context, which light to step into, or even whether they could converge to create a new light altogether.*

This presupposes that a host country is amenable to such a shift:

Thus, mutual accommodation is required for integration to be attained, involving the acceptance by both groups of the right of all groups to live as culturally different peoples. This strategy requires non-dominate groups to adopt the basic values of the larger society, while at the same time the dominant group must be prepared to adapt national institutions (e.g., education, health, labor) to better meet the needs of all groups now living together. (Berry, 1997, p. 11)

---

* In fact, an interesting example of this can be seen in the popular culture. Suro (1999) cited the existence of Banda music: "Banda originated with groups that regularly toured the U.S. and Mexico, picking up bits of music in both countries....The music, the dress and the dancing are neither Mexican nor American, but rather a constantly evolving mixture of the two. Banda is the anthem of a transnational space that is not only home to newcomers and the native born, but also serves as a way-station for Latinos who easily travel between neighboring nations" (pp. 30–31).

Wrong (2000) echoed this sentiment: "The pluralism and multiculturalism of American society create multiple social identities for individuals to acquire and cherish" (p. 15).

Moreover, recent research on ethnic identity formation and psychological health among second-generation adolescents suggests the appropriateness of this approach. Roberts et al. (1999) analyzed a cohort of second-generation adolescents from various ethnic backgrounds (European, Latino, and African American). In this study, they confirmed that those who retained a strong sense of ethnic identity "were associated positively with self-esteem, coping, sense of master, and optimism" (p. 310). Sam (2000) found similar outcomes: "The predictive ability of ethnic identity with respect to self-esteem and mental health appears in line with findings in previous research" (p. 19).

The implication of this is that ethnicity is not an undesirable attribute; it can help adolescents develop their senses of belonging, identity, and values. Zhou (1997) wrote about the challenges facing the children of immigrants:

> Results from the survey of immigrant children in San Diego and Miami revealed that, regardless of race/ethnicity, immigrant students who retained cultural and family identity tended to outpace others in school, including their native-born European-American peers, because their immigrant families reinforced the values of hard work and educational achievement. (p. 80)

Certainly those adolescents who are fully bilingual, who can communicate with their peers in English and their grandparents or extended family in their native language, are apt to find more access to social and normative supports within their ethnic community (Zhou, 1997).

Furthermore, Rumbaut (1997) noted in his research with adolescents of immigrants that

> change over time, therefore, has been not toward assimilative American identities (with or without a hyphen), but a return to the ancestral or immigrant identity....In any case, "becoming American" for these children of immigrants may well turn out to be a lifelong occupation. (p. 494)

Laroche et al. (1998) borrowed a page from classic Bowen language to describe this need to retain the old ethnic identity while developing a second sense of self in time and place that exists simultaneously: "Specifically implied by these concepts are the differentiation of oneself and one's group from others and the integration of oneself with members of one's own group and the integration of one's group with other groups in the large society" (p. 127).

Race, ethnicity, and culture are still only part of the picture. It is time to re-examine some of our attitudes on religion, spirituality, and faith, as well. Aponte (1996) identified this phenomenon:

> People are coming to therapy wanting not just relief from their anxieties, but answers to what makes a better or right way to live or die. They often come with nothing to live for, not just because they are depressed, but because existentially there is little of meaning in their lives. Having lost their community, religion, and family, they are often looking to the therapist for guidance, direction, and example. They are asking for values, purpose, and meaning—spirituality. (pp. 493–494)

Everyone is a version of the therapist. The students, employees, and clients who come into our sphere of influence are seeking greater awareness of themselves and of others. They want to be understood, heard, respected, and honored. They want to speak in Spanish, celebrate Kwanza, dance a Kachina, and sing an Irish ballad. They want to march in a St. Patrick's Day Parade, celebrate Pulaski Day, or enjoy a picnic on Juneteenth.

If we are to move beyond the religious, ethnic, and racial beliefs that have divided us, being culturally sensitive is necessary, but not sufficient. We must move beyond seeing differences as negatives that need to be transformed and view them as attributes that need to be embraced or, at the very least, tolerated. For surely, there will always be people who cannot tolerate these differences. They, too, are part of the diversity of life. To quote Sullivan (1999) again:

> In an increasingly diverse culture, it is crazy to expect that hate, in all its variety, can be eradicated. A free country will always mean a hateful country. This may not be fair, or perfect, or admirable, but it is reality, and while we need not endorse it, we should not delude ourselves into thinking we can prevent it. That is surely the distinction between toleration and tolerance. Tolerance is the eradication of hate; toleration is co-existence despite it. We might do better as a culture and as a polity if we concentrated more on achieving the latter rather than the former. We would certainly be less frustrated. (p. 113)

It is not that we must move beyond cultural diversity, as much as that we must empower cultural richness. This is how we can rebuild the bridge and widen it to carry subsequent generations into a brighter future. This may mean that we have to tolerate the bitter alongside the sweet, the spicy alongside the savory. We should begin to question the critics who want to paint only in black and white and the varying shades of gray in between. The world is full of color. To allow religion, culture, and ethnicity to be categorized into boxes labeled conservative or liberal, fundamentalist or freethinking, is to deny that color, is to deny our very humanity.

In 1956, Martin Luther King Jr. said:

> We stand today between two worlds...the dying old and the emerging new. Now I am aware that there are those who would contend that we live in the most ghastly period of human history....They would argue that we are retrogressing instead of progressing. But far from representing retrogression and tragic meaninglessness, the present tensions represent the necessary pains that accompany the birth of anything new. Long ago the Greek philosopher, Heraclitus argued that justice emerges from the strife of opposites, and Hegel, in modern philosophy preached a doctrine of growth through struggle. It is both historically and biologically true that there can be no birth and growth without birth and growing pains.

The metaphor is an apt one. America is still in labor. Those of us in positions of influence are the midwives. We need to help her regulate her breathing, to lose the fear and hysteria that is born of pain if we are to deliver a healthy baby who will carry on the ideals of this country over that bridge into the future.

To do that we must get beyond labels. We must move beyond racial, ethnic, and religious profiles. We must go beyond being culturally sensitive and begin to create the new America, an America that has been transformed from old ideas regarding social inequality to a new set of ideals regarding social equity and justice. Being culturally sensitive is necessary but not sufficient to take us to the next level of development. We must take collective steps across our bridges and seek common ground. Taking the common ground requires learning the intricacies and tact of renegotiating membership in one's own culture and finding new opportunities to negotiate across the boundaries that divide racial, ethnic, and cultural communities (Bruffee, 2002).

Common ground thinking is a dramatic paradigm shift that requires us to acknowledge our interdependence. Common ground thinking requires long-term commitments and support from not only individual citizens but from the institutions to which they belong. This is akin to establishing a new kind of bridge. A two-tier suspension bridge that has an upper and lower deck. A bridge that preserves the original framework that allows those who travel at a slower pace of individual or social growth to keep moving forward, while those who want to speed toward a more pluralistic future can do so unobstructed by fear or judgment. For the point is that the common ground of America is the bridge—the bridge between our historical past and the future which must be secured for all of us.

REFERENCES

Aponte, H. J. (1996) Political bias, moral values, and spirituality in the training of psychotherapists. *Bulletin of the Menninger Clinic, 60*, 488–502.

Bateson, G., Jackson, D. D., Haley, J., & Weakland, J. (1956). Toward a theory of schizophrenia. *Behavioral Science, 1*, 251–264

Berry, J. W. (1997). Immigration, acculturation, and adaptation. *Applied Psychology: An International Review, 46*, 5–68.

Biskupic, J. (1998, December 7). High court to review law aimed at gangs. *Washington Post*, A04.

Bruffee, K. A. (2002). Taking the common ground: Beyond cultural identity. *Change, 34*, 10–17.

Erikson, E. (1950). *Childhood and society.* New York: W.W. Norton.

Guillaume, P. (1991). *The double bind: The intimate tie between behavior and communication.* Retrieved December 5, 2000, from http://www.well.com/user/bbear/double_bind.html.

Hacker, A. (1992). *Two nations, black and white, separate, hostile, unequal.* New York: Ballantine Books.

Hardy, K. (1993). War of the worlds. *Family Therapy Networker, 17*, 50–57.

Harris, D. A. (1999). *Driving while black: Racial profiling on our nation's highways. An American Civil Liberties Union special report.* Available from http://www.aclu.org/profiling/report.

Jefferson, T. (1776). The declaration of independence. In L. Behrens & L. J. Rosen (Eds.), *Theme and variations: The impact of great ideas.* Glenview, IL: Scott, Foresman.

King, M. L., Jr. (1956, December 3). *Facing the challenge of a new age.* Presented at the First Annual Institute on Nonviolence and Social Change, Mongomery, AL.

Laroche, M., Kim, C., & Tomiuk, M. A. (1998) Italian ethnic identity and its relative impact on the consumption of convenience and traditional foods. *Journal of Consumer Marketing, 15*, 125–151.

Lords, E. (2001). Outrage continues over fraternities racially offensive costumes. *Black Issues in Higher Education, 18*, 10–11.

Martin, H. (2000, June 7). Inmate freed in Rampart scandal files lawsuit. *Los Angeles Times*, B3.

Paine, T. (1995). *Common sense.* New York: Barnes and Nobles Books (Originally published 1776).

Perlmann, J., & Waldinger, R. (1998). Are the children of today's immigrants making it? *Public Interest, 132*, 73–96.

Roberts, R. E., Phinney, J. S., Masse, L. C., Chen, Y. R., Roberts, C. R., & Romero, A. (1999). The structure of ethnic identity of young adolescents from diverse ethnocultural groups. *Journal of Early Adolescence, 19*, 310–323.

Rumbaut, R. G. (1997). Paradoxes (and orthodoxies) of assimilation. *Sociological Perspectives, 40*, 483–511.

Sam, D. L. (2000). Psychological adaptation of adolescents with immigrant backgrounds. *Journal of Social Psychology, 140*, 5–26.

Snyder, H., & Sickmund, M. (1999). *Juvenile offenders and victims, 1999 national report.* Available from http://www.ojjdp.ncjrs.org/facts/pubs-1.html.

Stephen, A. (1996). Ethnic cleansing, US-style. *New Statesman, 17,* 127.

Sullivan, A. (1999, September 26). What's so bad about hate? *New York Times Magazine,* 51.

Suro, R. (1999). Recasting the melting pot. *American Demographics, 21,* 30–32.

Taylor, S., Jr. (2000). Bigotry, baseball, and the magic of the marketplace. *National Journal, 32,* 140–141.

Wrong, D. (2000). Adversarial identities and multiculturalism. *Society, 37,* 10–15.

Young, A. (2000, January 11). Rocker has chance for redemption. *Atlanta Constitution,* A11.

Zhou, M. (1997). Growing up American: The challenge confronting immigrant children and children of immigrants. *Annual Review of Sociology, 23,* 63–95.

CHAPTER 2

CHILDREN'S PSYCHOLOGICAL EXPERIENCE OF ETHNICITY Implications for Interethnic Understanding and Cooperation

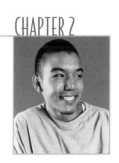

STEPHEN M. QUINTANA AND PATRICIA ALEMAN

This chapter reviews research on children's experiences of race and ethnicity. This review emphasizes developmental differences in how children understand and conceptualize their ethnicity-related experiences. These developmental differences have important implications for interracial and interethnic understanding and cooperation. This chapter also reflects children's experience through their voices, using interviews conducted with children and youth from several different ethnic and racial groups, including Mexican Americans in Texas and Arizona, African Americans in Chicago, transracially adopted Korean children, and international children from Korea and Latin American. These interviewees provide compelling, sometimes poignant, insights into children's experiences of race and ethnicity.

Ethnic or racial status has a profound effect on a child's life. During their lives, children will be classified into many different social statuses, including sex, race, sexual orientation, nationality, religion, and social class. Of these, only sex and race are fixed at birth, have clear biological components, and remain relatively permanent throughout life. These two forms of social status are critically important to children's lives, profoundly affecting social expectations of them. It is instructional to compare the roles that these two forms of social status have in children's development. Young children learn to identify the particularly important forms of social status early in life. Infants learn to identify others first by gender, then by race (Katz, 1983). Children are able to apply gender labels around

3 years of age (Brannon, 1996), and they learn to apply race labels slightly later, between 3 and 5 years of age (Aboud, 1987). Despite significant cross-cultural variation in composition of ethnic and racial groups, children have been shown to classify according to race at approximately the same age across cultures (Hirschfeld, 1994).

Clearly, an infant's ability to differentiate according to sex is important for adaptive and survival purposes. Males and females have different roles in the socialization and child-rearing activities of infants and preschool-age children (Katz, 1983). The importance of gender continues through adulthood when choosing playmates and romantic partners as children learn to follow strong social rules for behaviors, including mundane choices such as which restroom to use (Lobel, Bempechat, Gerwirtz, Shoken-Topaz, & Bashe, 1993). Hence, children's ability to differentiate according to sex serves important developmental functions for infants and young children. In contrast, why is racial classification learned so early in childhood? Why is it important for young children to differentiate according to racial groups?

Although infants' and young children's ability to discriminate caregivers according to gender may have evolutionary significance, there seems limited adaptive significance, in terms of physical survival, for children in learning racial classification at an early age. Children usually have intimate experiences with different sexes within families but have relatively little personal exposure to members of different races. Only in multiracial or biracial families do children have intrafamilial experiences with different races. Even in multiracial families, children may not be explicitly taught to label and differentiate according to race to the same extent that they are socialized to differentiate according to gender (Johnson, D. J., 1992). Gender labeling is usually associated with various toys, play activities, and clothes, but the major objects of a young child's life are not typically identified and associated with racial or ethnic status (Idle, Wood, & Desmarais, 1993; Lips, 1988).

Consequently, there may not be the evolutionary significance, familial experiences, and explicit socialization efforts associated with teaching children to differentiate among people according to race as there are for differentiating according to sex. Nonetheless, some physical and biological features of race and sex may aid children in learning to differentiate according to these social groups. These physical differences may help explain why children learn these social categories so early in their development (Katz, 1983). Nonetheless, when considering physical features of race, the obviousness of racial differences may not be as apparent as it seems (Hirschfeld, 1994). The biological reality of sex is rarely debated, given the chromosomal, physical, and hormonal correlates of sex. The biological significance of race, however, is in dispute (Yee, Fairchild, Weizmann, & Wyatt, 1993). Only a few physical implications of racial classification exist, with nearly as much individual difference across racial groups as within racial groups. Racial differences in psychological functioning, including performance on intellectual tests, are at best subtle and are likely to be associated more closely with opportunity or racism (Rowe, Vazsonyi, & Flannery, 1994). To many, racial differences are social constructions and fail to have the biological basis that is often assumed (García Coll et al., 1996).

Notwithstanding the relatively superficial nature of racial differences in physical characteristics, it is possible that children learn to classify according to race because of differences in appearance, including skin, eye, and hair color; hair texture; and facial features. Consider, however, the challenge for young children learning to associate these physical appearances with racial classification: These features vary widely within racial groups and even within an individual. Hair, eye, and skin coloration may vary dramatically for individuals who use tanning salons, hair dyes, or tinted contacts. Moreover, given the amount of contemporary and historical intermixing across races, there are relatively high proportions of multiracial individuals who defy strict categorization (Hirschfeld, 1994). The large proportion of multiracial individuals is in sharp contrast to the relatively straightforward classification of sex. In short, variations in the physical expression of racial heritage defy straightforward categorization and surely complicate children's ability to classify according to race based on physical appearances.

Adults socialized within a society may take for granted the apparent obviousness of racial differences in appearance, but to others, these differences may be more subtle. When I (Quintana) traveled to Guatemala, I had difficulty differentiating between the two racial groups (Mayan-descended and European-descended), because from my vantage, they differed only slightly: dark brown versus black hair, brown versus darker brown skin pigmentation, and slight differences in height and in facial features. Young children raised in Guatemala, however, can easily differentiate what they consider obvious racial differences (Quintana & de Baessa, 1996). A stranger to our culture might not find racial differences in our society as apparent as we have been socialized to believe.

There is little apparent purpose to learn to differentiate by race, children have relatively little personal exposure to members of different races, they receive little explicit tutoring in differentiating race, and the variation in the physical expression of racial heritage complicates the acquisition of racial classification for young children. Despite all these factors, children learn early that racial differences are important. Race is important to children because they are socialized to perceive it as important. This emphasis on children's socialization seems to result, in part, from the historical events shaping American society with respect to race relations and the ways the dynamics of race relations influence contemporary society. Years ago, Allport (1924, as cited in Milner, 1975) suggested that prejudice against blacks could not be explained by the purported degree of racial differences in valued traits (e.g., IQ). Analogously, the rate at which children develop race awareness cannot be explained exclusively by the perceptual obviousness of racial differences in physical features.

Children seem to be implicitly socialized about race—socialization that occurs by inference and nuance (Feagin & Vera, 1995). When explicit socialization about racial status occurs, particularly in the United States, these direct teachings may be inconsistent or contradictory to the implicit socialization about race (Feagin & Vera, 1995; Peters, 1985). That is, explicit teachings about race usually take the form of communicating the value of racial equality (Demo & Hughes, 1990; Spencer, 1983), whereas implicit socialization seems to imply inequalities among racial groups (Feagin & Vera, 1995; Gopaul-McNicol, 1995). This double bind in children's socialization is likely to be confusing and to reinforce the implicit message that racial status is an important characteristic in appraising others and self, but one that is infrequently directly discussed, undoubtedly creating confusion for children.

The problem is all the more complicated because children are often discouraged from discussing their observations about race (Feagin & Vera, 1995). White children are often told what to think about race. Ethnic and racial minority parents may have ambivalence about discussing the realities of racial prejudice with their children, given that their own recollections of racism may be difficult and painful.

Clearly, race and ethnicity are confusing aspects of children's lives for many reasons. Race relations are confusing matters for adults, and children do not have the benefit of adult logic with which to understand these complex, nuanced, and emotionally laden experiences.

CHILDREN'S DEVELOPMENTAL UNDERSTANDING OF RACE AND ETHNICITY

One of the most pernicious mistakes in working with children is assuming that they function like small adults. Children are wonderful mimics of adults—they often repeat words or terms that they do not understand. They experiment with roles and behaviors and watch how others respond to them long before they understand the consequences and meaning of their actions. Research has shown that children use racial terms long before they have a good understanding of race (Quintana, 1998). When hearing a child use a racial label or description, one may assume the child is referring to race—as adults understand the concept—when in fact, the child has a very limited understanding of race. Children's usage of racial terms is simply a reference to the appearance of skin coloration. One colleague described how a kindergartner explained the origin of an ethnic group: "Black children have two black parents; white children have two white parents, and brown [Mexican American] children have one black parent and one white parent." (G. Manaster, personal communication, 1994) A white child explained why some children of color, who lived down the street, should not be allowed to use playground equipment in the park: "They might use the slide and then their [skin] color might come off and get on other kids." In this example, the child was aware of negative connotations associated with race, but was able to justify the bias only using her developmental logic.

These two examples illustrate how children apply developmental logic when expressing their racial attitudes and thoughts. In both cases, the children had incomplete understandings of race and ethnicity, and their responses must be interpreted in light of their racial conceptions. For us to understand children's psychological experiences of race and ethnicity, we need to appreciate how they understand race. Research has identified four developmental levels in children's understanding of race and ethnicity (Quintana, 1998; see Table 2-1).

Preschool Years

Children acquire the ability to classify according to race at 3 to 5 years of age. When specifically prompted to sort pictures of people, they can classify reasonably accurately between 3 and 4 years of age. Children tend to sort by gender spontaneously—that is, without prompting—more often than by race (Hirschfeld, 1994). Interestingly, children's abilities to differentiate based on race according to affective dimensions seems to be better developed than their ability to cognitively differentiate. That is, they develop strong attitudinal biases about racial groups at an early age, before they have developed a cognitive understanding of race. For example, research by Williams and Morland (1976) indicated young children show clear differentiation among racial groups based on pejorative social descriptors (e.g., clean, dirty, smart, mean). These attitudinal differentiations develop sooner than the ability to differentiate racial groups reliably based on perceptual features (Williams & Morland, 1976). Indeed, children's tendency to demonstrate racial prejudice tends to reach its peak between ages 3 and 5—the degree of prejudice levels off or diminishes after 5 years of age (Aboud, 1987). The age-related reduction of prejudice is consistent across racial groups in North America and seems to be consistent in other regions of the world (Quintana, Ybarra, Gonzalez-Doupe, & de Baessa, 2000).

It is important to note that this prejudice tends to be biased consistently against darker complexioned racial groups (Williams & Morland, 1976). Young white chil-

Table 2-1

Children's Understanding of Ethnicity and Race:
Developmental Milestones and Implications for Intergroup Interaction

Age	Developmental Milestones	Strategies for Increasing Intergroup Interaction
Preschool Years	Children classify early according to race	Integrate and diversify preschool programs and activities
	External, physical manifestations of race seen as essence of race	Redress societal bias
	Racial/ethnic status believed to be impermanent	
	Children's racial attitudes independent of parental attitudes	
	Sensitive to societal bias	
	Dichotomous thinking about "good" and "bad" groups	
	Children's racial/ethnic bias infrequently expressed socially	
Early Childhood	Race/ethnicity understood as determined by ancestry	Provide information about history, customs, and characteristics of racial/ethnic groups
	Racial status viewed as permanent	
	Emphasis on primary cultural characteristics	Develop programs promoting interethnic cooperation
	Race/ethnicity seen as irrelevant in interpersonal relationships	Use cooperative learning groups
	Tend to advocate for equality across ethnicity, race, and social class	Use programs that emphasize similarities and differences across groups
	Negative racial/ethnic attitudes diminish	

dren tend to indicate strong positive views toward whites and less favorable views toward darker-complexioned racial groups (Doyle & Aboud, 1995). Children of color tend to show less of a prowhite/antiblack bias, but like white children, they tend to increase their esteem of darker complexioned racial groups by 6 or 7 years of age (Aboud, 1987).

It is important to note that prejudice in early childhood is measured by asking children to make attributions about fictitious persons, who are racially identified by dolls, pictorial representations, or verbal descriptions (Clark & Clark, 1940; Doyle & Aboud, 1995; Williams, Best, Boswell, Mattson, & Graves, 1975). It is

TABLE 2-1 (CONTINUED)

AGE	DEVELOPMENTAL MILESTONES	STRATEGIES FOR INCREASING INTERGROUP INTERACTIO
Middle/ Late Childhood	Understand social context of interracial relations Increased concern with ethnic/racial prejudice Greater awareness of social class disparity across race and ethnicity Racial/ethnic attitudes increasingly influence social behavior Potential for some insecurity in interracial relationships Increased concern with bias and prejudice of authority Greater willingness to consider ethnic differences	Teach social norms, roles, and values of different groups in multicultural education programs Encourage learning about how race/ethnicity affect self, peers, and social relationships Integrate schools Implement cooperative learning groups in multicultural education programs Address racial/ethnic bias and prejudice directly
Adolescence	Ethnicity subjectively and socially determined Formation of social cliques Pressure for conformity to group norms Tendency to stereotype outgroup members Increased importance of expressions of ethnic identity, pride, and group consciousness Increased questioning of authenticity of racial/ethnic group membership	Use multicultural curriculum Continue using cooperative learning groups Encourage participation of diverse groups in all school activities Encourage activities that develop racial pride and destigmatize outgroup members

encouraging to note that young children tend not to express their prejudice behaviorally to peers (Finkelstein & Haskins, 1983). Their prejudiced views tend to be of an abstract form, in the sense that they tend not to apply these prejudices within their peer groups. One researcher noted that immediately after an interview, a white boy with particularly strong racial prejudice spontaneously joined African American children on the playground (Porter, 1971). To this boy and other preschool children, race remains a concept with which they have affective connotations, but that has relatively few implications for daily social interactions. This developmentally induced form of prejudice against racial minority groups seems to stem from an interaction of developmental and socialization processes in the child's environment.

Young children have been found to think literally in black and white terms (Doyle, Beadet, & Aboud, 1988; Shiner, 1998). Children categorize features of the physical and social environment into dichotomous categories, in which good people are considered to possess only positive qualities, and bad people have only negative qualities. Consequently, children will exaggerate the positive qualities of good groups and consider only the negative qualities of bad groups. As children mature, their thinking becomes more flexible and complex, such that they understand that there may be positive aspects of bad things and vice versa (Shiner, 1998). This increase in cognitive flexibility has associated with reductions in prejudice (Doyle et al., 1988; Doyle & Aboud, 1995). These developmental factors help account for variations in ethnic attitudes, but do not account for the reasons children tend to develop prowhite/antiblack biases (Williams & Morland, 1976).

It would be tempting to blame parents for fostering prowhite/antiblack bias in children's attitudes, particularly because this bias appears before children are old enough to enter public schools. Research has shown, however, that children's racial attitudes are not associated with parental attitudes—parental racial attitudes are not predictive of children's attitudes until children reach adolescence (Aboud, 1993). Moreover, research has found that parents of color with strong racial pride nevertheless have children who have a prowhite/antiblack bias (Branch & Newcombe, 1980). Conversely, children's attitudes have been found to be sensitive to broader societal racial attitudes (Gopaul-McNicol, 1995). In ways that are not fully understood, children's racial attitudes reflect broad societal views that seem to be communicated primarily implicitly. Retrospective reviews of research (Aboud, 1987) suggest that there has been a general reduction in children's prowhite/antiblack bias over time, corresponding to major shifts in societal views, such as during the U.S. civil rights movement in the 1960s. Allport (1954) suggested that prejudice is "caught not taught" to young children, in that parents do not seem to teach their children to be prejudiced directly, but that children seem to be infected with the racial prejudice embedded in the society. We are no closer to understanding how societal bias is infectious to young children than Allport was in 1954.

Unfortunately, preschool-age children's racial attitudes seem somewhat immune to parental attempts to counteract the racial bias embedded in society. Interestingly, children's views of gender are similarly immune to parental efforts to promote less gender bias in children's preferences in playmates (Maccoby, 1990). Attempts to promote positive attitudes toward African American have had ironic effects in several studies (Branch & Newcombe, 1980; McAdoo, 1970). That is, these socialization efforts seem to have only sensitized children to the broader societal views of race, which resulted in the children developing stronger prowhite/antiblack attitudes than peers with parents who did not explicitly socialize their children about race.

Sadly, it appears that young children are very vulnerable to picking up society's racial bias before they even understand what race is. Indeed, Hirschfeld (1994) suggested that children learn about race first by picking up these affective attitudes, rather than with direct personal contact with other racial groups. Hence, our society's racial hierarchy seems so embedded and implicitly communicated as to render parental efforts impotent in counteracting the effect of society's racial bias on preschool children. When preschool-age children talk about race, they tend to focus on physical characteristics (Holmes, 1995). Children seem to conceptualize the external manifestations of race (i.e., skin, hair, and eye color, as well as diction) as the essence of race. The following excerpt from interviews with children is illustrative:

> Interviewer: What does it mean to be black?
> Child: It's just the color of your skin.

In speculating about others' racial prejudice, children suggested in interviews that prejudiced people dislike different skin colors. Children may coin their own terms to describe the physical features of race, such as "chocolate" and "vanilla" (Alejandro-Wright, 1985). One child responded to the question, "Could you become another race besides being black?" with "I could be brown." Children have been noted to refer to Africans Americans as "brown," rather than using the more common racial term "black," probably because brown is a more accurate way of describing skin pigmentation than "black" (Ramsey, 1987). Furthermore, children show confusion about the connection between skin color and race:

> Interviewer: Is there any way you could stop being Mexican American?
> Child: Maybe if I changed my skin color to be white.

> Interviewer: If you had white skin, would you still be Mexican American?
> Child: No.

> Interviewer: How would you describe a child who had one white parent and
> one black parent?
> Child: If they had twins one would be white and one would be black.

In another interview, a child indicated that you could change race by "going out into the sun" and getting a suntan. Clearly, external manifestations of race tend to be the focus of children's verbal descriptions of race and ethnicity.

Preschool-age children's psychological experiences of race are dominated by several trends: (a) Many children (particularly white children) express affective connotations associated with race in a way that stigmatizes racial minority groups; (b) children's racial cognitions tend to be categorical in nature, in that negative qualities of stigmatized groups are exaggerated, while positive qualities of nonstigmatized groups are emphasized; and (c) children's verbal reasoning about race suggests that they confuse the external, physical manifestations of race with the essence of racial status.

Implications for Interracial Cooperation

Racial differences do not seem to influence preschool-age children's social behavior (Finkelstein & Haskins, 1983) as young children seem to form friendships based on physical proximity rather than on demographic characteristics (Selman, 1980). Children's selection of playmates tends to be determined by who lives nearby, goes to the same preschool, does similar activities, or is friendly. Although racial differences do not seem to influence friendship formation directly, structural barriers prevent greater contact among racial groups during preschool. That is, racial segregation that occurs in neighborhoods, preschool programs, and incidental social contact may deprive children of substantial interracial experiences (García-Coll et al., 1996). Consequently, many children learn about other racial groups primarily through impersonal exposure, such as mass media (Gopaul-McNicol, 1995). The tendency to learn about racial differences at such psychological distances could influence children's attitudes and racial cognitions at later developmental stages.

To promote interracial cooperation during the preschool years, children need to be exposed to other racial groups. Through meaningful interactions in neighborhood and school settings, parents and teachers can provide additional opportunities for children to become acquainted with peers from different racial and ethnic groups. Interaction opportunities for interracial interaction include attending child care facilities with a diverse clientele, participating in heterogeneous playgroups of neighborhood children, participating in cultural activities representative of various cultures, and providing educational activities related to different groups. By fostering these opportunities during preschool years, children's exposures to different ethnic and racial groups will not be limited to superficial knowledge gained from the media or incidental contact.

Unfortunately, contact alone does not seem to reduce ethnic or racial bias in preschool children. Moreover, curricular programs exposing young white children to African American culture (songs, heroes, etc.) and engaging them in play activities (e.g., coloring) related to race have not been shown to reduce racial bias (McAdoo, 1985). Some research suggests that white children's racial attitudes and preferences can be made to be less biased against African Americans if they are exposed to operant conditioning (e.g., awarding candy or money contingent on children's responses) of children's attitudes toward the colors white and black (Williams & Morland, 1976). These same procedures were, however, ineffective for modifying African American children's racial attitudes and preferences (McAdoo, 1985; Williams & Morland, 1976). Unfortunately, young children's racial attitudes appear somewhat intractable. The most effective means for reducing preschool children's racial biases may be to ameliorate racial bias within the broad society.

Early Childhood

During the early elementary-school grades, children's understanding of race and ethnicity becomes transformed in several ways. Children begin to understand that racial status extends beyond its external manifestations. Children no longer see skin color or physical features as the defining features of race. Instead, they understand that some nonobservable features are associated with determining racial status, such as parents' racial status. At first, children's understanding of how parents determine a child's racial status may be incomplete, as illustrated by interviews with two children:

> Interviewer: Is there any way that this [mixed race] child could only be Mexican or only Anglo?
> Child: If she asks her parents and they say she could, then she'd be just one.

> Child: If the parents' divorce and then if [one parent] marries someone of the same kind...then she would be just Mexican.

Eventually, children develop the understanding that ancestry defines race and ethnicity:

> Interviewer: What does it mean to be African American?
> Child: It means your ancestors are from Africa.

> Interviewer: What does it mean to be Mexican American?
> Child: It means your parents were born in Mexico and you were born in America.

Concomitant with the understanding that race is determined by ancestry, children realize that racial status cannot be changed by modifying superficial physical characteristics and that race is a permanent status:

> Interviewer: Could you ever change from being black?
> Child: You could change your skin color, but you would still be black.

This process is analogous to children's understanding of the permanence of gender: Those children who have knowledge of gender differences in genitalia also understand that superficial changes in appearance (e.g., hair, clothing) do not affect gender status. With an accurate definition of race and ethnicity, children use racial labels in a manner consistent with adults using, for example, the term *black* instead of *brown* to refer to African Americans (Quintana, 1998).

Children's psychological experiences of race and ethnicity seem to be influenced by their adopting a literal understanding. That is, their conceptualization of race is similar to a dictionary definition of race. They conceptualize racial status to be an artifact of one's history and seem relatively unaware of aspects of racial group membership that are not directly implicated by the literal features of race. To illustrate:

> **Interviewer:** Do you prefer to be friends with someone who is white or Mexican American or would it matter?
> **Child:** No. Why would what [ancestry] your parents are matter what kind of friend you are?

In other words, ethnic group membership is conceived to affect one's past, but does not affect contemporary events, such as interethnic friendships or relationships (Quintana, 1994). In Quintana's (1994) research interviews, the only contemporary events that children perceive race or ethnicity to influence tend to be celebrations (e.g., Cinco de Mayo, Kwaanza) or other customs that are literally associated with ethnicity or race (e.g., eating Mexican food, speaking Spanish):

> **Interviewer:** How are white and Mexican-American children different?
> **Child:** Mexican children eat Mexican food, come from Mexico and speak Mexican [Spanish].

Interestingly, interviews with African American children at this stage of development indicated they associated a legacy of slavery as being literally connected to racial status. The following are responses from three different African American children:

> **Interviewer:** What does it mean to be African American?
> **Child:** It means your ancestors were from Africa, and they were brought over as slaves.

> **Interviewer:** What does it mean to be white?
> **Child:** That you didn't have to be sent from Africa [and] that you used to treat the black people wrong.

> **Interviewer:** Why do you like being African American?
> **Child:** Because there aren't slaves anymore.

In these and other interviews with African American children at this level, the legacy of slavery was perceived not to influence contemporary interracial relations. When asked, African American children at this level of development denied any difference between same-race and different race relationships. In a sense, African American children denied that past historical events could influence current events.

Implications for Interracial Cooperation

The literal view children bring to understanding racial differences is similar to the literalness they bring to their conceptualization of social class and other forms of social status (Leahy, 1983). Children perceive people of different social classes to differ only in the amount of money they have in their bank accounts or in their pockets and not to differ in any other ways, such as personality or values.

Interestingly, along with this literalness is a strong commitment to equality. Children in elementary school tended to be strong proponents of an equal distribution of wealth regardless of merit, relative to other developmental periods (Leahy, 1983). Similarly, children of this age also advocated equality among racial groups. A large majority of children interviewed expressed no racial or ethnic bias in friendship preferences. This emphasis on egalitarianism stems in part from the literalness with which they view race: (a) Race is an artifact of history, (b) racial differences tend to be limited to infrequent events related to customs and holidays, and (c) history has little implication for contemporary relationships. These features of children's literal view of race may help explain why negative attitudes associated with racial or ethnic differences diminish during this age period (Doyle & Aboud, 1995).

In addition, this literalness may encourage positive attitudes toward sociodemographic differences. When asked what benefits exist for interethnic or interracial relations, children interviewed for Quintana's (1994) research referred to learning cultural knowledge, skills, or customs: "I could teach them [white Americans] Spanish," "I could learn about their culture," or "I teach them about my culture." Moreover, parents seem to have fewer reservations about their children's interethnic friendships during early childhood than in later developmental levels, in part because interethnic peers are seen as less dangerous or less of a corrupting influence on their own children. In short, many features are associated with this developmental level that make children at this age responsive to programs promoting interethnic cooperation.

During early childhood, multiple factors can contribute to interracial cooperation. Children emphasize primary cultural differences, conceptualize race in a historical perspective, and appreciate human similarities. Educators can take advantage of these unique circumstances of this developmental period through the use of multicultural education programs. These allow educators to provide children with knowledge specific to ethnic and racial groups. This knowledge may promote greater interracial understanding and have positive effects on inter-group attitudes (Banks, 1988, 1993). For the programs to succeed, they should be specifically tailored for this developmental period. Lessons concerning primary cultural difference between groups, such as histories, languages, holidays, foods, and other customs, should be incorporated into the curriculum. Not only should the differences among the groups be taught, the similarities across cultural groups should be emphasized. In addition to incorporating specific lessons related to culture and ethnicity, examples from a variety of groups should be used to illustrate key concepts in different subject areas (Banks, 1993).

Two developmental characteristics associated with early childhood—commitment to equality and lack of racial or ethnic bias in friendships—provide additional opportunities for educators to promote interracial cooperation. To facilitate additional interracial interactions and friendships, teachers can use cooperative learning groups, which can be heterogeneous mixes of students across race, gender, and ability level. Examples of cooperative groups include Student Teams–Achievement Divisions (STAD) and Teams-Games-Tournament (TGT) (Slavin, 1995). For each of these teaching methods, a small group of children work together to achieve a common goal. In STAD, children work together to complete worksheets. The team score is based on the improvement of each student's score, and the team is rewarded for improvement in a class newsletter. In TGT, students compete against other teams in academic tournaments. Each child competes with other children at the same academic level. Each child's score contributes to the team score. (For additional information concerning cooperative groups, see Slavin, 1979, and DeVries, Edwards, & Slavin, 1978.)

To be successful, these cooperative groups need to include Allport's (1954) four conditions for positive intergroup contact. First, in cooperative learning groups, all individuals must have equal status. Second, activities within cooperative learning groups must promote cooperation, rather than competitiveness, among group members. The groups should not be able to achieve the goal without the contribution of all the group members (Bossert, 1989; Johnson, D. W., & Johnson, 1992; Sherif & Sherif, 1966). Third, positive interaction among the members of different racial groups must be sanctioned and encouraged by authority (e.g., teachers, principals). Fourth, all participants must work toward a common goal. When these conditions are met, the team obtains positive group interactions and academic improvements. In general, participants are more likely to have friends outside their own ethnic or cultural groups than they would in classrooms not using cooperative learning groups (Slavin, 1983a, 1983b, 1985).

Also, several studies suggested that implementation of cooperative learning groups results in improvements in majority-minority friendships (Slavin, 1995; Slavin & Oickle, 1981). These friendships may lead to additional reinforcement of the similarities among groups (Schofield, 1995). Because of some developmental features (i.e., commitment to egalitarianism), this age group may represent a critical period to promote positive intergroup interactions.

One caveat is in order with respect to the potential for instilling positive intergroup interactions during this developmental period. The literalness associated with understanding race and ethnicity seems to come at the cost of denying many interracial differences. At this age period, the only differences children tend to associate with race are those characteristics that are literally connected to racial or ethnic culture (e.g., eating Mexican food, learning African traditions, and speaking Spanish). These differences are generally considered primary cultural differences because the cultural differences derive from the culture of origin and are particularly prevalent in recent immigrants (Ogbu, 1994). These cultural differences may seem glamorous or exotic, or have an international flavor.

Conversely, children at this developmental period may have difficulty accepting and embracing secondary cultural characteristics. Secondary characteristics are those ethnic characteristics that develop as coping responses to interracial contact, such as those cultural characteristics that developed in response to slavery and are passed down generationally (Ogbu, 1994) or those coping responses common to victims of racism and prejudice (Allport, 1954; Crocker & Major, 1989). Rather, children at this developmental period become akin to humanists appreciating human similarity and individuality, primarily embracing only superficial cultural differences, such as cultural celebrations or culinary preferences. The challenge for this developmental age is to be able to accept, or at least understand, ethnic and racial differences in social customs or cultural values, particularly ones that might contradict their own customs and values. Consequently, it may be possible to introduce differences in primary and secondary cultural characteristics in cooperative learning groups, particularly after the groups become cohesive during an initial period of emphasizing similarity (Pettigrew, 1998).

Middle Through Late Childhood

As children mature, the innocence or naïveté associated with race that is characteristic of early childhood diminishes. During this period, children make observations about racial dynamics beyond the academic or dictionary-like understanding of race and ethnicity found earlier in childhood. Children become akin to sociologists, in that they integrate independent observations about racial differences into their conceptions of race. Children also become aware of subtle differences in social activity across race. Children observe that peers of other groups may have certain behavioral patterns, language preferences, and social characteristics, depending on their race. The following are excerpts from three children:

> Interviewer: How are your friendships different with children who are your race/ethnicity and those who are not?
> Child: I speak Spanish with my Mexican American friends and speak English with whites.

> Child: If I go [with] black friends, we play outside, like jump rope, but if I go with a white friend, we go to the mall or play computer games.

> Child: My white friends talk differently than black friends, I can hear the difference.

In the United States and elsewhere, racial groups differ in social class. During middle childhood, children comment on the connection between social class and race (Quintana, 1994). A Mexican American child responded to the question: "What does it mean to be white?" with "To live in a better part of town." Another child said, "They live in a bigger house and have maids." A third child responded to this question by observing differences in public services received: "In my neighborhood, they don't fix the streets, but in white neighborhoods, all the streets are nice." Children also cite social class as a reason why someone might have negative feelings about their race. Below are examples from two African American children:

> Interviewer: Why might someone not like being black?
> Child: They don't have the things that other races have...money, fancy cars.

> Child: White people have all the clean stuff, and black people have the dirty stuff.

More generally during middle childhood, children appreciate the social implications of ethnicity and race. Children conceptualize race to be more than just reflective of one's ancestry or the occasional celebration, but to have implications for everyday social activity. Children recognize that forming friendships with ethnically similar peers may be somewhat easier than with peers from other ethnic groups. They are also aware that ethnic differences may result in conflict and misunderstanding between individuals. The following are responses from African American children to the question, "Would it be easier to make friends with white children, black children, or would it [race] not make a difference?"

> Child: It could be harder to be friends with the white child, because we could be playing and then she might see some of her white friends and run off with them.

> Child: Like if I hang around a white person, they might walk away.

Child: If I ask a white person [to do something together], they might be doing something with a white person.

When directly queried, children perceived that both same- and different-raced peers would have ethnocentric preferences for social relationships (Quintana, Vera, & Cooper, 1999). Hence, children perceive their peers to be ethnocentric, making them cautious and insecure when entering cross-race friendships.

Although admitting that there may be initial barriers to forming interethnic friendships, many children at this developmental level were optimistic that once formed, interethnic relationships would function similarly to intraethnic relationships: "Once we were friends there'd be no difference [between same-race and different-race friendships]."

Poignantly, most children from ethnic minority groups spontaneously mention that they or their peers have been the target of prejudice, usually by adults.

Interviewer: What would it be like to spend the night at a white family's house?
Child: It wouldn't make a difference to me, but I couldn't be sure how the parents feel towards Mexican Americans.

Interviewer: Why are some children prejudiced?
Child: Their parents raise them that way.

Interviewer: Has that kind of thing [interethnic conflict] ever happened to you?
Child: Yes, I had a teacher that was prejudiced against Mexican kids. She was nicer to the white kids and stricter with the Mexican kids.

Child: I went over to a [white] friend's house, and his mother whispered in his ear that Mexican kids were not the kind of kids to hang around.

These quotes illustrate how children at this developmental level understand the social implications of race and ethnicity. They must be wary of members of other ethnic groups who may be prejudiced toward them. This awareness has developmental costs and benefits. One benefit is that relative to younger children, they can better interpret experiences involving prejudice by not making internal attributions for these unpleasant and painful experiences (Crocker & Major, 1989). The developmental cost is that they no longer naïvely trust members of other groups who are in authority, such as teachers or police.

Implications for Interracial Cooperation
This developmental level poses additional challenges for interracial cooperation and understanding. Children no longer conceive of ethnicity as an artifact of the past, but as having an effect on mundane social relations. Children, particularly

children of color, may be suspicious of and sensitive to the interethnic attitudes of others. This vigilance adds another layer to interethnic interactions. More troubling is research suggesting that children may be more likely to act on their ethnic prejudice, in terms of social preferences, than at earlier developmental periods (Aboud, 1992). Earlier in development, racial prejudice did not seem to influence interracial relations. During this developmental period, however, children's racial attitudes affect their social behavior to a greater extent. For example, white children who are biased will avoid contact with children of other racial groups (Schofield, 1982). This research supports children's apprehensiveness about the potentially fragile nature of interethnic relationships illustrated in the earlier interview excerpts. On the other hand, children are developing the ability and willingness to consider ethnic differences more than younger children were. This ability, developed under nurturing situations, could allow them to achieve a level of interethnic understanding that may not have been possible earlier in childhood. Of course, this ability is double-edged, because the willingness to consider ethnic differences may be associated with an increase in negative evaluations of these differences.

Educators need to be mindful of these developmental characteristics when designing curricula for multicultural education programs. In addition to teaching about the norms, roles, and values of different groups (Triandis, Bontempo, Villareal, Asai, & Lucca, 1988), children need opportunities to integrate knowledge gained from their observations of society. This integration may be facilitated through discussions or written assignments that encourage children to learn about and understand how ethnicity and culture affects them, their peers, and others in different ethnic and cultural groups. In particular, course material related to social and economic issues associated with race and ethnicity should be integrated into the curriculum and class discussions.

In regard to social interactions, children in middle to late childhood are better able to understand and conceptualize the effect of ethnic differences on peer interactions. They recognize that forming friendships with ethnically similar peers may be somewhat easier than with peers from other groups because they are aware that ethnic differences can contribute to conflict and misunderstanding among individuals. This awareness may make children more cautious in developing cross-ethnic friendships and apprehensive during initial stages of these relationships. Because children perceive same ethnic friendships to be easier and less anxiety provoking than cross-ethnic friendships, they may begin to segregate themselves by ethnicity and race (Patchen, 1982; Schofield, 1979). Children are more likely to have friends of the same ethnicity than friends from other ethnicities (Schofield, 1991). Children of similar cultural and ethnic groups may sit near each other during lunch and only play with each other during recess. Extracurricular activities in schools may be racially segregated (Scherer & Slawski, 1979; Sullivan, 1979). Moreover, children at this age may be more vulnerable to peer pressure and may be encouraged by peers to discriminate or express prejudice according to race or ethnicity (Blanchard, Lilly, & Vaughn, 1991; Patchen, 1982). This trend toward increased racial and ethnic segregation, as well as increased peer influence, combine to perpetuate ethnic and racial conflict during this period.

To promote positive interactions, educators need to desegregate school lunchrooms, playgrounds, and extracurricular organizations. For example, children tend to sit near others who are similar to them during lunch (Schofield, 1979; Schofield & Sagar, 1977). School personnel can contribute to greater intergroup interaction by assigning children to particular seating arrangements in class and during recreational activities. This allows children the opportunity to interact with others and form friendships (Byrne, 1961; Schofield, 1982, 1989). By having children interact with diverse people within multiple settings, teachers can promote intergroup friendships. Educators need to implement cooperative learning groups within multicultural education programs through the use of cooperative learning groups.

In cooperative groups, new social categories may be developed that are not based on typical categories such as ethnicity, socioeconomic status, and language (Brewer & Miller, 1984; Vanbeselaere, 1987). Research suggests that these new social identities attenuate bias about other groups (Gaertner & Dovidio, 1986; Gaertner, Mann, Murrell, & Dovidio, 1989). This reduction in bias can promote enhanced interethnic friendships (Aronson & Gonzales, 1988; Slavin, 1983a, 1983b, 1985). Also, techniques that reduce prejudice can be used to help students develop more egalitarian values. These techniques include dividing students into arbitrary groups and having them experience discrimination on the basis of arbitrary distinction (Byrnes & Kiger, 1990; Weiner & Wright, 1973), acting out cases of discrimination that can occur in school settings (Breckheimer & Nelson, 1976), and role playing being a member of another group (Smith, 1990). Each of these activities can increase children's ability to take the perspective of ethnically or racially different peers.

Adolescence

As children enter secondary schools, peer groups tend to become even more segregated. Early adolescence is especially marked by the formation of social cliques, which provide pressure for conformity to group norms. The enhancement of ingroup cohesion within cliques often comes at the cost of positive relations and attitudes toward outgroups (Sherif & Sherif, 1966). At about this same time, youth develop the cognitive ability to infer the perspective of a group (Selman, 1979). To explain, younger children tend see groups as collections of individuals, each with his or her own individual perspective. Conversely, adolescents are able to conceive of groups as social units. This ability to assume a group perspective can enhance ingroup cohesion. The emergent quality of this social cognitive ability seems to be associated with the tendency to exaggerate ingroup sameness and outgroup difference (Selman, 1979). The tendency to stereotype outgroup members during early adolescence has been widely observed (Quintana, 1994, 1998). Not surprisingly, many adolescent cliques are ethnically and racially homogenous (Schofield, 1982). Moreover, the cliques may be even further subdivided into cultural groups within ethnic groups, such as Mexican-oriented (first-generation immigrants) and Mexican-American (second- or later-generation immigrant) groups (Matute-Bianchi, 1986).

During adolescence, the psychological experience of ethnicity is often closely tied to involvement in an ethnic group. Earlier in development, ethnicity was determined objectively (i.e., by heritage). In adolescence, however, ethnicity is also subjectively and socially determined (Quintana, 1994). That is, a person's ethnicity or race is only partly determined by his or her birth status. Equally important as these objective makers of race are subjective and social experiences with ethnic and racial groups. To illustrate, researchers asked youth to describe long-term influences of interracial contact:

> Interviewer: How would a black child adopted by white parents be different than one adopted by black parents?
> Child: She'd be white because she lives with them.

> Interviewer: How would hanging around an all-white group for a year or more affect an African American child?
> Child: From being around people who are different colors than her, like she could get their ways.

> Interviewer: What would it be like to be the only black kid on an all white soccer team?
> Child: He would have to get used to the way white people act.

These quotes illustrate that youth understand that a person's racial status, determined objectively, may be of less social significance than how the person expresses his or her racial or ethnic identification. These youth indicate awareness that lifestyles, values, and behavioral patterns are associated with racial and ethnic enculturation. They recognize that people adopt the cultural patterns of the groups with which they affiliate themselves.

Youth may question the authenticity of an individual who may be a member of an ethnic group, but who does not overtly identify with the ethnic group. Derogatory names such as "Oreo," "coconut," "banana," and "apple" refer to people who are nominally African American, Latino, Asian American, and American Indian, respectively, but who fail to show pride in and identification with their ethnic or racial group. Ethnic minority individuals who acculturate to the dominant group risk peer pressure and derision (Aboud, 1992). One African American youth indicated pressure he would receive from his racial group in response to having white friends, when he suggested his black peers might say to him, "Yo Hersey, why are you hanging around white friends?" The following is another example of this intraracial pressure:

> **Interviewer**: What would it be like to be the only black child on an all-white soccer team?
> **Child**: The black people would probably think I don't like black people, [they'd think] I want to be white.

On the other hand, members of an ethnic group may extend honorary membership for someone from another ethnic group who identifies with them, as indicated by the following quote from an African American interviewee: "Some white girls at my school try to act black, we respect them and their ways." To further complicate matters, youth are aware of perceptions of them by other groups, as illustrated in the excerpts from interviews with two African American youth:

> **Interviewer**: Do you like having friends who are white?
> **Child**: Yes, because if you are not racist you should like being friends with all races.

> **Child**: If I was friends with just blacks, they'd [white peers] think I was racist.

Clearly, youth struggle with pressure and impressions that others have of them based on their interracial and intraracial friendships and activities. Many youth feel caught between their loyalty to their ethnic or racial group and their interest in forming interethnic or interracial relationships.

The development of ethnic identity and ethnic pride are important maturational tasks during adolescence (Phinney, 1989). Some youth of color may move through racial identity stages (Cross, 1995), such that they progress from stages of relative unawareness of racial prejudice in society to an awakening of this bias. The following interview excerpt illustrates a youth's keen awareness of discrimination:

> **Interviewer**: What would it be like to play on an all-white soccer team?
> **Child**: They wouldn't treat you like you wanted to be treated….[they'd treat you] dirty, rude, they treat me impolite, too.

This awareness of the racial and ethnic bias within society for youth of color leads to an immersion into the activities of, ideology of, and identification with their ethnic or racial group (Helms, 1995). At this immersion stage, there may be a marked reversal of the prowhite/antiminority attitudes purportedly characteristic of earlier stages of development (Helms, 1995). During this immersion, racial pride is strengthened, and children explore and commit to their racial identification. Examples of this sense of racial pride are reflected in the following responses youth gave to the question, "What does it mean to be black?"

> Child: It means you should respect who you are, what you do, and don't let anybody put you down because of your skin color, and black is a wonderful color to be because I'm proud to be black.

> Child: It means to be proud about who you are and what you are.

> Child: It means to stand up for your rights, and don't let nobody judge who you are. Just believe in yourself.

Concomitant with the development of ethnic and racial identity is the development of an ethnic group consciousness. Youth often interpret social and political events according to this ethnic group consciousness. Consequently, interracial interactions are perceived to be not just interactions between individuals, but between racial groups as well. The history of relations between the groups is used as a filter to interpret interethnic interactions. Youth are keenly aware of how actions of individual members of their ethnic or racial group are perceived to reflect on the entire group:

> Interviewer: Why do some people not like people who are African American?
> Child: Because if a black person did something to them, they'll say all of the other black people will do the same thing.

> Child: Because in school somebody was messing with you that's a black person and that white person might [see the interaction and] not like the rest of the blacks.

> Interviewer: Why do some people not like people who are Mexican American?
> Child: If one [Mexican] did something, it's like all the Mexicans in the world did everything bad.

This sense of ethnic group consciousness can also promote the ingroup cohesion that is important to youth. There is a sense that other members of the ethnic group share important ideological, experiential, and value positions:

> Interviewer: Why do you like having Mexican American friends?

Child: They are Mexican too. They know. They do the same thing you do, come from the same background, and know where you stand.

Child: Mexican Americans stick together, stand by each other, protect each other.

Clearly, a sense of ethnic belongingness is important to many youth, particularly those who are of color. The development of ethnic identity and ethnic group consciousness have important implications for interracial interactions.

Implications for Interracial Cooperation

Adolescents tend to group themselves homogeneously. Social cliques, school organizations, and extracurricular activities are often divided by ethnic and cultural lines (Patchen, 1982). Often in schools, students of one ethnicity or culture tend to participate in only certain organizations and activities. Different groups may congregate in specific activities, with minimal interaction with other groups (Collins, 1979; Sullivan, 1979). This self-segregation makes it difficult for students to form friendships with youth from other ethnic and racial groups (Schofield, 1991; Stephan, 1978). Also, peers may often encourage youth to discriminate against other ethnic and cultural groups (Blanchard et al., 1991; Patchen, 1982). Ethnic segregation in social and academic settings, as well as peer influence, accentuate discrimination during adolescence and hinder interactions among youth from different ethnic, racial, cultural, or socioeconomic groups (Slavin, 1995).

To promote desegregation of schools and social groups, educators should implement multiple strategies. These should include use of a multicultural curriculum, use of cooperative learning groups, and encouragement of participation in different school activities. To increase understanding and attenuate exaggeration of group characteristics, multicultural education should incorporate activities that provide students with opportunities to learn about the characteristics and views of other groups. Examples of such activities include acting out cases of discrimination that can occur in school settings (Breckheimer & Nelson, 1976) and role-playing being a member of another group (Smith, 1990).

In cooperative groups, youth develop new social categories that are not based on typical grouping categories such as ethnicity (Brewer & Miller, 1984; Levine & Campbell, 1972; Schofield & McGivern, 1979). These new social identities help to relieve bias about other groups (Gaertner & Dovidio, 1986; Gaertner et al., 1989). Because cooperative activities provide students with opportunities to reduce bias while recognizing similarities between groups, these activities may lead to newly perceived similarities between people (Schofield, 1995). Also, cooperative learning groups may lessen stereotypes (Schofield, 1995), through participants' viewing members of other groups as individuals rather than as a stereotypical representation of a group (Judd & Park, 1988; Ryan, Judd, & Park,

1996). Once students perceive other groups as similar to their group, they have a greater tendency to develop relationships between different groups during the cooperative group activities (Miller & Harrington, 1992). In general, cooperative learning groups provide students with the opportunity to form friendships outside their own ethnic or cultural groups.

Other methods of promoting positive group interactions among groups of youth include desegregating school activities and organization. One method of desegregating schools is by encouraging all students to participate in extracurricular activities that support positive group interactions, such as band and theater (Schofield, 1995). Research has found that children who play sports are more likely to have cross-ethnic friendships and more positive racial attitudes (Hallinan & Teixeira, 1987; Patchen, 1982; Slavin & Madden, 1979). In addition to encouraging participation, educators should help reduce barriers that prevent some children from participating. Barriers include economics as well as transportation issues. Many low-income children are unable to pay for activity costs, such as instruments, uniforms, or costumes. Also, some children have difficulty finding transportation between the activities and home. Overcoming these economic barriers may promote greater interactions among children of different ethnic, racial, and economic backgrounds.

It may be tempting to assume, in the interest of intergroup cooperation, that all forms of segregation should be discouraged. In relation, it may be assumed that racial pride suppresses interest in forming relationships with members of other racial groups. Some research, however, shows that the reverse may be true (Quintana et al., 1999). This research indicated that children who were low in racial pride tended to endorse segregation strategies at higher rates than children who were high in racial pride. Indeed, use of segregation strategies seemed to have been attempts by children of color to repair racial pride that had been assaulted by racial discrimination. Segregation may offer some refuge from racial discrimination and may offer opportunities to instill pride in a stigmatized group. Conversely, those children in Quintana et al.'s (1999) study who were most comfortable with their racial status expressed the most interest in forming interracial relationships. Consequently, interracial cooperation may be promoted by encouraging activities that support the development of racial pride. It is important to note that these activities need not be segregated—rather, celebrations and recognitions of minority cultures may be even more powerful if they are culturally integrated. These kinds of activities, which if integrated may promote forms of racial pride in minority groups, encourage interracial contact and understanding of minority cultures by ethnic majority youth. These conditions could set the stage for enhancement of interracial friendships.

CONCLUSION

Remarkable changes occur in children's understanding of race and ethnicity through the school years. Children start off with rather naïve, confused conceptions of ethnicity and race and leave adolescence with sophisticated understandings of the social implications of race and ethnicity. Earlier emphasis on objective markers of ethnicity and race, such as skin color, yield to greater emphasis on to subjective features, including ethnic identity, expression of racial pride, and ingroup and outgroup social affiliations. In essence, each stage of development brings a new dimension to children's definition of ethnicity and race. Children in early childhood add a literal dimension (i.e., understanding of heritage and some literal features of culture) to the physical definition typical of pre-school-age children. During middle childhood, children add a social dimension to their understanding of the literal features of ethnicity. During adolescence, youth incorporate the importance of subjective features (e.g., ethnic affiliation and expression of pride) to the essentially objective definition of ethnicity that was in operation throughout most of childhood.

Educators, service workers, and other professionals should be conversant in each of these dimensions to respond in a developmentally sensitive manner to children. The biggest lesson of the research interviews is that children and youth have much to say about ethnicity and race in their lives. Children, particularly adolescents, felt that their exploration of these issues had been hampered by an apparent taboo in our society against having frank, honest, and personally engaging discussions about difficult issues involved in ethnicity and race. Dialogues about race and ethnicity typically occur only with like-minded peers, with the attitudes and misconceptions expressed in these contexts rarely, if ever, being challenged. Some discussions about race and ethnicity can occur in integrated settings resulting in learning by members of ethnic minority and majority groups alike.

Research has consistently and powerfully indicated the success of desegregation programs that include Allport's (1954) four essential ingredients in many different contexts, such as the armed forces and public housing (Pettigrew, 1998). Research also suggests that programs that fail to include these four components often result in interracial conflict. It is important, therefore, to note that intergroup contact in and of itself will not necessarily lead to positive effects. Rather, the four essential ingredients are believed to promote intergroup cooperation because they allow participants to (a) learn about the other groups, (b) get reinforcement for participants' changing their behavior toward members of other groups, (c) develop positive affective ties and form personal friendships, and (d) reappraise their ingroup standards, realizing that their customs and norms are not the only legitimate ones (Pettigrew, 1998).

Research has been able to reconcile an apparent conflict in the literature. Specifically, it has been known that intergroup contact is facilitated when group differences are not made salient and where similarities among individuals are emphasized. Intergroup contact situations in which group differences are not salient, however, has not resulted in prejudice against the other group. That is, when group differences are minimized, members of the other group are seen as not being representative of their larger group, which means that attitudes toward them as individuals are not generalized to their group. Conversely, intergroup contact that makes group differences salient results in positive attitudes being generalized to the larger outgroup. In these latter situations, participants in the contact situation are seen as representatives of their respective groups and thereby, the attitudes can be generalized.

Pettigrew (1998) recommended a solution to this apparent dilemma: The initial stages of intergroup contact can minimize group differences, but over time group differences can become more salient. For example, an interracial club may begin by emphasizing the common interests that all members share. As the club develops cohesion, racial differences may be increasingly emphasized so that members can generalize their positive feelings about fellow club members beyond members of the club. Programs designed to increase intergroup cooperation and understanding need to include Allport's (1954) four conditions to be successful. Moreover, these programs can be more powerful by successfully challenging participants to recognize and learn about group differences. The research about children's psychological experiences of ethnicity and intergroup contact indicates the complexity of designing programs to promote intergroup cooperation and understanding. This research and theory, by managing this complexity, also provides reason for optimism for the efficacy of these efforts.

REFERENCES

Aboud, F. E. (1987). The development of ethnic self-identification and attitudes. In J. S. Phinney & M. J. Rotheram (Eds.), *Children's ethnic socialization* (pp. 32–55). Newbury Park: Sage.

Aboud, F. E. (1992). Conflict and group relations. In C. U. Uhlinger & W. W. Hartup (Eds.), *Conflict in child and adolescent development. Cambridge studies in social and emotional development* (pp. 356–379). New York: Cambridge University Press.

Aboud, F. E. (1993). The developmental psychology of racial prejudice. *Transcultural Psychiatric Research Review, 30,* 229–242.

Alejandro-Wright, M. N. (1985). The child's conception of racial classification: A socio-cognitive model. In M. B. Spencer, G. K. Brookins, & W. R. Allen (Eds.), *Beginnings: Social and affective development of black children* (pp. 185–200). Hillsdale, NJ: Erlbaum.

Allport, G. W. (1954). *The nature of prejudice.* Cambridge, MA: Addison-Wesley.

Aronson, E., & Gonzales, A. (1988). Desegregation, jigsaw, and the Mexican American experience. In P. A. Katz & D. A. Taylor (Eds.), *Eliminating racism: Profiles in controversy* (pp. 301–314). New York: Plenum Press.

Banks, J. S. (1988). *Multiethnic education: Theory and practice.* Boston: Allyn & Bacon.

Banks, J. S. (1993). Multicultural education for young children: Racial and ethnic attitudes and their modification. In B. Spodek (Eds.), *Handbook of research on the education of young children* (pp. 236–250). New York: Macmillan.

Blanchard, F. A., Lilly, T., & Vaughn, L. A. (1991). Reducing the expression of racial prejudice. *Psychological Science, 2,* 101–105.

Bossert, S. T. (1989). Cooperative activities in the classroom. In E. Z. Rothkopf (Ed.), *Review of research in education* (Vol. 15, pp. 225–250). Washington, DC: American Education Research Association.

Branch, C., & Newcombe, N. (1980). Racial attitudes of black preschoolers as related to parental civil rights activism. *Merrill-Palmer Quarterly, 26,* 425–428.

Brannon, L. (1996). *Gender: Psychological perspectives.* Allyn and Bacon: Boston.

Breckheimer, S. E., & Nelson, R. O. (1976). Group methods for reducing racial prejudice and discrimination. *Psychological Report, 39(3),* 1259–1268.

Brewer, M. B., & Miller, N. (1984). Beyond the contact hypothesis: Theoretical perspectives on desegregation. In N. Miller and M. B. Brewer (Eds.), *Groups in contact: The psychology of desegregation* (pp. 281–302). Orlando, FL: Academic Press.

Byrne, D. (1961). The influences of propinquity and opportunities for interaction on classroom relationships. *Human Relations, 14,* 63–69.

Byrnes, D. A., & Kiger, G. (1990). The effect of a prejudice-reduction simulation on attitude change. *Journal of Applied Social Psychology, 20,* 341–356.

Clark, K. B., & Clark, M. P. (1940). Skin color as a factor in racial identification and preferences in Negro children. *Journal of Negro Education, 19,* 341–350.

Collins, T. W. (1979). From courtrooms to classrooms: Managing school desegregation in a Deep South high school. In R. C. Rist (Eds.), *Desegregated schools: Appraisals of an American experiment* (pp. 89–114). New York: Academic Press.

Crocker, J., & Major, B. (1989). Social stigma and self-esteem: The self-protective properties of stigma. *Psychological Review, 96,* 608–630.

Cross, W. E., Jr. (1995). The psychological of nigrescence: Revising the Cross model. In J. G. Ponterotto, J. M. Casas, L. A. Suzuki, & C. M Alexander (Eds.), *Handbook of multicultural counseling* (pp. 93–122). Thousand Oaks, CA: Sage.

Demo, D. H., & Hughes, M. (1990). Socialization and racial identity among black Americans. *Social Psychological Quarterly, 53,* 361–374.

DeVries, D. L., Edwards, K. J., & Slavin, R. E. (1978). Biracial learning teams and race relations in the classroom: Four field experiments on Teams-Games-Tournament. *Journal of Educational Psychology, 70,* 356–362.

Doyle, A., & Aboud, F. E. (1995). A longitudinal study of white children's racial prejudice as a social-cognitive development. *Merrill -Palmer Quarterly, 41,* 209–228.

Doyle, A. B., Beadet, J., & Aboud, F. E. (1988). Developmental patterns in the flexibility of children's ethnic attitudes. *Journal of Cross Cultural Psychology, 19,* 3–18.

Feagin, J. R., & Vera, H. (1995). *White racism.* Routledge: New York.

Finkelstein, N. W., & Haskins, R. (1983). Kindergarten children prefer same-color peers. *Child Development, 54,* 502–508.

Gaertner, S. L., & Dovidio, J. F. (1986). The aversive form of racism. In J. F. DoDovidio & S. L. Gaertner (Eds.), *Prejudice, discrimination, and racism* (pp. 61–89). New York: Academic Press.

Gaertner, S. L., Mann, J., Murrell, A., & Dovidio, J. F. (1989). Reducing intergroup bias: The benefits of recategorization. *Journal of Personality and Social Psychology, 57,* 239–249.

García Coll, C., Crnic, K., Lamberty, G., Wasik, B. H., Jenkins, R., García , H. V., et al. (1996). An integrative model for the study of developmental competencies in minority children. *Child Development, 67,* 1891–1914.

Gopaul-McNicol, S. (1995). A cross-cultural examination of racial identity and racial preference of preschool children in the West Indies. *Journal of Cross-Cultural Psychology, 26,* 141–152.

Hallinan, M. T., & Teixeira, R. A. (1987). Students' interracial friendships: Individual characteristics, structural effects and racial differences. *American Journal of Education, 95,* 563–583.

Helms, J. (1995). An update of Helms' white and people of color racial identity models. In J. G. Ponterotto, J. M. Casas, L. A. Suzuki, & C. M Alexander (Eds.), *Handbook of multicultural counseling* (pp. 181–198). Thousand Oaks, CA: Sage.

Hirschfeld, L. A. (1994). The child's representation of human groups. *Psychology ofLearning and Motivation, 31,* 133–185.

Holmes, R. M. (1995). *How young children perceive race.* Thousand Oaks, CA: Sage.

Idle, T., Wood, E., & Desmarais, S. (1993). Gender role socialization in toy play situations: Mothers and fathers with their sons and daughters. *Sex-Roles, 28,* 679–691.

Johnson, D. J. (1992). Developmental pathways: Toward an ecological theoretical formulation of race identity in black-white biracial children. In M. P. P. Root (Ed.), *Racially mixed people in America* (pp. 37–49). Newbury Park, CA: Sage.

Johnson, D. W., & Johnson, R. T. (1992). Positive interdependence: Key to effective cooperation. In R. Hertz Lazarowitz & N. Miller (Eds.), *Interaction in cooperation groups* (pp. 174–199). Cambridge, UK: Cambridge University Press.

Judd, C. M., & Park, B. (1988). Outgroup homogeneity: Judgements of variability at the individual and group levels. *Journal of Personality and Social Psychology, 54,* 778–788.

Katz, P. A. (1983). Developmental foundation of gender and racial attitudes. In R. Leahy (Ed.), *The child's construction of social inequality* (pp. 41–78). New York: Academic Press.

Leahy, R. L. (1983). The child's construction of social inequality: Conclusions. In R. L. Leahy (Ed.), *The child's construction of social inequality* (pp. 41–78) New York: Academic Press.

Levine, R. A., & Campbell, D. T. (1972). *Ethnocentrism: Theories in conflict, ethnic attitudes, and group behavior.* New York: John Wiley & Sons.

Lips, H. M. (1988). *Sex & gender: An introduction.* Mountain View, CA: Mayfield.

Lobel, T. E., Bempechat, J., Gewirtz, J. C., Shoken-Topaz, T., & Bashe, E. (1993). The role of gender-related information and self-endorsement of traits in preadolescents' inferences and judgments. *Child Development, 64,* 1285–1294.

Maccoby, E. E. (1990). Gender and relationships: A developmental account. *American Psychologist, 45,* 513–520.

Matute-Bianchi, M. E. (1986). Ethnic identities and patterns of school success and failure among Mexican-descent and Japanese-American students in a California high school: An ethnographic analysis. *American Journal of Education, 95,* 233–255.

McAdoo, J. L. (1970). *An exploratory study of racial attitude change in black preschool children.* Ph.D. dissertation, University of Michigan, Ann Arbor. (University Microfilms 71-4677).

McAdoo, J. L. (1985). Modification of racial attitudes and preferences in young black children. In H. P. McAdoo & J. L. McAdoo (Eds.), *Black children: Social, educational and parental environments* (pp 243–256). Newbury Park, CA: Sage.

Miller, N., & Harrington, H. J. (1992). Social categorization and intergroup acceptance: Principles for the design and development of cooperative learning teams. In R. Hertz-Lazarowitz & N. Miller (Eds.), *Interaction in cooperation groups* (pp. 203–227). Cambridge, UK: Cambridge University Press.

Milner, D. (1975). *Children and race.* Harmondsworth, UK: Penguin.

Ogbu, J. U. (1994). From cultural difference to differences in cultural frame of reference. In P. M. Greenfield & R. R. Cocking (Eds.), *Cross-cultural roots of minority child development* (pp. 365–392). Hillsdale, NJ: Lawrence Erlbaum.

Patchen, M. (1982) *Black-white contact in schools: Its social and academic effects.* West Lafayette, IN: Purdue University Press.

Peters, M. E. (1985). Racial socialization of young black children. In H. P. McAdoo & J. L. McAdoo (Eds.), *Black children: Social, educational and parental environments* (pp 159–173). Newbury Park, CA: Sage.

Pettigrew, T. F. (1998). Intergroup contact theory. *Annual Review of Psychology, 49,* 65–85.

Phinney, J. S. (1989). Stages of ethnic identity development in minority group adolescents. *Journal of Early Adolescence, 9,* 34–49.

Porter, J. D. R. (1971). *Black child, white child: The development of racial attitudes.* Cambridge, MA: Harvard University.

Quintana, S. M. (1994). A model of ethnic perspective taking ability applied to Mexican-American children and youth. *International Journal of Intercultural Relations, 18,* 419–448.

Quintana, S. M. (1998). Children's developmental understanding of ethnicity and race. *Applied & Preventive Psychology, 7,* 27–45.

Quintana, S. M., & de Baessa, Y. (1996, March). *Autoestima, preferencia, y concocimiento etnico en niños Quichés* [Ethnic self-esteem, preference, and knowledge in Quiché children]. Guatemala City, Guatemala Fondo de las Naciones Unidas para la Infancia, UNICEF.

Quintana, S. M., Vera, E., & Cooper, C. (1999, August). *African-American children's racial identity and inter-racial coping strategies.* Poster presentation at the American Psychological Association, Boston, MA.

Quintana, S. M., Ybarra, V. C., Gonzalez-Doupe, P., & de Baessa, Y. (2000). Cross-cultural evaluation of ethnic perspective-taking ability in two samples: US Latino and Guatemalan Ladino children. *Cultural Diversity and Ethnic Minority Psychology, 6,* 334–351.

Ramsey, P. G. (1987). Young children's thinking about ethnic differences. In J. S. Phinney & M. J. Rotheram (Eds.), *Children's ethnic socialization* (pp. 56–72). Newbury Park: Sage.

Rowe, D. C., Vazsonyi, A. T., & Flannery, D. J. (1994). No more than skin deep: Ethnic and racial similarity in developmental process. *Psychological Review, 101,* 396–413.

Ryan, C. S., Judd, C. M., & Park, B. (1996). Effects of racial stereotypes on judgement of individuals: The moderating role of perceived group variability. *Journal of Experimental Social Psychology, 32,* 71–103.

Scherer, J., & Slawski, E. (1979). Color, class, and social control in an urban school. In R. C. Rist (Ed.), *Desegregated schools: Appraisals of an American experiment* (pp. 117–153). New York: Academic Press.

Schofield, J. W. (1979). The impact of positive structured contact on intergroup behavior: Does it last under adverse condition? *Social Psychology Quarterly, 42,* 280–284.

Schofield, J. W. (1982). *Black and white in school: Trust, tension or tolerance?* New York: Praeger.

Schofield, J. W. (1989). *Black and white in school: Trust, tension, or tolerance?* (2nd ed.). New York: Teacher College Press.

Schofield, J. W. (1991). School desegregation and intergroup relations: A review of the research. In G. Grant (Ed.), *Review of research in education* (Vol. 17, pp. 335–409). Washington, DC: American Educational Research Association.

Schofield, J. W. (1995). Promoting positive intergroup relations in school settings. In W. D. Hawley & A. W Jackson (Eds.), *Toward a common destiny: Improving race and ethnic relations in America* (pp. 257–289). San Francisco: Jossey-Bass.

Schofield, J. W., & McGivern, E. P. (1979). Creating interracial bonds in a desegregated school. In R. G. Blumberg & J. Roye (Eds.), *Interracial bonds* (pp. 106–119). Bayside, NY: General Hall.

Schofield, J. W., & Sagar, H. A. (1977). Peer interaction patterns in an integrated middle school. *Sociometry, 40,* 130–138.

Selman, R. L. (1979). *Assessing interpersonal understanding: An interview and scoring manual in five parts constructed by the Harvard-Judge Backer Social Reasoning Project.* Boston: Harvard-Judge Baker Social Reasoning Project.

Selman, R. L. (1980). *The growth of interpersonal understanding: Developmental and clinical analyses.* San Diego, CA: Academic Press.

Sherif, M., & Sherif, C. W. (1966). *Groups in harmony and tension.* New York: Octagon.

Shiner, R. L. (1998). How shall we speak of children's personalities in middle childhood? A preliminary taxonomy. *Psychological Bulletin, 124,* 308–332.

Slavin, R. E. (1979). Effects of biracial learning teams on cross-racial friendships. *Journal of Educational Psychology, 71,* 381–387.

Slavin, R. E. (1983a). *Cooperative learning.* New York: Longman.

Slavin, R. E. (1983b). When does cooperative learning increase student achievement? *Psychological Bulletin, 94,* 429–445.

Slavin, R. E. (1985). Cooperative learning: Applying contact theory in desegregated schools. *Journal of Social Issues, 41,* 45–62.

Slavin, R. E. (1995). Enhancing intergroup relations in schools: Cooperative learning and other strategies. In W. D. Hawley & A. W. Jackson (Eds.), *Toward a common destiny:Improving race and ethnic relations in American* (pp. 291–314). San Francisco: Jossey-Bass.

Slavin, R. E., & Madden, N. A. (1979). School practices that improves race relations. *American Educational Research Journal, 16,* 169–180.

Slavin, R. E., & Oickle, E. (1981). Effects of cooperative learning teams on student achievement and race relations: Treatment by race interactions. *Sociology of Education, 54,* 174–180.

Smith, A. (1990). Social influence and antiprejudice training programs. In J. Edwards & R. S. Tindale (Eds.), *Social influence processes and prevention, Vol. 1. Social psychological applications to social issues* (pp. 183–196). New York: Plenum Press.

Spencer, M. B. (1983). Children's cultural values and parental children rearing strategies. *Developmental Review, 3,* 351–370.

Stephan, W. (1978). School desegregation: An evaluation of predictions made in *Brown v. Board of Education. Psychological Bulletin, 85,* 217–238.

Sullivan, M. L. (1979). Contacts among cultures: School desegregation in a poly-ethnic New York City high school. In R. C. Rist (Ed.), *Desegregated schools: Appraisals of an American experiment* (pp. 201–204). New York: Academic Press.

Triandis, H. C., Bontempo, R., Villareal, M. J., Asai, M., & Lucca, N. (1988). Individualism and collectivism: Cross cultural perspectives on self-ingroup relationships. *Journal of Personality and Social Psychology, 54,* 323–338.

Vanbeselaere, N. (1987). The effects of dichotomous and cross social categorization upon intergroup discrimination. *European Journal of Social Psychology, 17,* 143–156.

Weiner, M. J., & Wright, F. E. (1973). Effects of understanding arbitrary discrimination upon subsequent attitudes toward a minority group. *Journal of Applied Social Psychology, 3,* 94–102.

Williams, J. E., Best, D. L., Boswell, D. A., Mattson, L. A., & Graves, D. J. (1975). Preschool racial attitude. *Educational and Psychological Measurement, 35,* 3–18.

Williams, J. E., & Morland, J. K. (1976). *Race, color, and the young child.* Chapel Hill, NC: University of North Carolina Press.

Yee, A. H., Fairchild, H. H., Weizmann, F., & Wyatt, G. E. (1993). Addressing psychology's problem with race. *American-Psychologist, 48,* 1132–1140.

CHAPTER 3

WHITE ANTIRACIST IDENTITY DEVELOPMENT
Implications for Multicultural Education

CHRISTINE CLARK

Racism cannot simply be removed from cultural, social, and political arenas by calling for its abolition or by appealing to calls for justice. Because of the entrenched nature of the ideology of whiteness, racism remains an active part of the cultural, social, and political configuration of group relationships that characterize life in the United States (Omi & Winant, 1994). Although dismantling racial constructs remains a future goal, facilitating critical dialogue about these constructs is valuable to the ultimate realization of this goal. This chapter undertakes such dialogue by exploring the progression from racist to antiracist thought and action by whites in the United States and by examining the implications of this progress for multicultural education pedagogy (Clark & O'Donnell, 1999).

BACKGROUND ON WHITE ANTIRACIST IDENTITY DEVELOPMENT

The progression of thinking regarding white antiracist identity development in the United States can be traced through nine major phases from the 1400s to the present day. The phases are: (1) active and passive racism, (2) liberalism and colorblindness, (3) white identity development theory, 4) negative effects of racism on racists, (5) people of color as researchers on white identity, (6) social construction of race and whiteness, (7) critical white studies, (8) white fetishism, and (9) race traitors and new abolitionism. Because this progression weaves in and out of various academic disciplines, fitting neatly into none, it is hard to trace. Furthermore, because the notion of white antiracist identity development is antithetical to the preservation of white supremacy inherent in society as we know it, many of the details of this progression have been obscured throughout history (Ignatiev & Garvey, 1996). Therefore, although this progression is detailed in a developmental manner in this chapter, it is convoluted in practice.

Active and Passive Racism

According to the literature bases in race-related education and training, *active racism* can be defined as the persistent belief in the biological or intellectual superiority of white people. Active racism is also said to describe the deliberate, often physically violent, discriminatory acts perpetrated by active racists against people of color.

Passive racism can be defined as acquiescence to active racism. Passive racists may not articulate the active racist's belief of biological superiority or deliberately engage in discriminatory acts against others in the name of active racism. By not taking an affirmative stance against active racism, however, passive racists facilitate active racist thought and action.

Beginning at least as early as the 1400s, Western European scientists set out to prove biological superiority and inferiority based on race (as well as ethnicity, socioeconomic class, and sex). Despite the fact that their research repeatedly disproved their hypothesis of biological superiority of the white race, they preferred to forge their research, rather than acknowledge results that contradicted this hypothesis (Gould, 1996).

To examine these scientists' motives, researchers must explore the historical context in which they lived. In the 1400s and earlier, Western Europeans voraciously engaged in territorial conquest under the auspices of manifest destiny, the bringing of "civilization" to the "uncivilized" in the name of a higher power (Loewen, 1995; Miller, 1996; Takaki, 1993; Zinn, 1970, 1980). If the masses of Western Europeans thought that Africans and Native Americans were their biological equals, it is unlikely that they would have condoned the ruthless pillage of these people, as well as their homes, communities, and life resources (Loewen, 1995; Miller, 1996; Takaki, 1993; Zinn, 1970, 1980). By socially constructing people of color as less than whites, the tyranny waged against them could be easily rationalized as being for their own good and then dismissed as nothing more than an act of "taming" (Loewen, 1995; Miller, 1996; Takaki, 1993; Zinn, 1970, 1980).

The fictional notion of biological superiority and inferiority based on race, as well as the "scientific" research on which this notion claims to be based, has been comprehensively reviewed, vehemently interrogated, and exhaustively debunked. Despite this, the notion remains reified (Gould, 1996; Herrnstein & Murray, 1994). Most relevant to multicultural education, evidence of its reification can be seen in the persistent use of standardized testing (Bigelow, 1999a, 1999b). Although standardized testing was originally developed to assess student academic weaknesses so that educational accommodations could be made to resolve the weaknesses, it was quickly co-opted for use as a gate-keeping mechanism (Gould, 1996). That is, what was designed as an evaluation instrument is now used as an admission criterion. This means that rather than aiding in the determination of how to educate a student, it is being used to determine if a student should even have access to certain kinds of education (Bigelow, 1999a, 1999b).

For example, one question on a current standardized aptitude test used in pre-K-12 schools asks students to look at a picture depicting five different houses and determine what is missing from them (Gould, 1996). Many students do not live in houses, but rather apartments, hogans, trailer homes, shelters, and so forth. As a result, these students are less prepared to answer this question. Certainly, however, their ability to answer this question has nothing to do with their aptitude for learning (Bigelow, 1999a, 1999b). Yet, missing the answer to this question lowers their overall test score, leading them to be characterized as of lesser aptitude. The implications of this characterization are far reaching. They affect students' self-confidence, determine their access to certain courses, and influence educator attitudes toward them (Nieto, 2000).

In this example, it is clear that the active and passive racism of the 1400s persists today even in education. For this reason, multicultural education suggests alternatives to standardized testing. In particular, it favors portfolio assessment and other nonstandardized forms of assessment of cognitive and noncognitive abilities.

Liberalism and Colorblindness

According to the academic research bases in multicultural education and related fields, liberalism is characterized by the belief that all people, regardless of race, are equally capable. Liberals generally believe that racism existed in the past and persists today and that this disadvantages people of color. Liberals generally do not recognize that in disadvantaging people of color, however, racism advantages white people (Hardisty, 1996). In this way, liberalism can be recognized as a form of passive racism. As a result, liberals generally do not support affirmative action, because they perceive it to actually give an advantage to people of color *over* whites rather than to attempt to give an advantage to people of color to a degree *equal to* whites (Clark & O'Donnell, 1999; Hardisty, 1996).

Instead of through affirmative action, liberals believe that the way to rectify racism is to reward individuals based on merit (Hardisty, 1996). This is because liberals believe that racism is the problem of individuals, a case of "a few bad apples spoiling the bushel," instead of an institutionally produced and reproduced systemic problem (Hardisty, 1996). In rewarding individuals based on merit, liberals argue, everyone must be colorblind. That is, they must ignore, or pretend not to see, a person's color to recognize their capabilities (Lipsitz, 1995). This perspective fails to acknowledge that capabilities are assessed via standards (Bigelow, 1999a, 1999b; Gould, 1996). Given the previous discussion of standardized assessment, it becomes clear that meritocracy is also predicated on active racism, however masked. Unmasked, meritocracy can be seen as a way for white people to "help" people of color to achieve in ways that (a) white people recognize as worthwhile; (b) make white people feel comfortable; (c) do not threaten white people psychologically, ideologically, politically, economically, or physically; and (d) guarantee that white people will remain in the majority of those who are well-educated and professionally employed (Bell, 1992, 1995; Carter, 1990; Goldberg, 1990; Kovel, 1984).

In the 1960s and 1970s, educators commonly remarked that because they were colorblind, they treated all of their students the same (Carter & Goodwin, 1996). To a lesser extent, this proclamation is still heard today. Educators who espouse the liberal colorblind philosophy believe it is possible to ignore or not notice color, although research has proven the contrary (Banks, 1997; Banks & Banks, 1997; Nieto, 2000). They also believe that treating everyone the same means treating everyone equitably. Multicultural education argues the opposite, that to treat students equitably, their individual needs must be recognized and addressed in a unique fashion (Nieto, 2000). In this way, weaknesses become strengths, and all students develop a shared core knowledge base (Clark, 1993). Treating every student the same means reproducing weaknesses over and over again, essentially guaranteeing that those who come into the classroom with the most weaknesses leave the same way and vice versa (Banks, 1997; Banks & Banks, 1997; Nieto, 2000). This, in turn, guarantees the reproduction of the status quo. Multicultural education argues that to rectify racism, differences based on race, as well as other social identity group memberships, must be acknowledged and affirmed in the curriculum so that truly equitable educational outcomes for all students can be achieved (Hooks, 1993; Howard, 1993; Kinchloe & Steinberg, 2000; Mathison & Young, 1995; Paley, 1979).

WHITE IDENTITY DEVELOPMENT THEORY

Formal research on racial identity development emerged in the 1970s and continues today (Bollin & Finkel, 1995; Bonnett, 1996; Bowser & Hunt, 1981; Dennis, 1981; Helms, 1984; 1995; Hardiman, 1979, 1982; McIntosh, 1983, 1992; Rowe, Bennet, & Atkinson; 1994; Tatum, 1992; 1994; Terry, 1981). Racial identity development theory attempts to describe a process by which an individual develops identity based on their racial group membership, or how their racial group membership influences their identity development. Specialized research on specific racial group identity development emerged from the larger body of research on racial identity development in general (Bowser & Hunt, 1981). Research on white racial identity development was pioneered by Hardiman (1979) and Helms (1984).

Hardiman's (1982) research postulates a model of white racial identity development that is sociopolitically rooted, drawing from the field of social justice education, whereas Helms's (1995) research delineates a model of white racial identity development that is more psychosocially located, based on thinking in the fields of counseling, psychology, human services, and applied behavioral sciences. Because multicultural education is grounded in sociopolitics, the Hardiman model is more relevant to the discussion at hand (Nieto, 1998, 2000).

This model suggests that there are four major stages in the racial identity development of white Americans: (1) acceptance of racism, in which acceptance may be active, initiating a racist act, or passive, going along with a racist act; (2), resistance to racism, in which resistance may be passive, avoiding a racist act, or active, confronting a racist act; (3) redefinition; and (4) internalization (Hardiman, 1982).

The model argues that all white Americans, by virtue of their socialization in the institutionally racist United States, come, to some degree very early in life, to actively and passively accept racism. According to the model, one is born into this stage and may function within it for one's whole life (Hardiman, 1979, 1982).

Movement into subsequent stages is developmental and may occur in one of two ways: via informal experiences—circumstantial, usually traumatic, and highly emotionally charged events that have consciousness shattering effect, or via formal experiences—deliberate interaction designed to influence attitudes or behavior. Informal experiences are more likely the catalysts in engendering movement from stage one to stage two (someone in the acceptance of racism stage does not generally enroll in a racism awareness seminar unless they are mandated to do so), whereas formal experiences are more likely the catalysts in producing movement beyond stage two (Hardiman, 1979, 1982).

A circumstantial, traumatic event causes an individual, almost overnight, to rethink his or her whole existence. The individual sees how naive he or she has been and becomes angry at their own shortsightedness. In short, the individual moves into resisting racism, first passively and then later, if the rethinking and associated anger persist, more actively (Hardiman, 1979, 1982).

Once some of the anger subsides, if it does, the individual may begin to seek out ways to redefine racial identity not as only good (a characteristic of a person in the acceptance stage) or as only bad (a characteristic of a person at the resistance stage), but as an integration of both good and bad (Hardiman, 1979, 1982).

Movement into internalization occurs when the individual is able to integrate racial identity with all other identities vis-à-vis socioeconomic class, gender, sexual preference or orientation, and so forth. At this stage, the individual is committed to facilitating other people's movement through the model (Hardiman, 1979, 1982).

The major critique of both Hardiman's (1979) and Helms's (1984) models from the perspective of multicultural education is that they are linear, modernistic, and positivistic (Hidalgo, F., Chávez Chávez, & Ramage, 1996; Kinchloe, Pinar, & Slattery, 1994). That is, they suggest an all-too-neat developmental progression from the first stage to the last. In reality, people may have parts of their identity in all the stages, with perhaps a dominant stage (Clark, 1999). Or, people may have parts of their identity in stages not identified by the models. For example, the models do not address the role of spirituality in the identity development process (Clark, 1999). Furthermore, many people find that the models do not describe their racial identity development experiences. This is not because they are resistant to antiracist identity development, but simply because the models have omissions. For example, the models do not permit identity development that progresses in a circular fashion, in which a similar situation may be encountered many times, but each time from a new vantage point that takes into account learning gleaned from past encounters (Carter, 1990; Clark, 1999).

A more recent critique of these models is that they perpetuate active racism (Ignatiev, 1996; Novik, 1995; Powell, 1996; Scheurich, 1993; Sleeter, 1993a; Wellman, 1993). According to the models, for white people to develop an antiracist identity, they must come to understand that being white is "okay" if one is a "good white person." The models define a good white person as one who has progressed through the model (Hardiman, 1982; Helms, 1995). In this way, the models perpetuate attachment to a white identity and, in so doing, perpetuate white supremacy (Novik, 1995). This is because white people who move through the models become as preoccupied with their status as white antiracists as Ku Klux Klan members become with their status as white racists (Ignatiev & Garvey, 1996). In the end, the system of privileges afforded both groups based on racial identity persists (López, 1996). This will be addressed in greater detail in the next section.

NEGATIVE EFFECTS OF RACISM ON RACISTS

In the 1980s, thought regarding antiracist identity development was marked by a sharp shift (Bowser & Hunt, 1981). The impetus for this shift came from research out of which this thought emerged 10 years earlier, educational psychology, from which the following plea was made: "Perhaps sociologists will oblige us by dropping their preoccupation with the alleged pathologies of Black America and study the very real, corroding sickness of White America" (Young, 1969, p. 87). During this decade and continuing today, researchers began to look at the negative effect of being racist on whites, rather than the negative effect of racism on people of color (Dennis, 1981). In particular, educational psychologists began to look at how racism makes whites sick by trapping them in a personal and political pathology that makes them believe they are better than people of color, a kind of delusions-of-grandeur-based psychosis (Terry, 1981).

Critiques of this perspective have been lobbied by progressive lawyers (Jenkins, 1994). These lawyers fear that if racism is made into a bona fide mental illness, then white people who kill, rape, torture, and assault people of color will claim, as a psychiatric defense, that they suffer from racism and, therefore, can not be held accountable for their actions (Jenkins, 1994; Kairys, 1990).

Despite this critique, multicultural education does believe that the key to rectifying power imbalances based on race, among other things, in society is to rectify them in the curriculum (Bartolomé, 1994; Hidalgo, N., 1993; Pinar, 1993; Sleeter, 1996; Sleeter & McLaren, 1995). For example, if white people learn, from prekindergarten to graduate school, only about the important contributions people who look like them have made to every subject area, and on the other hand, only about the servitude of people who look different, how will they come to value others as they value themselves (Clark, forthcoming)? Furthermore, how will they come to question their own value as they question the value of others? Multicultural education teaches that everyone has glorious and not-so-glorious pasts and presents (Clark, 1993). In this way, all students learn that they are no more important, but also no less important, than anyone else.

PEOPLE OF COLOR AS RESEARCHERS ON WHITE IDENTITY

Rodríguez (1999) suggested that people of color take an interest in studying white people, especially with respect to race, racial identity development, and white antiracist identity development. He pointed out that precisely because of racism, white people have controlled not only their own representation in history and modern-day mass culture, but also that of people of color. Although people of color have begun to reclaim control of their own representations, they have not yet embarked on the journey to claim control of even small aspects of the representations of whites (Fiske, 1994; Takaki, 1987, 1993).

In essence, Rodríguez is advocating that people of color tell history by inserting whites into the history of people of color and depict whites in the present-day in the context of a colorcentric everyday life. Rodríguez suggested that people of color should analyze white people anthropologically, sociologically, psychologically, and so forth. In this way, white privilege is contested both in terms of content and process, furthering the rectification of power imbalances in the curriculum and society discussed previously (Clark, forthcoming).

Multicultural education supports Rodríguez's point of entry into debate by articulating the need for people of color to be designers and implementers of curriculum in every discipline (Clark, forthcoming). The erosion of affirmative action can be seen as a backlash against the reclamation and reconfiguration of historical and modern-day representations of people of color and whites, by people of color, from a colorcentric reference point (Guiner, 1994; Hall, 1991, 1996; Harris, 1993; Shohat & Stam, 1994). This is necessary to maintain the status quo representations of both required to perpetuate active racism and, therefore, white supremacy (Bonnett, 1996; Hall, 1991, 1996).

SOCIAL CONSTRUCTION OF RACE AND WHITENESS

Also in the 1990s, the notion of race as a social construct emerged (Gallagher, 1994; Goldberg, 1990; Keating 1995; López, 1996; Lott, 1993). Anthropologists have long struggled to identify reliable indicators of race in skin color, hair type, body structure, and so forth, to no avail (Takaki, 1987, 1993). That is, any indicator identified was always found across so-called racial groups and, therefore, could not be used to predictably distinguish one from another (Takaki, 1993). In response to this research, anthropologists have generally shifted away from the simplistic, yet constantly reified, notion of race as any kind of scientific indicator of specific group membership (Allen, 1994).

At the same time that anthropologists arrived at this conclusion, López was emerging as a pioneer in the field of critical legal theory (CLT). CLT is a branch of jurisprudence that critiques the law for Eurocentric bias and studies the implications deriving from this (Flagg, 1993; Kairys, 1990). López used CLT to analyze racial identity development vis-à-vis the law. What he has found was that as anthropologists' arguments reifying race eroded, legal ones emerged in their place to maintain white supremacy (López, 1996).

According to López (1996), during the period following the Emancipation Proclamation of 1865 (the theoretical ending of legalized slavery) through to the 1950s, the government developed and enforced a little-known immigration requirement to prevent primarily Asian immigration to the United States. This requirement forced immigrants to the United States to prove that they were either "of African ancestry" or "white." The language here is crucial. Would-be immigrants were *not* forced to prove that they were black or of European ancestry; or black or white; or of African ancestry or European ancestry. Although proving ancestry is a fairly concrete endeavor, although not always easily accomplished, proving that one is a color is certainly not. How does one argue, in a court of law, that one is white? Although López cited a number of plaintiffs, only a very small number were ever granted a day in court. The rest were dismissed based on the plaintiff's "obvious inability" to successfully prove African ancestry or whiteness. It should be noted that of the cases cited, in none did the plaintiffs try to argue that they were of African ancestry. Although this may have been perceived as a harder thing to prove, it is more likely because Asian immigrants to the United States did not want to deliberately subject themselves to Jim Crow segregation (López, 1996).

In a particularly landmark case cited, an Asian plaintiff's white anthropologist expert witness made a scientifically compelling argument, and his white lawyer made an equally compelling political one, as to why he was white, only to have the judge rule against them all (López, 1996). Defending the ruling, the judge argued that although the plaintiff may be white anthropologically or politically, he did not *look* like what "common knowledge" tells "Americans" a white person looks like, and, therefore, he would not be allowed to immigrate (López, 1996).

Race, no longer attributable to a biological reality, became a social construct— a fabrication of legal argument designed to perpetuate the notion of race as a biological reality, and hence, of biological superiority and inferiority based on racial group membership (Gould, 1996; López, 1996). In demystifying race in this way, López's (1996) work set a new precedent for how white antiracist identity development would be characterized. In essence, his work led to a break from discussing white antiracist identity development in terms of white people, instead framing it in terms of the ideology of whiteness.

In essence, López argued that there is no such thing as white people, rather only people who are identified as white based on their appearance and behavior in certain contexts. To illustrate this point, López pointed out that often people identified as white are not even of Western European ancestry, whereas people who are Western European are mistaken as people of color. Hence, white antiracist identity development in this context challenges people identified as white to change their behavior so that their appearance will not automatically afford them white privilege (Ignatiev & Garvey, 1996). In this way, white supremacy is said to erode. This is because once agents of the state (e.g., the police, judges, lawmakers) are stripped of the ability to identify people as white ideologically (i.e., based on the assumption of allegiance to white supremacy predicated on appearance and behavior in certain contexts), the system of rewards these agents are empowered to afford "white" people no longer has exchange value in the state. That is, whiteness is no longer valuable (López, 1996).

This conceptualization of white antiracist identity development is meaningful to multicultural education because it can be applied across social identity group memberships. That is, if race is a social construct, then what about ethnicity, sex, gender, sexuality, and so forth (Sleeter & McLaren, 1995)? In this way, the concept of social construction can be used in multicultural education to further problematize social identity group configurations—their etiology, the degree to which they exist as mere reifications, their exchange value in the context of Eurocentric society, and the effect of their deconstruction on school and society (Cruz, 1996; Harris, 1993; Shohat & Stam, 1994; Sleeter & McLaren, 1995).

CRITICAL WHITE STUDIES

The field of critical white studies (CWS) has emerged in academia in the last five years (Delgado & Stefancic, 1997; Stowe, 1996) from critical race theory (CRT), which came out of critical legal studies (CLS) (Delgado, 1995; Delgado & Stefancic, 1997; Kairys, 1990). CLS can be understood as a new conceptualization of legal jurisprudence, which challenges the Eurocentric notion that the law is a blunt instrument, unbiased and neutral (Kairys, 1990). CLS further challenges the notion that any imperfection in the law is a function of the players within the legal system and the prejudices that they, as individuals, bring to the interpretation and application of the law and the enforcement of the legal system (Kairys, 1990).

CLS, when applied to issues of race exclusively (i.e., separate from the sexist, classist, homophobic aspects of Eurocentrism) is called CRT (Delgado, 1995). Critical race theorists critically examine the law for its specific biases based on race. For example, in the 1950s, Congress enacted the Racketeering Influence and Corrupt Organizations (RICO) statutes and the Greaser Act specifically targeting Italian and Mexican Americans, respectively (Jenkins, 1994; Miller, 1996). In the late 1980s and into the 1990s, Congress expanded RICO and the Greaser Act into what are now referred to as Gang laws, specifically targeting Latino (Mexican, Puerto Rican, and Central and South American) and black (African American and West Indian) male teenagers (Jenkins, 1994; Miller, 1996). Critical race theorists argue that since the founding fathers conceptualized the Constitution, no such statutes, acts, or laws have ever been developed to specifically target whites and white collar criminals (perceived as nonethnic), or what CRT calls corporate gangs and corporate organized crime (Jenkins, 1994; Miller, 1996). If written and then applied without bias, the RICO statutes, Greaser Act, and Gang laws would all find the founding fathers to be repeat offenders (Franklin, 1966; Jenkins, 1994; Miller, 1996; O'Brien, 1996).

CWS is the application of CRT to the antiracist identity development process of people identified as white. CWS literature is oriented to challenging white privilege toward the eradication of racism of white Americans in two ways.

First, many texts examine how the concept of whiteness is constructed to ensure social, political, and economic benefits for whites (López, 1996; Roediger, 1991). For example, this vein of CWS informs multicultural education by encouraging it in its growth to interrogate white privilege more vehemently. Although multicultural education has always required students to challenge their propensities to prioritize what is normative to them (i.e., their own social identity group memberships), CWS asks multicultural education to challenge white students to do this with greater resolve (Nieto, 1998; Pinar, Reynolds, Slattery, & Taubman, 1995; Rosenberg, 1997; Sleeter, 1993b). Because multicultural education grew out of the civil rights movement and ethnic studies research, it was conceived with a focus that prioritized race and socioeconomic class issues in the context of discussing other issues (i.e., gender, sexuality, language, etc.; Nieto, 2000). CWS suggests that multicultural education programs revisit race with more direct critical resolve to engage all students in the contestation of whiteness and the eradication of white privilege (Delgado & Stefancic, 1997).

Second, other texts argue that social and political arrangements may only benefit middle- and upper-class whites and, hence, call for the abolition of whiteness altogether (Ignatiev & Garvey, 1996; Roediger, 1991, 1994). That is, the attention focused on race and the problem of whiteness diminishes the attention necessary for forging interracial allegiances, especially across the working class (Ignatiev & Garvey, 1996; McLaren, 1999).

White Fetishism

Because the field of CWS is growing so rapidly, critics have begun to talk about the phenomenon of "white fetishism" (McLaren, 1999; Nakayama & Krizek, 1995). Simply put, critics wonder if the surge of interest in even critical white studies by leftists genuinely committed to antiracist struggle is but another way dialogue becomes recentered on whiteness (Clark & O'Donnell, 1999; McLaren, 1999). Even dialogue that seriously problematizes whiteness and its social construction taken to an extreme, by dominating the discourse at multicultural education conferences, in multicultural education textbooks, and in the multicultural education classroom, puts whites and their issues at the center again and again (Clark & O'Donnell, 1999).

Clearly, the argument for focusing on eroding white student resistance to multicultural education by prioritizing white identity issues in the multicultural education classroom is compelling (Chávez Chávez, 1995). But as compelling as this argument is, it is also problematic. It exacerbates white supremacy by putting whites and whiteness at the center again—yet another expression of white fetishism. That is, it makes concepts related to whiteness the standard for learning even in the multicultural education classroom where, at least theoretically, the argument has been that surely in this kind of classroom, students of color will finally find their issues and identities centered (Nieto, 2000). This is not said, however, to support a view of multicultural education as compartmentalized ethnic studies curriculum for only students of color, but rather to encourage the ongoing political interrogation of whiteness in the multicultural education classroom (Clark & O'Donnell, 1999).

This said, by integrating the white fetishism critique and the CWS perspective, a dynamic tension is created, from which one can teach about race and whiteness in the multicultural education classroom (Allen, 1994; Clark & O'Donnell, 1999).

RACE TRAITORS AND NEW ABOLITIONISM

The race traitor and new abolitionism philosophy asks, "How did 'white people' become white?" (Ignatiev, 1995). Furthermore, what was the incentive for them to give up being ethnic and become white (Ignatiev, 1995; Niles & Olson, 2000)? The answers to these questions lie in the exchange value of whiteness.

Leaving ethnicity (i.e., Italianness, Irishness, Frenchness, etc.) and, in some cases, race (i.e., Latinoness) behind, affords a person or a people greater access to participation in the social, political, and economic aspects of U.S. society (Giroux, 1996; Roediger 1991, 1994; Segrest, 1994). This is because the exchange value of whiteness has its foundation in white supremacy. Consciously or subconsciously, choosing to ignore or deny nonwhite Anglo Saxon aspects of identity in an effort to assume white Anglo Saxon ones increases human worth (López, 1996). This is because whiteness is a commodity exchanged for social, political, and economic rewards. Giroux (1996) and McLaren (1995), however, have argued that all things nonwhite and Anglo Saxon have been so demonized by white Anglo Saxon control over historical and modern-day representations of these things, that people who embody these nonwhite and Anglo Saxon things have been made fugitive from their ethnicity and race. That is, they run from who they are because who they are has been socially constructed as bad and are, therefore, socially, politically, economically, and psychologically costly. The process by which ethnicity and race are abandoned, then, is not conscious or unconscious per se. Rather, it is the function of deliberate and insidious torture, manifest in the representational master narrative that attacks a person's or people's ethnic and racial psyche—eating away at their cultural pride and infusing self-hatred (Giroux, 1996; McLaren, 1995).

The race traitor and new abolitionism philosophy, articulated by Ignatiev and Garvey (1996), contends that

> the key to solving the social problems of our age is to abolish the white race. Until that task is accomplished, even partial reform will prove elusive, because white influence permeates every issue in U.S. society, whether domes-

tic or foreign....Race itself is a product of social discrimination; so long as the white race exists, all movements against racism are doomed to fail. (p. 10)

Along the same lines, Cone (1986) argued that

if whites expect to be able to say anything relevant to the self-determination of the black community, it will be necessary for them to destroy their whiteness by becoming members of an oppressed community. Whites will be free only when they become new persons—when their white being has passed away and they are created anew in black being. When this happens, they are no longer white, but free. (p. 97)

McLaren (1999), however, cautioned that

becoming non-white is not a "mere" choice, but a self-consciously political choice, a spiritual choice, and a critical choice. To choose blackness or brownness merely as a way to escape the stigma of whiteness and to avoid responsibility for owning whiteness is still very much an act of whiteness. To choose blackness or brownness as a way of politically disidentifying with white privilege and instead identifying and participating in the struggles of non-white peoples is an act of transgression, a traitorous act that reveals a fidelity to the struggle for justice. (p. 43)

Contrary to the philosophy of the white racial identity development, the race traitor and new abolition philosophy suggests that because races exist in a zero sum relationship to one another, the celebration of whiteness in any way, promulgates the desecration of brownness and blackness. Even the celebration of whiteness in the context of white antiracist identity development serves to reinforce white supremacy (McLaren, 1999). In fleshing out this philosophy, McLaren (1999) argued that

the celebration of whiteness in any form is inseverably linked to the peripheralization and demonization of non-whites. White identity serves implicitly as the positive mirror image to the explicit negative identities imposed on non-whites (López, 1996). Even in the case of white U.S. citizens who claim European American identity as a way of avoiding the white versus non-white opposition, such a move is actually based on the double negative of not being non-white. (p. 43)

The race traitor and new abolitionism philosophy does not embrace multicultural education (Ignatiev & Garvey, 1996), nor does it recognize social identity group memberships other than race (i.e., language, sexuality, gender, etc.) that are integral to multicultural education as legitimate sites of sociopolitical struggle (Niles & Olson, 2000). Despite this, the race traitor and new abolitionism philosophy is still relevant to multicultural educators in furthering the problematization of race, racism, whiteness, racial identity development, and white antiracist identity development. Multicultural education requires critical reflection as the basis for informed social action to end injustice (Sleeter, 1996). By providing a deeper and richer body of thought on these concepts, reflection on them will be likewise deepened and enriched. As a result, social justice action promises to consider (a) the complexities of white antiracist identity development; (b) the dire nature of social, political, economic, and psychological realities that persist and grow even more dire with each moment that white supremacy lingers; and (c) the relationship between these two things. The commission of traitorious and abolitionistic acts vis-à-vis white supremacy is foundational to a sociopolitically conceptualized multicultural education (McLaren, 1995; Nieto, 2000; Sleeter, 1996).

IMPLICATIONS OF WHITE ANTIRACIST IDENTITY DEVELOPMENT FOR MULTICULTURAL EDUCATION

Multicultural education is the most contemporary conceptualization of the field of teacher education. It can be described as

> a process of comprehensive school reform and basic education for all students. It challenges and rejects racism and other forms of discrimination in schools and society and accepts and affirms the pluralism (ethnic, racial, linguistic, religious, economic, and gender, among others) that students, their communities, and teachers reflect. Multicultural education permeates the school's curriculum and instructional strategies, as well as the interactions among teachers, students, and parents, and the very way that schools conceptualize the nature of teaching and learning. Because it uses critical pedagogy as its underlying philosophy and focuses on knowledge, reflection, and action (praxis) as the basis for social change, multicultural education promotes democratic principles of social justice. (Nieto, 2000, p. 207)

Multicultural education is a basic, pervasive, antiracist process that is important for all students. It provides education for social justice and critical pedagogy or simply good pedagogy (Nieto, 2000). An important component of multicultural education is education that is multicultural. Education that is multicultural applies the theory and practice of multicultural education across academic levels and disciplines through the comprehensive process of multicultural curriculum transformation. A multiculturally transformed curriculum does for students of color, white female students, and working-class students, among others, what the "canon" does for white, middle-class, male students. That is, it affirms them. The canon affirms white, middle-class, male students in terms of what it teaches, how it teaches it, and how it evaluates learning on it. In so doing, it privileges white, middle-class, male students above all other students; it gives them an advantage. A multiculturally transformed curriculum affirms all students, thereby leveling the playing field. Multicultural curriculum transformation addresses the development of multiculturally oriented curricula content, pedagogical approaches, and methods of evaluating student learning and teaching effectiveness. It also addresses the building of positive relationships between pre-K–12 and higher education faculty and their increasingly diverse bodies of students, and the creation of more supportive educational environments in which that interaction can occur.

Given that more than 90% of all pre-K–12 and higher education faculty, as well as teacher education undergraduate students and doctoral students across disciplines, are white, white antiracist identity development has a number of implications for multicultural education (Chávez Chávez, 1995, 1998; Clark & O'Donnell, 1999). These implications converge on strategies for reducing student resistance to multicultural education.[*] These strategies are discussed in the context of an autobiographical case study and a review of best pedagogical practices.

STUDENT RESISTANCE TO MULTICULTURAL EDUCATION

Most multicultural educators have worked with students who are resistant to multicultural education. In particular, the idea that no one social issue (e.g., racism) or social group membership (e.g., race) is more important than another (e.g., sexual orientation) is generally difficult for all students to embrace, as they tend to feel the issue or group membership they prioritize should be the one everyone does (Nieto, 1998). Student opposition to and nonengagement with multicultural issues is a common topic of discussion among multicultural educators (Chávez Chávez & O'Donnell, 1998; Hooks, 1993; McCarthy & Critchlow, 1993). Narrowing the discussion of the ideas embedded in multicultural education to issues of race, and more specifically antiracism, the composition of students who are not receptive also narrows, converging around almost exclusively white students.

To move the research on student resistance to multicultural education into a discourse of positiveness, the question, What about white students who do not resist multicultural education? emerges. What might be the experiences that cause

---

[*] Faculty resistance to multicultural education will be discussed herein in the context of faculty pre-K–12 and higher education experience as students. A discussion of faculty resistance to multicultural curriculum transformation, a related topic, can be found in the "Multicultural Curriculum Transformation Across Disciplines" (Clark, forthcoming).

or at influence this disposition to develop in whites? How did they move from a racist to an antiracist consciousness? Can these experiences be simulated in a classroom context?

In a previous study (Clark & O'Donnell, 1999), white multicultural educators, who as white students had championed multicultural education even when their white classmates desecrated it, detailed their experiences, the processes of transformation in their racial identity development as white people to an antiracist consciousness, and the implications of this transformation for their work as multicultural educators. The following recounts excerpts from this chapter author's autobiographical case study.

An Autobiographical Case Study: Antiracist Racism and the Struggle to Become More Fully Human*

I was raised to be an antiracist, not an antiracist racist. Although these two things may look very similar at a superficial level, the difference between them is vast and significant. Both confront injustice, but antiracists avoid confronting their own privilege when such confrontation calls them into question, when it costs them something personally.

Antiracists do not own the inevitability of their racism. They believe that in confronting injustice to the degree that they do, they cannot be a racist. They believe the practice of confrontation signifies the antithesis to racism.

Antiracist racists know that even in the practice of confrontation of injustice, they are still racist, and ownership of this inevitability is not sociopathic; it is not in the "Of course I'm a racist, everybody is, so what's the big deal" vein. Rather, it embodies an honest experience of the complexities of the racism occupying one's psyche mediated with a profound commitment to the lifelong confrontation and attempted eradication of it from one's psyche. No matter the terms and context of the struggle, the antiracist racist is forever engaged.

Seeing

To grow up in Grosse Point, Michigan, was to grow up in one of the whitest places in the world. Had it not been for the African American woman my mother hired as a maid, it is likely that I would not have seen, much less had any significant contact with any person of color until I was almost 6, by which time, I understand, my personality would have already been fundamentally established. Strangely, although I believe my mother's unacknowledged and deep-seated racism and classism led to this occurrence, I will be eternally grateful that it did, for I am certain that,

---

* The notion of "struggle to become more fully human" comes from Freire (1980). Most of these excerpts are from the case study previously titled "The Secret: White Lies Are Never Little," published in *Becoming and Unbecoming White: Owning and Disowning a Racial Identity* (Clark & O'Donnell, 1999).

as a result, I became more engaged in the struggle to become an antiracist racist than I ever would have been had this woman not come into my life.

I do not remember a time in my life before Mrs. A was a part of it. Mrs. A was originally from Tennessee. She moved to Detroit with her family. Part of the racism inherent in my relationship with Mrs. A is that she knew everything about me and my family, and to this day, I know virtually nothing about hers. What I do know, such as the fact that she was originally from Tennessee, I learned as an adult, long after the last time I ever saw her.

My mother hired Mrs. A as a maid, a cleaning woman, on the recommendation of some other white family in the area for whom she had worked. Mrs. A came from inner-city Detroit by bus to a stop in the suburbs near where we lived. From there, she walked to and from our house. On occasion, my mother or father picked her up at the stop in our car and brought her to our house and then took her back to the stop at the end of her work day. Usually, this was when the weather was bad, when it was dark outside, or when she did not feel well. Perhaps on occasion, they even did it just to be nice.

My parents' relationship with Mrs. A was very kind, but still very racist. The distance between employer and employee, between white and black, between colonialist and the object of colonialization, was mediated in one very significant way. They called Mrs. A, a woman at least 15 years their senior, "Mary," and she called them "Mr." and "Mrs." To add insult to injury, as a 2-, 3-, and 4-year-old child, I, too, called this woman, at least 55 years my senior, "Mary." When my mother or father talked to my sisters and I about Mrs. A in her absence, we all called her "Mary," so I know our behavior was sanctioned at the institutional level in the family. My mother has said that this was what Mrs. A was comfortable with, as if Mrs. A could have honestly said otherwise without fear of some kind of reprisal. When challenged that she could still have called her "Mrs. A" and had us do so as well, my mother, like so many other typical antiracists, is quick to blame these relationships of power on "the times."

In retrospect, I am horrified by what I know this behavior perpetuated. An African American colleague later told me how important it was to his mother that he and his siblings show respect by referring to all African American people, but especially older African Americans, as "Mr." or "Mrs.," "sir" or "ma'am," or "Mr." or "Miss" plus the person's first name, if they did not know the person's last name. The history his mother conveyed to his siblings and him underlying this non-negotiable request was that adult African American men and women have so often been referred to by white adults, even by white children, without a title, by first name, or worse, by a diminutive or racial epithet, that they were to be given the utmost respect by their own community, especially by children.

I remember Mrs. A as an extremely warm and loving woman who, when she scolded me, never made me feel humiliated in the way I remember feeling when my mother or father did. She was firm but kind and always seemed more comfortable expressing both sentiments with appropriate physical affection. I know that I romanticized the kind of mother I imagined Mrs. A was to her own children in wishing I could be one of them. And yet today, I know as a result of having this feeling about her that I learned that working-class parents (and parents of color) can be better parents than those with greater means (or who are white), who often substitute material things for interpersonal interaction and call it an expression of love.

My specific memories of Mrs. A are few: She taught me to tie my shoes, and she begrudgingly played hide-and-seek with me, all the while complaining that I was wasting her time, keeping her from her work, not to mention making more work for her by messing other things up in an effort to hide. It is these general impressions of her that have meant the most. When we moved, as a going-away gift she gave me a Santa Claus doll animal that, of course, had a white face and blue eyes. It also had a music box inside. With all of the unfixed boundaries around race that existed in my 5-year-old mind at the time, I named the doll, which I still have, after her. This, coupled with my desire to be her child, illustrates the luxury I enjoyed as a white child in thinking about race unconsciously or rather in not thinking about it at all; as a white child, I had the luxury of not having become raced yet, of not knowing that I was raced, and for that matter, that she was raced, too, and what that meant.*

Ironically, around the same time that I was experiencing myself as unraced, or rather not experiencing myself as raced, two critical incidents occurred in my life that forced me to experience and see myself as gendered. I remember the exact moment that I developed a consciousness of myself as a girl, mediated with a consciousness of how men see women as less than men; even 4- and 5-year-old boys somehow understand that they have institutional power and that this power legitimizes their actions against girls. The first time I was 4; the second time, 5. The first time, there were two boys; the second time there were five, all age peers, all upper-middle-class and white, boys whom I considered my friends and playmates.

In both instances, the boys premeditated isolating and cornering me, then pulled my pants down against my will to view my vagina. A week before the first incident, the same two boys tried to drop a brick on my head when I followed them behind a garage to play. This failing, they chained me to a tree, where I

---

* Consciousness and unconsciousness are complex concepts. The notion of unconscious conscious or conscious unconscious (Chávez Chávez, 1998) as employed here is a reference to the affirmation or denial of metacognition, respectively. As a child, I metacognitively affirmed the existence of racism in my unconscious consciousness; I knew it existed. As an adult, I might metacognitively deny that I benefit from racism, refuse to acknowledge my privilege.

remained for three hours until one of my older sisters, who came looking for me at dinnertime, helped me escape.

What is significant about these incidents with respect to my racial identity development is that they raised my awareness about being female, about being "other." Before the first incident, the two boys involved in it were just playmates, and in some vague way, male. Afterward, they were not only not playmates, but in a very confrontative fashion, they were boys and I was a girl. Although I did not immediately understand the parallel to race, this incident set the groundwork for me to see, to grow race conscious, to become white, to become an antiracist racist, not just an antiracist.

Perhaps most significant about my relationship with Mrs. A was how important and unique it was for me and how unimportant and usual I imagine it was for her. I now think of myself as having been just one more spoiled white child who, in enjoying all the attention that I did from her and the benefits I derived from it, took time away from her own children. Because racism exists and is so congruently mediated with classism, she worked for my parents to provide basic support for her family. I imagine that had she and her husband had the same opportunities that my mother and father did, she would rather have been home with her own children than with me. Ironically, and despite the somewhat antifeminist contradiction, my mother could have been home with me instead of Mrs. A.

My oldest sister sent me the book *My Soul is Rested: The Story of the Civil Rights Movement in the Deep South* (Raines, 1977) a few years ago. It is an autobiography of a white man who grew up in the segregated South with, like us and so many other white children from slavery to the present, an African American maid. He subsequently became heavily involved in the civil rights movement and attributes his consciousness in becoming so involved to the presence of this African American woman in his life as a child. My sister and I agree that Mrs. A had a similar effect on our consciousnesses. This is what is so hard to reconcile: Out of some of the most racist historical circumstances, antiracist racist consciousness emerges.

In this way, even as a young child, I experienced myself as in opposition to the collusion in and maintenance of the boundaries of racism, while simultaneously sensing I was inextricably involved in their perpetuation. By never owning my whiteness, the persistence of my racism, and the requirement to confront these boundaries even when it cost me what I was never supposed to allow it to, I remained unraced; without consciousness of culture, norms, and ethnicity; uncritically conscious; forever disengaged with the real, not pathological other; forever patrolling borders, never deconstructing them; and thus eroding the institutionalization of discrimination these borders protect.

Choice

When my family moved to Ohio, our neighborhood was still predominantly white, but not all white. I remember African American families within a block, including the Leverts, of the musical groups "The O'Jays," and "Levert." The public elementary school that I attended was African American and white. It was 1968, and the civil rights movement was hot. The junior and senior high schools in our district abutted the elementary school play yard. As a result, we were heavily influenced by the actions of the "big kids." We saw them interracially dating, so we did, to the degree that first through sixth graders date. Interracial relationships were at least as common as same-race dating. The first three age peers that I can remember as boyfriends were all African American. Although my peers and I experienced ourselves as choosing to cross borders around sexual taboos by having sex, choosing to cross borders around racial taboos by interracially dating, and choosing to cross both kinds of borders in having interracial sex, the extent of our actual choice in doing these things must be juxtaposed with the influence of the big kids. I do not ever remember thinking, "Why am I having sex?," "Why am I interracially dating?," and so forth. I only remember that these were the things to do, so this raises the question of how much choice was involved. Nonetheless, we crossed these borders, at least publicly, as never before in history.

Perhaps one of the most significant racist contradictions in white society is the characterization of an extremely attractive and desirable man as "tall, *dark*, and handsome." My father has always been considered such, especially the dark, part because of his so-called olive-complexioned skin, which allowed him to tan so well. White people head to the beach and to tanning beds in droves to brown, despite the real danger of skin cancer. Whites jokingly compare themselves to African American people in measuring the progress of their tans. We romanticize the virility of a darkly tanned white man, racistly sexualize the virility of an authentically brown African American man, but make taboo the establishment of relationships between white women and African American men whether constructed around "jungle fever" (sexual attraction based on racist sexual stereotypes) or something more significant. We say dark is handsome, but we construct it as the opposite when it is taken to its logical conclusion in blackness.

Interracial platonic friendships were also common in grade school. The choice involved in the development of these relationships was more genuine, predicated on personality similarities and common interests rather than fad and superficiality. My best female friend, Sue, was African American. Sue and I were inseparable and were best friends with another pair of interracial best friends, Robin, who was African American, and Cathy, who was white. The four of us were the girl athletes in the school and the gym teacher's pets.

Robin, Cathy, and I all lived within 10 houses of each other. Sue lived about three miles away in an area that I frequented when shopping with my mother. It was a "blacker" section of town, although still fairly middle-class. The four of us had sleepovers often but always at Robin's, Cathy's, or my house. Sue and I had sleepovers even more often but always at my house.

I remember going to Sue's house only one time. It was very nice, though I sensed in some unconsciously conscious[3] way that it was decorated in a race- and class-related culturally different fashion, African American and middle-class. It had shag carpet and comfortable chrome and leather furniture in the living room, which we were actually allowed to use, unlike at my house, where we were relegated to the basement or my bedroom. There were family pictures every-where. I think Sue's mother might have been a single parent. The fact that I was not sure, as a colleague pointed out, speaks volumes about the racist construc-tion of our friendship. As with Mrs. A, Sue's life outside of school was as much a mystery to me then as it is today.

I called my mother from Sue's house that day to ask to spend the night. I remember the call as if it were yesterday. My mother was unwavering in saying no, no matter how much I begged. It was as if a definitive steel door between me and the experience I perceived at the time might have facilitated my coming to know the secret of antiracist racism was slammed in my face. Here, the choice to not cross a border was made for me; still, I felt responsible. Of course, Sue could come to our house but I could not stay there—period, end of discussion. In retro-spect, I imagine that the reason I was not allowed to stay had something to do with racist, classist assumptions about parental permissiveness. The irony is that Sue's mother was far stricter than my own.

I remember Sue's mother was watching me on the phone to see what my mother would say when I asked, as if she was waiting to confirm a suspicion. I knew at the time by the most subtle and, considering the circumstances, extraordinarily polite innuendo that Sue and her mother took my mother's refusal to be evidence of her and, probably by association, my racism. Of course, they were right. In this instance, we reeked of racism. I also knew, again by innuendo, that by not being able to cross this border at this time, whatever open invitation I had enjoyed with Sue had been revoked. Our friendship was never quite the same after this inci-dent and altogether disintegrated when we entered junior high school, where the race borders among the girls were constructed in concrete.

In contradiction, I also remember two white friends that I had, Susan and Peggy. They both lived about three blocks away. They were more middle class, like Sue, and although the exterior of their houses were as nice as ours (and Sue's), inside was another story—they were always a mess. Furthermore, there was never any supervision when I went to either house—sex, drugs, you name it—not to mention the racial epithets that abounded from their parents' mouths when they occasionally made an appearance. My mother always expressed strong disapproval when I went to visit, and especially sleep over, at these two friends' houses because, I believe, of the racist attitudes to which she suspected I would be exposed. But, she never took the choice of whether I would interact with these friends and cross the class boundaries between us away from me as she had with Sue. I am not sure she knew the extent of the disarray or lack of supervision in Susan's or Peggy's home, but what is interesting is that she did not assume anything in this regard one way or another. What is significant is that she did not know the extent of the order, cleanliness, and strict supervision at Sue's house either, but she assumed the contrary. Had Sue lived in a predominantly white middle-class neighborhood instead of a predominantly African American middle- or even upper-middle-class one, I believe none of this would have ever emerged as an issue. Hence, I learned that my mother's standard of class approval was higher for people of color than it was for whites and that my ability to border cross or not was predicated on this racist standard.

Learning to respect borders as an antiracist racist grew out of these experiences. The enduring pain of the racist betrayal I perpetrated against Sue and her mother serves as a constant reminder to me of the complexities of border politics and has acted as a thermometer for me in all subsequent relationships in discerning whether, when, and in what way it is appropriate to cross the border.

Responsibility

A consequence of becoming an antiracist racist is that associations with whites become difficult at the same time people of color do not always, nor in my opinion should be expected to, embrace you. There is an element of longing to belong somewhere that goes with the commitment to antiracist racist struggle.

Clearly, the antiracist racist responsibility in border walking is phenomenally complex. Often, whites trusted as allies by people of color are let in, able to cross borders in ways that allow them to at least observe if not sometimes participate in, aspects of other life that they would not otherwise come to know. I believe that sometimes we are trusted when we are not ready for, or do not yet fully understand, the responsibility this trust entails. I also believe that sometimes we are let in too far.

For example, perceived as both a nonally and an ally, I have been called "white girl," "honky," "cracker," "white bread," "*blanquita*," "*gringita*," and so forth. As a nonally, I understand this naming to mean that I may not cross the border. As an ally, I understand this naming to mean that I may now, or already have been allowed to cross the border. But, as an antiracist racist, I also understand that in neither context may I use theoretically comparable names for people of color to insult or to embrace. This is part of the "power + prejudice = 'ism" equation (Jackson, 1976). Although all people have prejudice, not all people have access to power at the institutional level in society to enforce these prejudices and create "isms." Racial prejudice and racism are distinguished by the institutional power associated with the latter but absent from association with the former. By virtue of being white and because whites have had disproportionate access to institutional power in the United States, the racial prejudice toward people of color that all whites are socialized, consciously and unconsciously, to essentially embrace is necessarily entrenched in and enforced by our political, economic, and social structures. According to this equation, seemingly parallel actions on the part of a white person and a person of color have different effects. For me to be called a honky by a person of color is simply not the same thing as my calling a person of color a "nigger" or a "spic." My actions are reinforced exponentially by the racism of the superstructure, whereas those of a person of color toward me are not; hence, the latter carries less effect.

I have also been told that I am "black by injection" or called "*negrita*." Again, I understand this naming to mean that I have been allowed to cross the border. I take such naming as an enormous compliment and an expression of support for my being an antiracist racist, which carries with it an enormous responsibility to never forget that I am white and never sell out my commitment to antiracist racist work.

In my last 10 years as a multicultural education professor, I have had an increasing number of white students who express a sense of being let in even further. They have African American friends who call them the theoretically reclaimed version of nigger, "niggah," or "my niggah," as in "my brutha'," "my homeboy," "my homie," and "homecrunch," meaning my good friend. I have students engage in discussion about ingroup and outgroup naming, during which we debate if, even with ingroup naming, terms, phrases, or symbols can be reclaimed from their derogatory etiology and used instead to affirm pride in group membership. I believe that even ingroup naming in the spirit of reclamation is evidence of some kind of internalized self-hatred. I know I feel this about myself when I exchange the word *bitch* with other women in a so-called affectionate fashion. At the same time, I do not presume to tell members of ingroups of which I am not a member how to refer to each other. I do point out to my students, however, that virtually no negative terms, phrases, or symbols are aimed at insulting men as a group, nor have I ever heard white people greet each other with self-directed racially derogatory language like, "Howdy, honky," though the converse is quite common, such as, "what'z up, niggah?" Taken collectively, white male privilege absents white men from this phenomenon, which should make the rest of us think long and hard about why this is.

I have come to draw a line when these same white students go on to tell me that they are also allowed to use the term *niggah* or derivations of it, toward their African American friends. Whites should never be let in this far, nor should we want to be. Respect for the other must involve an understanding of the historical and present-day violence it references. If I am really someone's friend or ally, and if I am really an antiracist racist, this is not a border I would ever cross.

IMPLICATIONS

In discussing myself as an antiracist racist, I am often asked to explain why I am only talking about white people as racist. Certainly people of color are racist or, at least in light of the power plus prejudice equation, have race prejudice too. I find this argument to be at the crux of the race problem. The history of race-related thought has always focused on people of color: how *they* are, what *they* do, what *they* do not do, and so forth. This serves to justify and reinforce the racist attitudes of whites (Dennis, 1981; Terry, 1981). When people of color or an antiracist racist suggest that we refocus that thought onto white people—how *we* are, what *we* do or do not do that perpetuates racism—the white response is indignant. It is amazing just how uncomfortable whites become when asked to look at ourselves and our behavior in relationship to this problem. With lightning speed, we preach to people of color to take responsibility for this and for that, but we fail to hold ourselves to the same standard. We do not practice what we preach. We do not take responsibility for interrupting the individual racist thoughts we have and for the individual and collective racist acts that we initiate and in which we participate, including, both inadvertently and deliberately, socializing children in our racist image.

At least in a consciously unconscious way, I believe white people know we benefit from racism even if we are disadvantaged by being poor, non-English-speaking, female, physically disabled, and so forth. We do not want to admit this benefit, however, because then we might have to go on to admit that it is unjust, at least in the context of a so-called democracy, to enjoy this benefit at the expense of others. But this assumes that becoming an antiracist racist is worse than a zero sum game and that whites must give up all benefit for people of color to gain any. This is why so many white people believe my ongoing struggle to be an antiracist racist must be, at best, a function of altruism gone awry. My profound commitment to this struggle does not permit me to belittle my colleagues in this struggle, both people of color and whites, by engaging in it as nothing more than a glorified "do-gooder." Although I benefit from racism, I benefit a whole lot more from being an antiracist racist. It is in my self-interest, the self-interest of all whites as well as people of color, to engage in a struggle against racism. If I work in cooperation with all people toward a common goal, we all benefit.

I often struggle with how best to get my students, as well as everyone else, to see institutional discrimination so that they will make the choice to take responsibility for ending it. The following are my suggestions for this:

- Be open, look at yourself first, and engage in self-critique.

- Have others take a look at you, and allow yourself to be critiqued by others.

- Critique white people.

- Challenge yourself, leave your comfort zone, and seek out experiences that involve taking intellectual and emotional risks.

- Ask yourself what it would mean for you if the experiences and perceptions that others have of the world, with which you have historically disagreed, were true.

- Interrogate the notion of privilege deriving from superiority, do not allow yourself this rationalization, and seek other explanations.

- Recognize the seductive nature of privilege and the mechanisms in society that encourage you to passively accept it and not to question it or act against it. Fight the constant risk of being co-opted by white supremacy.

- Refuse to enjoy the luxury afforded whites who choose not to deal with racism 24 hours a day, seven days a week.

- Educate yourself, knowing that intellectual understanding of racism is never the same as organic experience of it. You can never be an expert on someone else's experience .

- Ask yourself if you would have had the same experience in whatever situation if you were not white; how might a person of color have felt or been treated in the same instance, place, circumstance?

- Do not expect others to educate you.

- Expect whites to reject you.

- Do not expect people of color to accept you.

- Expect to be lonely.

- Develop antiracist racist allies to help you stay strong.

- Struggle to understand the sociopolitical context of oppression. Understand that we cannot just all get along because of the historically constructed and constantly perpetuated opportunity structures in society that disadvantage some while privileging others based on group membership. Recognize that this must be understood before we can begin dialogue and action about getting along. Recognize that this action must begin with the interrogation, reparation, and eradication of oppression.

- Always interrupt oppression in some way. Develop a repertoire of strategies for doing this most effectively in any and every context.

- Deal with the individual not their group membership. At the same time, do not disregard the importance of group membership for the individual.

- Find common ground.

- Ask someone how they feel about or what they think about something.

- Be committed, stay committed, do not give up, never give up.

- Treat others with dignity and respect; do not allow yourself to lose respect others nor for others to lose it with you.

- Struggle to become more fully human.

CONCLUSION

The struggle to become more fully human is integrally linked with the antiracist racist struggle; I would argue that the former informs the latter. But neither struggle can be clearly defined—that is, there is no one way to engage in these struggles or integrate them. Rather, each of us has to decide what these struggles mean to us and engage in them accordingly. I have defined these struggles as being guided by the principles of seeing, choice, and responsibilities, what others have called "the ontological," "the epistemological," and "the axiomatic" or the "to know," the "to be," and the "to know how to do the right thing" (Chávez Chávez, 1998). Whatever guiding principles we name for ourselves, the ultimate test of our level of engagement in these struggles is our willingness to maintain our commitment to them even when it costs us something personally. We need to begin to ask ourselves, how much is enough? Does, for example, one individual really need 40 billion dollars? Should insurance companies control health care decisions, turning health maintenance into sickness management? Should there be restrictions on, penalties for, or elimination of corporate capital flight? When will we become fully human enough to embrace these questions? Furthermore, when will we act in accordance with our answers to these questions toward the realization of full humanness for everyone? It is toward these ends that this autobiographical case study is directed.

ANALYSIS

This case study illustrates the process by which one white student turned multicultural educator moved from a racist to an antiracist consciousness. Combining the learning from this case study with that from a literature review, three primary pedagogical practices emerge as best for facilitating movement through this process: (1) problem-posing pedagogy and reflective journaling, (2) whiteness instead of racism as a point of entry into debate, and (3) creating oppositional spaces to fight for equality and social justice (Bidell & Lee, 1994; Carter, 1990; Carter & Goodwin, 1996; Clark & O'Donnell, 1999; Frankenberg, 1993; Gaertner, 1976; Giroux, 1992, 1993, 1996, 1997; Gorski, 1998; Haymes, 1995; Hidalgo, 1993; Howard, 1993; Lawrence, 1997; Lawrence & Bunche, 1996; McIntyre, 1997; McLaren, 1995; Powell, 1996; Sleeter, 1993a, 1996; Sleeter & McLaren, 1995).

Problem-Posing Dialogue and Reflective Journaling

Problem-posing dialogue is a pedagogical approach in which educators ask students carefully crafted questions in relationship to course content to elicit critically conscious, as opposed to pat, responses (Freire, 1980, 1990). In using problem-posing dialogue, educators exchange the notion of teaching as *telling* for teaching as *showing*. That is, instead of teachers giving students information, they guide students to discover it (Freire, 1980, 1990).

To engage students in problem-posing dialogue, educators must give up the notion of teaching as mastery (Freire, 1980, 1990). As classrooms become increasingly diverse, the reality that students will undoubtedly have more knowledge about particular subjects than educators do simply because of their different life experiences must be confronted. Educators should not assume, however, that students have this knowledge simply because of their experiences (Nieto, 2000). This recognizes the reciprocity of the teaching/learning relationship.

Given this, it makes more sense to think of educators as facilitators of the process of learning who actively involve students in this process (Freire, 1980, 1990). To do this, educators must ask students what they already know about a particular subject to make sure that the information is new to students and challenges them. Next, students must have demonstrated that they already have knowledge about many things of which they may be unaware. In addition, educators must ask students what they want to learn about a subject (Freire, 1980, 1990).

With this mindset and information in hand, educators can engage students in problem-posing dialogue by asking them questions that cause them to think critically, relative to knowledge that they already possess, to arrive at answers about this body of information. In this way, educators no longer look on students, and they no longer see themselves, as empty receptacles into which deposits of information are made. Instead, students become critical agents in their own education (Freire, 1980, 1990). In this way, students are made responsible and take responsibility for their own learning.

In the context of facilitation, educators must think consciously and carefully about their power and how it advantages some student perspectives while disadvantaging others (in both positive and negative ways, as well as deliberate and inadvertent ways). Educators must think about how their voices as facilitators can silence students or encourage them to speak (Zúñiga, Nagda, & Sedvig, forthcoming).

Reflective journaling involves students in the thoughtful, written recording of their daily reactions to their multicultural educational experience (Connelly & Clandnin, 1990). Reflective journaling is like keeping a diary, but in addition to recording reactions to experiences, students record self-critical analyses of their reactions (Connelly & Clandnin, 1990). In particular, having students alternate between recording general reactions to each class and responding to specific problem-posing questions that emerge in each class encourages them to engage in self-critique regarding their own identity development process.

Both problem-posing dialogue and reflective journaling facilitate student movement from racist to antiracist consciousness. Important, specific, problem-posing questions to garner responses from students of any race, whether in the context of the dialogue or the journaling, are:

- Why did you take this class? What did you hope would come out of it? What did you hope you would get out of it?

- What does it mean to you for someone to be white? How do you experience whiteness in yourself or in others?

- What does it mean to you to be racist? Would you call yourself a racist? Why or why not?

- What relationship, if any, do you see between whiteness and racism?

- What do the phrases *individual racism, cultural racism,* and *institutional racism* mean to you?

- What does it mean to you for a white person to be labeled a racist? Are all white people racist? If so, why? If not, how do you distinguish those who are from those who are not?

- What do you think is the role, if any, of whites in addressing racism?

- How do you view white people or other white people in relation to yourself?

- How do you view white people who appear to be racist because of their words or actions, in relation to yourself?

- What do you do or not do that is racist?

- How are you a part of the problem?

- How do you understand the notion of white privilege?

- How do you understand the concept of the exchange value of whiteness in relationship to the notion of white privilege?

- How do you understand the phrase the *transparency of whiteness*?

- What role, if any, do whites have in educating each other about racism and white privilege?

- Do people of color have a responsibility to educate whites about racism and white privilege or do they bear the burden of having to do this? Both? Neither? Why or why not?

- What do you think the relationship is, if any, between racism and fear?

- Do you think that white people fear people of color? If so, what do you think causes this fear? What do you think, if anything, can get white people past this fear?

- What can you do or change to reduce or eliminate racism? How are you a part of the solution?

- Important specific questions to garner answers from students of color to are:

- Is there anything you want to hear from white people about racism? If so, what? If not, why?

- Do you feel like you are being forced to deal with this topic, like it or not? That is, is this just another approach for trying to get white people to understand racism that promises to give people of color hope for change, but will likely change things very little?

- Can you trust a white person with whom you are closest with regard to race issues as much as you could trust a person of color you just met? Why or why not?

Whiteness Instead of Racism as a Point of Entry into Debate

Giroux (1997) examined the pedagogical complexities posed by whiteness as a social construct for multicultural educators and stated:

> I am concerned about what it means educationally for those of us who engage in an antiracist pedagogy and politics to suggest to students that whiteness can only be understood in terms of the common experience of white domination and racism. What subjectivities or points of identification become available to white students who can only imagine white experience as monolithic, self-contained, and deeply racist? What are the pedagogical and political stakes in rearticulating whiteness in anti-essentialist terms as part of a broader new discourse of ethnicity, so that white youth can understand and struggle against the long legacy of white racism while using the particularities of "their own culture as a resource for resistance, reflection, and empowerment?" (Hall, 1991, p. 57).
>
> At the same time, there are too few attempts to develop a pedagogy of whiteness that enables white students to move beyond positions of guilt or resentment. There is a curious absence in the work on whiteness regarding how students might examine critically the construction of their own identities in order to rethink whiteness as a discourse of both critique and possibility. Educators need to connect whiteness with a new language of ethnicity, one that provides a space for white students to imagine how whiteness as an ideology and social location can be progressively appropriated as part of a broader politics of social reform. Theorizing the relationship between ethnicity and identity enables students to both locate themselves in society and construct temporary points of belonging and orientation. Central to such a task is the political and pedagogical challenge of refashioning an antiracist politics that informs a broader, radical, democratic project. (p. 314)

Giroux (1997) concluded that multicultural education pedagogy vis-à-vis white antiracist identity development must distinguish between *whiteness* and *people identified as white.* In this way, white student resistance to antiracist education is reduced, as multicultural educators engage with white students against whiteness, instead of with racism against them. That is:

> Analyzing whiteness opens a theoretical space for teachers and students to articulate how their own racial identities have been shaped within a broader racist culture and what responsibilities they might assume for living in a present in which whites are accorded privileges and opportunities (though in complex and different ways) largely at the expense of other racial groups (p. 314, emphasis added).

At the core of reducing student resistance to multicultural education and, more specifically, white student resistance to the antiracist piece of multicultural education, is the notion of making the other *us*, and not *them* (Rorty, 1989). In the multicultural education classroom, all students feel like the other from time to time, but white students feel like the other most of the time (Clark & O'Donnell, 1999). Ironically, the multicultural education classroom is one of the few contexts in which whites ever feel like the other (Clark & O'Donnell, 1999). People of color not only feel like the other, but are, in fact, marginalized, virtually all of the time (Omi & Winant, 1994). In fact, for people of color, the multicultural education classroom is one of the few places that they are not marginalized all the time (Nieto, 2000). Given this, multicultural educators have the difficult task of balancing white students' needs to always feel like *us*, with the needs of students of color to not always feel like *them* (Giroux, 1997). Creating the right mix of challenge and affirmation for all students is paramount to the development of white antiracist consciousness (Clark & O'Donnell, 1999). Because no formula or recipe for creating this mix exists, multicultural educators must practice dialogical trial and error over the duration of each course, to arrive at the unique combination of challenge and affirmation that will develop in every student the predisposition to develop an antiracist identity (Clark, 1999).

Creating Oppositional Spaces to Fight for Equality and Social Justice

No one incident or revealed contradiction will make students shed their blinders to the realities of racism and white privilege (Clark & O'Donnell, 1999). Only a series of incidents and revealed contradictions, informal (inadvertently experienced) and formal (sought out), enable students to see (Hardiman, 1982). Toward this end, the multicultural education classroom must become an oppositional space, in which educators and students can come together to fight for equality and social justice (Giroux, 1997). That is, it must become a space in which prejudice and discrimination are the common enemies and educators and students join forces to figure out how to eradicate prejudice in themselves and in the context of discipline-specific study and professional practice.

In these spaces, prejudicial thought and discriminatory action can be openly contested via critique and self-critique. Educators and students alike can view themselves as "works in progress" toward a shared goal. Trangressions in this progress are challenged, but forgiven. Successes are championed, but in a tempered fashion. The focus is on the process, learning how to engage across social identity group boundaries with dignity and respect as true equals in every regard. In learning this, educators and students, across race and other social identity group memberships, can join together in the work, begun hundreds of years ago, to continuously reconceptualize and reconfigure society in an ever more socially just fashion (Giroux, 1997).

It is in the nakedness of these spaces then, that educators and students come to understand that to persist in being racist, they have to continue to believe the following:

- Racism is a pathology of the individual racist only, not a function of a racist culture and political structure;

- whiteness is normal and American;

- people of color are other and, as such, are abnormal and deficit; and

- Eurocentric schooling teaches the absolute truth (Clark & O'Donnell, 1999).

To become antiracist, they have to

- be exposed to educational experiences (books, newspapers, films, speakers, and so forth) outside the Eurocentric norm;

- engage with people of color in books, newspapers, films, and in person (by chance in public spaces, in alternative classrooms, and so forth); and

- engage with antiracist whites in books, newspapers, films, and in person.

In short, they must get a multicultural education (Clark & O'Donnell, 1999). It is important to point out that the maintenance of a racist identity requires a person to do nothing. They must simply continue to think and behave as they always have (Hardiman, 1982). On the other hand, the development of an antiracist identity requires a tremendous amount of hard work, at both the levels of thought and action, sustained over a lifetime (Clark & O'Donnell, 1999). Educators and students should remind themselves of this whenever spaces created feel overwhelmingly oppositional and the fight for equality and justice feels more like a war.

CONCLUSION

As this chapter has detailed, white antiracist identity development is a complex process. But, as the case study illustrates, it can be achieved. That is, whites can be positively transformed by their experiences so that they realize that the benefits of being antiracist far outweigh the benefits of being racist (Clark & O'Donnell, 1999). Structuring multicultural educational experiences that encourage engagement in the process of antiracist identity development is equally complex (Clark & O'Donnell, 1999). Through innovative pedagogical practices, however, multicultural educators can engender student involvement in the curriculum (Nieto, 2000). Lifelong commitment to the promotion of racial understanding (among other forms, such as ethnic and religious) in the United States and beyond is at the core of unlocking these complexities.

REFERENCES

Allen, T. W. (1994). *The invention of the white race: Racial oppression and social control.* London: Verso.

Banks, J. A. (1997). *Teaching strategies for ethnic studies* (6th ed.). Boston: Allyn and Bacon.

Banks, J. A., & Banks, C. A. M. (1997). *Multicultural education: Issues and perspectives* (3rd ed.). Boston: Allyn and Bacon.

Bartolomé, L. (1994). Beyond the methods fetish: Toward a humanizing pedagogy. *Harvard Educational Review, 64,* 173–194.

Bell, D. (1992). *Faces at the bottom of the well: The permanence of racism.* New York: Basic Books.

Bell, D. (1995). Racial realism—After we're gone: Prudent speculations in America in a post-racial epoch. In R. Delgado (Ed.), *Critical race theory: The cutting edge* (pp. 2–8). Philadelphia: Temple University Press.

Bidell, T., & Lee, E. (1994). *Developing conceptions of racism among young white adults in the context of cultural diversity coursework.* (ERIC Document Reproduction Service, No. ED 377 270)

Bigelow, B. (1999a, Summer). Standards and multiculturalism. *Rehtinking Schools,* 6–7.

Bigelow, B. (1999b, April). Why standardized tests threaten multiculturalism. *Educational Leadership,* 37–40.

Bollin, G. G., & Finkel, J. (1995). White racial identity as a barrier to understanding diversity: A study of preservice teachers. *Equity and Excellence in Education, 28*(1), 25–30.

Bonnett, A. (1996). Anti-racism and the critique of white identities. *New Community, 22*(1), 97–110.

Bowser, B. P., & Hunt, R. G. (Eds.). (1981). *Impacts of racism on white Americans.* Beverly Hills, CA: Sage.

Carter, R. (1990). The relationship between racism and racial identity among white Americans: An exploratory investigation. *Journal of Counseling & Development, 69,* 46–50.

Carter, R., & Goodwin, L. (1996). Racial identity and education. In L. Darling-Hammond (Ed.), *Review of research in education* (pp. 164–173). Washington, DC: American Education Research Association.

Chávez Chávez, R. (1995). *Multicultural education in the everyday: A renaissance for the recommitted.* Washington, DC: AACTE.

Chávez Chávez, R. (1998). Engaging the multicultural education terrain: A holographic montage for engagers. In R. Chávez Chávez and J. O'Donnell (Eds.), *Speaking the unpleasant: The politics of (non)engagement in the multicultural education terrain* (pp. 102–124). New York: State University of New York Press.

Chávez Chávez, R., & O'Donnell, J. (Eds.). (1998). *Speaking the unpleasant: The politics of (non)engagement in the multicultural education terrain.* New York: State University of New York Press.

Clark, C. (1993). *Multicultural education as a tool for disarming violence: A study through in-depth participatory action research.* Unpublished dissertation, Unversity of Massachusetts, Amherst.

Clark, C. (1999). The secret: White lies are never little. In C. Clark and J. O'Donnell (Eds.), *Becoming and unbecoming white: Owning and disowning a racial identity* (pp. 92–110). Westport, CT: Greenwood.

Clark, C. (forthcoming). *Multicultural curriculum transformation across disciplines.* Diversity Digest.

Clark, C., & O'Donnell, J. (Eds.) (1999). *Becoming and unbecoming white: Owning and disowning a racial identity.* Westport, CT: Greenwood.

Cone, J. H. (1986). *A black theology of liberation.* New York: Orbis Books.

Connelly, F. M., & Clandnin, D. J. (1990). Stories of experience and narrative inquiry. *Educational Researcher, 19*(5), 2–14.

Cruz, J. (1996). From farce to tragedy: Reflections on the reification of race at century's end. In A. Gordon and C. Newfield (Eds.), *Mapping multiculturalism* (pp. 19–39). Minneapolis, MN: University of Minnesota Press.

Delgado, R. (Ed.). (1995). *Critical race theory: The cutting edge.* Philadelphia: Temple University Press.

Delgado, R., & Stefancic, J. (Eds.). (1997). *Critical white studies: Looking behind the mirror.* Philadelphia: Temple University Press.

Dennis, R. (1981). Socialization and racism: The white experience. In B. P. Bowser & R. G. Hunt (Eds.), *Impacts of racism on white Americans* (pp. 112–127). Beverly Hills, CA: Sage.

Fiske, J. (1994). *Media matters.* Minneapolis, MN: University of Minnesota Press.

Flagg, B. (1993). "Was blind, but now I see": White race consciousness and the requirement of disciminatory intent. *Michigan Law Review, 9*(1), 953–1017.

Frankenberg, R. (1993). *White women, race matters: The social construction of whiteness.* Minneapolis, MN: University of Minnesota Press.

Franklin, V. P. (1966). *Black self-determination, a cultural history of the faith of the fathers.* Westport, CT: Lawrence Hill.

Freire, P. (1980). *Pedagogy of the oppressed.* New York: Seabury Press.

Freire, P. (1990). *Education for critical consciousness.* South Hadley, MA: Bergin & Garvey.

Gaertner, S. (1976). Nonreactive measures in racial attitude research: A focus on "liberals." In P. Katz (Ed.), *Toward the elimination of racism* (pp. 183–211). New York: Pergamon Press.

Gallagher, C. A. (1994). White construction in the university. *Socialist Review, 94,* 165–187.

Giroux, H. A. (1992). *Border crossings: Cultural workers and the politics of education.* New York: Routledge.

Giroux, H. (1993). *Living dangerously: Multiculturalism and the politics of difference.* New York: Peter Lang.

Giroux, H. (1997). Rewriting the discourse of racial identity: Toward a pedagogy and politics of whiteness. *Harvard Educational Review, 67*, 285–320.

Giroux, H. A. (1996). *Fugitive cultures: Race, violence, and youth.* New York: Routledge.

Goldberg, D. T. (1990). The social formation of racist discourse. In D. T. Goldberg (Ed.), *Anatomy of racism* (pp. 295–318). Minneapolis, MN: University of Minnesota Press.

Gorski, P. (1998). *Racial and gender identity in white male multicultural educators and facilitators: Toward individual processes of self-development.* Unpublished dissertation, University of Virginia.

Gould, S. J. (1996). *The mismeasure of man* (2nd ed.). New York: W.W. Norton.

Guiner, L. (1994). *The tyranny of the majority: Fundamental fairness in representative democracy.* New York: Free Press.

Hall, S. (1991). Old and new identities, old and new ethnicities. In A. D. King (Ed.), *Culture, globalization and the world system* (pp. 41–68). Binghamton, NY: State University of New York Press.

Hall, S. (1996). New ethnicities. In D. Morley and K.-H. Chen (Eds.), *Stuart Hall: Critical dialogues in cultural studies* (pp. 441–449). New York: Routledge.

Hardiman, R. (1979). *White identity development.* Amherst, MA: New Perspectives.

Hardiman, R. (1982). *White identity development: A process model for describing the racial consciousness of white Americans.* Dissertation Abstracts International, 432, 104A University Microfilms No. 82–10330.

Hardisty, J. (1996). My on-again, off-again romance with liberalism. *Brown Papers, 2*(7), 27–35.

Harris, C. I. (1993). Whiteness as property. *Harvard Law Review, 106*, 1709–1791.

Haymes, S. N. (1995). Educational reform: What have been the effects of the attempts to improve education over the last decades? (Response essay). In J. L. Kincheloe & S. R. Steinberg (Eds.), *Thirteen questions: Reframing education's conversation* (2nd ed., pp. 239–250). New York: Peter Lang.

Helms, J. E. (1984). Toward a theoretical explanation of the effects of race on counseling: A black and white model. *Counseling Psychologist, 12*(4), 153–165.

Helms, J. E. (1995). An update of Helms's white and people of color racial identity models. In J. G. Ponterotto, J. M. Casas, L. A. Suzuki, & C. M. Alexander (Eds.), *Handbook of multicultural counseling* (pp. 23–37). Thousand Oaks, CA: Sage.

Herrnstein, R. J., & Murray, C. (1994). *The bell curve: Intelligence and class structure in American life.* New York: Free Press.

Hidalgo, F., Chávez Chávez, R., & Ramage, J. (1996). Multicultural education: Landscape for reform in the 21st century. In J. Sikula & E. Guyton (Eds.), *Handbook of teacher education* (pp. 761–778). New York: Macmillan.

Hidalgo, N. (1993). Multicultural teacher introspection. In T. Perry & J. Fraser (Eds.), *Freedom's plow* (pp. 99–106). New York: Routledge.

Hooks, b. (1993). *Teaching to transgress: Education as the practice of freedom.* New York: Routledge.

Howard, G. (1993). Whites in multicultural education: Rethinking our role. *Phi Delta Kappan, 75*(1), 36–41.

Ignatiev, N. (1995). *How the Irish became white.* New York: Routledge.

Ignatiev, N. (1996). Editorial. In N. Ignatiev & J. Garvey (Eds.), *Race traitor* (pp. 3–5). New York: Routledge.

Ignatiev, N., & Garvey, J. (Eds.) (1996). *Race traitor.* New York: Routledge.

Jackson, B. (1976). *Black identity development.* Amherst, MA: New Perspectives.

Jenkins, M. (1994). Fear of the "gangsta": Policy responses to gang activity in the city of Boston. *Dissertation Abstracts International,* 9500590.

Kairys, D. (Ed.) (1990). *The politics of law: A progressive critique.* New York: Pantheon Books.

Keating, A. L. (1995). Interrogating "whiteness," (de)constructing "race." *College English, 57,* 907–924.

Kinchloe, J., Pinar, W. F., & Slattery, P. (1994). A last dying chord? Toward cultural and educational renewal in the South. *Curriculum Inquiry, 24,* 407–436.

Kinchloe, J., & Steinberg, S. (2000). *Changing multiculturalism: New times, new curriculum.* London: Open University Press.

Kovel, J. (1984). *White racism: A psychohistory.* New York: Columbia University Press.

Lawrence, S. (1997). Beyond race awareness: White racial identity and multicultural teaching. *Journal of Teacher Education, 48,* 108–117.

Lawrence, S., & Bunche, T. (1996). Feeling and dealing: Teaching white students about racial privilege. *Teaching and Teacher Education, 12,* 531–542.

Lipsitz, G. (1995). The possessive investment in whiteness: Racialized social democracy and the "white" problem in American studies. *American Quarterly, 47,* 369–387.

Loewen, J. W. (1995). *Lies my teacher told me: Everything your American history textbook got wrong.* New York: New Press.

López, I. H. (1996). *White by law: The legal construction of race.* New York: New York University Press.

Lott, E. (1993). White like me: Racial cross-dressing and the construction of American whiteness. In A. Kaplan & D. E. Pease (Eds.), *Cultures of United States imperialism* (pp. 474–498). Durham, NC: Duke University Press.

Mathison, C., & Young, R. (1995). Constructivism and multicultural education. *Multicultural Education, 2*(1), 7–10.

McCarthy, C., & Critchlow, W. (Eds.). (1993). *Race identity and representation in education.* New York: Routledge.

McIntosh, P. (1983). *Interactive phases of curricular development.* Wellesley: Center for Research on Women.

McIntosh, P. (1992). White Privilege and male privilege: A personal account of coming to see correspondences through work in women's studies. In P. H. Collins & M. Andersen (Eds.), *Race, class and gender: An anthology* (pp. 102–118). Belmont, CA: Wadsworth.

McIntyre, A. (1997). *Making meaning of whiteness: Exploring racial identity with white teachers.* New York: State University of New York Press.

McLaren, P. (1995). *Critical pedagogy and predatory culture.* London and New York: Routledge.

McLaren, P. (1999). Unthinking whiteness, rethinking democracy: Critical citizenship in gringolandia. In C. Clark & J. O'Donnell (Eds.), *Becoming and unbecoming white: Owning and disowning a racial identity* (pp. 10–55). Westport, CT: Greenwood.

Miller, J. G. (1996). *Search and destroy: African-American males in the criminal justice system.* New York: Cambridge University Press.

Nakayama, T. K., & Krizek, R. L. (1995). Whiteness: A strategic rhetoric. *Quarterly Journal of Speech, 81,* 291–309.

Nieto, S. (1998). From claiming hegemony to sharing space: creating community in multicultural courses. In R. Chávez Chávez & J. O'Donnell (Eds.), *Speaking the unpleasant: The politics of resistance in the multicultural education terrain* (pp. 33–57). New York: State University of New York Press.

Nieto, S. (2000). *Affirming diversity: The sociopolitical context of multicultural education* (3rd ed.). White Plains, NY: Longman.

Niles, C., & Olson, J. (Eds.). (2000). *The New Abolitionist, 3*(2/3), 1–12. Available from http://www.newabolition.org.

Novik, M. (1995). *White lies, white power: The fight against white supremacy and reactionary violence.* Monroe, ME: Common Courage Press.

O'Brien, C. C. (1996). Thomas Jefferson: Radical and racist. *Atlantic Monthly, 233*(5), 53–74.

Omi, M., & Winant, H. (1994). *Racial formations in the United States from the 1960s to 1990s.* New York: Routledge.

Paley, V. G. (1979). *White teacher.* Cambridge, MA: Harvard University Press.

Pinar, W. F. (1993). Notes on understanding curriculum as a racial text. In C. McCarthy & W. Crichlow (Eds.), *Race, identity and representation in education* (pp. 117–134). New York: Routledge.

Pinar, W. F., Reynolds, W. M., Slattery, P., & Taubman, P. M. (1995). *Understanding curriculum.* NY: Peter Lang.

Powell, R. (1996). Confronting white hegemony. *Multicultural Education, 4*(2), 12–15.

Raines, H. (1977). *My soul is rested: The story of the civil rights movement in the deep South.* New York: Penguin Books.

Rodríguez, R. (1999). The study of whiteness. *Black Issues in Higher Education, 16*(6), 20–25.

Roediger, D. (1991). *The wages of whiteness.* London: Verso Press.

Roediger, D. (1994). *Toward the abolition of whiteness.* London: Verso Press.

Rorty, R. (1989). *Contingency, irony, and solidarity.* New York: Cambridge University Press.

Rosenberg, P. M. (1997). Underground discourses: Exploring whiteness in teacher education. In M. Fine, L. Weis, L. C. Powell, & L. M. Wong (Eds.), *Off white: Readings on race, power, and society* (pp. 79–89). New York: Routledge.

Rowe, W., Bennet, S. K., & Atkinson, D. R. (1994). White racial identity models: A critique and alternative proposal. *Counseling Psychologist, 22*, 129–146.

Scheurich, J. J. (1993). Toward a white discourse on white racism. *Educational Researcher, 22*(8), 5–10.

Segrest, M. (1994). *Memoir of a race traitor.* Boston, MA: South End Press.

Shohat, E., & Stam, R. (1994). *Unthinking eurocentrism.* New York: Routledge.

Sleeter, C. E. (1993a). Advancing a white discourse: A response to Scheuirch. *Educational Researcher, 22*(8), 13–15.

Sleeter, C. E. (1993b). How white teachers construct race. In C. McCarthy & W. Critchlow (Eds.), *Race identity and representation in education* (pp. 157–171). New York: Routledge.

Sleeter, C. E. (1996). *Multicultural education as social activism.* New York: State University of New York Press.

Sleeter, C. E., & McLaren, P. (1995). Introduction: Exploring connections to build critical multiculturalism. In C. E. Sleeter & P. McLaren (Eds.), *Multicultural education, critical pedagogy, and the politics of difference* (pp. 5–32). New York: State University of New York Press.

Stowe, D. W. (1996). Uncolored people: The rise of whiteness studies. *Lingua Franca, 6*(6), 68–77.

Takaki, R. (1987). *From different shores: Perspectives on race and culture in America.* Boston: Little, Brown.

Takaki, R. (1993). *A different mirror: A multicultural history of America.* Boston: Little, Brown.

Tatum, B. D. (1992). Talking about race, learning about racism: The application of racial identity development theory in the classroom. *Harvard Educational Review, 62*(1), 1–24.

Tatum, B. (1994). Teaching white students about racism: The search for white allies and the restoration of hope. *Teachers College Record, 95*, 462–476.

Terry, R. (1981). The negative impact of white values. In B. P. Bowser & R. G. Hunt (Eds.), Im*pacts of racism on white Americans* (pp. 35–47). Beverly Hills, CA: Sage.

Wellman, D. (1993). *Portraits of white racism* (2nd ed.). New York: Cambridge University Press.

White, D. G. (1985). *Ain't I a woman?: Female slaves in the plantation South.* New York: W. W. Norton.

Young, W. (1969). *Beyond racism.* New York: McGraw-Hill.

Zinn, H. (1970). *The politics of history.* Boston: Beacon Press.

Zinn, H. (1980). *A people's history of the United States.* New York: Harper & Row.

Zúñiga, X., Nagda, B., & Sedvig, T. D. (forthcoming). *Intergroup dialogues: A practice model for cultivating student engagement across differences.* Unpublished paper.

CHAPTER 4

Educating Citizens for a Diverse Democracy
How Students Learn from Diversity in College

Jeffrey F. Milem, Paul D. Umbach, and Marie P. Ting

> *The literacy required to live in a civil society, the competence to partici-*
> *pate in democratic communities, the ability to think critically and act*
> *deliberately in a pluralistic world, the empathy that permits us to hear*
> *and thus accommodate others, all involve skills that must be acquired.*
> —Barber (1992, p. 4)

Unless you are a bit of a "news junkie," or unless you were paying particularly close attention to national events in the fall of 2000, it is quite likely that you missed what was arguably one of the more important news stories of that time. Airing on a number of evening television news broadcasts and buried somewhere in most major newspapers across the country were stories reporting that California had become what the news journalists described as a "majority minority" state.

At first glance, these terms seem contradictory. By definition, one could argue, how can a minority also be a majority? The reporters were telling us that people of color, who have traditionally been described as minorities in our country, had grown to be a larger portion of the population of California than white people, who have traditionally been described as the majority. California is now the third of our 50 states that can be described as majority minority—both Hawaii and New Mexico have been populated predominantly by people of color since they entered the Union. (The District of Columbia is also inhabited primarily by people of color.) The phenomenon that we observe in these three states will be descriptive of the rest of our country in the lifetimes of anyone who is currently of college age or younger. Sometime in the next 50 to 60 years, demographers tell us that the United States will become a nation that is majority minority.

The implications of these population shifts for our nation are quite powerful. No other country in the world is (or ever has been) as racially and ethnically diverse as the United States. We are truly a multicultural nation. This increasing diversity presents our democracy with great challenges and tremendous opportunities, as the rest of the world is watching us closely to see how we respond. By looking at our nation's history, we can see that we have not been successful in incorporating diverse people into American society. A critical analysis of our nation's history reveals abundant evidence of systematic, prolonged efforts to exclude many people of color from full participation in our democracy.

Over the past few decades, many college and university leaders recognized the great challenges and tremendous opportunities inherent in our society's growing diversity, and they began to change the educational missions of their institutions to respond to these challenges. Educators embrace diversity on their college campuses because they realize that it provides prospects for teaching and learning that more homogeneous settings do not. Increasingly, administrators are rewriting college and university mission statements to affirm diversity's important role in enhancing teaching and learning in higher education. Many in the higher education community argue that teachers and administrators have a unique responsibility to develop in students the knowledge, skills, and competencies they need to be active members of a society that is increasingly diverse and inextricably connected to a global community.

This chapter explores the ways that college students' engagement with diversity provides opportunities to develop skills, traits, and insights that assist them in becoming effective citizens in an increasingly diverse democracy. Knowing how to comfortably and effectively engage with diverse people is a skill that all citizens of our country, and, indeed, our world must have. A growing body of research shows that exposure to diversity in college enhances the learning and development of students across a range of important educational outcomes, including important democracy and citizenship outcomes.

Before we discuss how colleges and universities can assist students in developing the skills that help them become more effective citizens, we return to the two themes addressed above. First, the chapter summarizes demographic data and trends to illustrate how diverse our nation is. Next, we give a brief historical overview of how our nation has addressed issues of racial and ethnic diversity. The chapter concludes with a discussion of how interactions college students have with diverse populations and ideas enhance their learning and development.

The Changing Face of the United States

Changes in the racial and ethnic diversity of the population of the United States are evident throughout our nation's history. In examining trends and demographic projections, it is clear that the racial and ethnic composition of the United States will change even more dramatically over the next 50 years. Sometime after the middle of this century, the United States will become almost a majority minority nation.

Although whites made up three-quarters of the U.S. population in 1990, they will be only slightly more than half of the U.S. population in 2050. Between 1990 and 2050, Latinos, Asian Americans, Native Americans, and African Americans will show dramatic increases in their populations (258.3%, 269.1%, 83%, and 69.5%, respectively), whereas the white population will show only a small increase (7.4%). Additional evidence of growth in the population of people of color in the United States can be seen in the projected proportional increase for people of color in the total population (see Table 4-1). By the year 2050, Latinos will make up one-fourth of our country's population—up from less than one-tenth of the population in 1990. Moreover, by the year 2005, the population of Latinos in the United States will be larger than the African American population, making Latinos the largest population of people of color in our country. The proportion of Asian Americans in the United States is expected to increase by nearly 300% during this time period from 2.8 percent of the total population in 1990 to 8.2 percent in 2050.

Regional Changes in Demographics

Although these changes in population will be most profound in particular parts of the country, they will be evident in every region of the United States. Between 1995 and 2025, the white population will account for only one-fifth of the increase in the nation's population in every region of the country except the Northeast, where the number of whites is projected to decline during this time period.

Latinos will account for the largest proportion of population growth in every region of the country except the South (see Table 4-2). The most notable increases in this population will occur in the Northeast and West, where Latinos will account for 70.1% and 54.4% of population growth respectively. Half of the gains in the Latino population will occur in the West, whereas just slightly more than 30% of this growth will occur in the South.

In the Midwest, Northeast, and South, African Americans will account for approximately one-quarter of the total population increase. Within the African American population, the greatest effect of growth will take place in the South, where 64.1% of the increase in African Americans will occur. The percentage growth in Asian Americans will exceed that of whites in the Northeast and West. The West will account for 56.2% of the increase in the Asian American population, with the Northeast accounting for 19.4% of the growth. Native Americans are projected to account for only a small percentage of the increase in the population of the United States in all four regions of the country. Of the increases that do occur in the Native American population, however, 47.7% will occur in the West, 24.5% in the South, and 23.9% in the Midwest.

TABLE 4-1

Projected Distribution of the Population by Race/Ethnicity (in percentages)

YEAR	NATIVE AMERICAN	ASIAN AMERICAN	AFRICAN AMERICAN	LATINO	WHITE
1990	0.7	2.8	11.8	9.0	75.6
1995	0.7	3.3	12.0	10.2	73.6
2000	0.7	3.9	12.2	11.4	71.8
2005	0.8	4.4	12.4	12.6	69.9
2010	0.8	4.8	12.6	13.8	68.8
2020	0.8	5.7	12.9	16.3	64.3
2030	0.8	6.6	13.1	18.9	60.5
2040	0.9	7.5	13.3	21.7	56.7
2050	0.9	8.2	13.6	24.5	52.8
% Change from 1995 to 2050	83.0	269.1	69.5	258.3	7.4

Source: U.S. Bureau of the Census (1996, p. 60).

TABLE 4-2

Projected Distribution of Population Gains of Regions by Ethnicity Groups: 1995 to 2025 (in percentages)

REGION	TOTAL	NATIVE AMERICAN	ASIAN AMERICAN	AFRICAN AMERICAN	LATINO	WHITE
United States	100.0	1.1	16.5	16.5	44.3	21.6
Northeast[a]		0.5	39.1	25.2	70.1	
Midwest	100.0	2.7	15.5	25.4	31.4	25.0
South	100.0	0.7	6.1	25.8	32.2	35.2
West	100.0	1.3	22.8	3.1	54.4	18.4

Source: United States Bureau of the Census (1996, pp. 14–15).
[a] *Percentages do not add to 100 because of the declining size of the white population in the Northeast.*

Changes in the States

By examining the population predictions state by state, we can see that the proportional representation of people of color will increase in all 50 states (see Table 4-3), although different populations will increase in different states. The largest percentage increases in the African American population will take place in Georgia, Texas, Florida, Maryland, and Virginia. California, Texas, Florida, New York, and Arizona will experience the greatest increases in the Latino population. California, New

York, New Jersey, Texas, and Hawaii will witness the largest growth in the Asian American population. New Mexico, Oklahoma, Arizona, Minnesota, and Montana will experience the largest population gains of Native Americans.

Although all states will experience greater racial and ethnic diversity in the coming years, the effect of these trends will be felt quite profoundly in selected states. By the year 2050, Alaska, Arizona, Florida, Maryland, New Jersey, New York, and Texas are likely to join Hawaii, New Mexico, California, and the District of Columbia as majority minority states.

In addition, even states that are nearly all white (e.g., Idaho, Indiana, Iowa, Minnesota, Montana, Wisconsin, and Wyoming) will become significantly more diverse by 2025. In Iowa, for example, the proportion of Asian Americans and Latinos is predicted to double between 1995 and 2025 (from about 5% to nearly 10%).

These data and population trends suggest dramatic increases in diversity that will hold considerable significance for anyone who will attend college in the next 25 to 50 years. The dramatic demographic shifts occurring across the United States require college students to develop a new set of skills that will prepare them to participate fully and successfully as citizens of a diverse democracy and to be more competitive in a global economy, which demands workers who can successfully interact with diverse people and cultures.

HISTORICAL OVERVIEW

Although the previous section argued that we can learn a great deal by looking ahead at the increasing diversity of the United States, it is also important to look back at its history for other important lessons. The United States was founded by immigrants and their descendants, who share a common bond with subsequent generations of immigrants. Most came from somewhere else in the world seeking the promise of a better life for themselves and their families. In 1783, George Washington declared that "the bosom of America is open to receive not only the opulent and respectable stranger, but the oppressed and persecuted of all nations and religions, who we shall welcome to a participation of all our rights and privileges" (George Washington Papers).

At first glance, we might assume that Washington and the other founders believed that the United States was a nation where all were welcome to participate and enjoy the benefits of democracy. If we take a critical look at its history, however, it is fair to argue that the founding fathers had a rather limited view of whom the beneficiaries of democracy should be. Clearly, Washington did not intend for his remarks to apply to women or people of color. It was only recently that steps were taken to grant women and people of color the full rights and privileges of citizenship. A close examination of some past legislation indicates

TABLE 4-3

Projected Distribution of State Populations by Race/Ethnicity: 1995 and 2025 (in percentages)

STATE	YEAR	TOTAL*	AFRICAN AMERICAN	NATIVE AMERICAN	ASIAN AMERICAN	LATINO	WHITE
Alabama	1995	4,257	25.5	0.4	0.7	0.8	72.7
	2025	5,231	26.1	0.4	1.1	1.2	71.2
Alaska	1995	612	4.2	15.0	4.6	4.1	72.1
	2025	891	4.4	10.7	21.7	6.6	56.7
Arizona	1995	4,274	3.4	5.7	1.9	20.3	68.7
	2025	6,562	4.3	5.1	3.0	31.5	56.2
Arkansas	1995	2,486	15.8	0.6	0.6	1.1	81.9
	2025	3,062	15.3	0.7	1.0	2.2	80.8
California	1995	32,176	7.5	0.9	11.3	28.6	51.7
	2025	50,755	6.8	0.8	17.9	41.8	32.8
Colorado	1995	3,777	4.3	0.9	2.2	13.4	79.1
	2025	5,278	5.9	1.2	3.8	20.2	69.0
Connecticut	1995	3,308	9.1	0.2	2.0	7.5	81.2
	2025	3,825	12.8	0.3	4.5	15.0	67.4
Delaware	1995	717	18.3	0.3	1.7	2.6	77.1
	2025	869	22.9	0.2	3.1	5.5	68.2
District of Columbia	1995	563	62.5	0.2	3.0	6.6	27.7
	2025	666	58.0	0.0	4.4	12.0	25.7
Florida	1995	14,306	14.5	0.3	1.5	13.7	70.0
	2025	21,306	16.7	0.4	2.5	23.2	57.2
Georgia	1995	7,223	28.0	0.2	1.6	2.1	68.2
	2025	9,913	33.5	0.2	2.5	3.5	60.3
Hawaii	1995	1,244	2.3	0.5	60.7	8.0	28.5
	2025	1,845	2.3	0.4	64.9	10.1	22.3
Idaho	1995	1,170	0.5	1.4	1.1	6.2	90.9
	2025	1,755	1.0	1.8	1.7	11.7	83.9
Illinois	1995	11,901	15.2	0.2	3.0	9.2	72.4
	2025	13,612	16.0	0.3	5.3	16.7	61.7
Indiana	1995	5,813	8.1	0.2	0.8	2.0	88.8
	2025	6,568	9.4	0.3	1.5	3.7	85.1
Iowa	1995	2,848	2.0	0.3	1.2	1.6	94.9
	2025	3,047	3.0	0.5	2.5	3.2	90.9
Kansas	1995	2,577	6.1	0.9	1.6	4.4	87.0
	2025	3,136	7.9	1.1	2.7	9.0	79.3
Kentucky	1995	3,863	7.1	0.2	0.6	0.7	91.4
	2025	4,319	7.9	0.2	1.1	1.3	89.5
Louisiana	1995	4,360	31.7	0.5	1.2	2.4	64.2
	2025	5,158	35.8	0.5	2.2	4.4	57.0
Maine	1995	1,241	0.4	0.5	0.6	0.5	98.0
	2025	1,424	0.6	0.5	1.3	1.4	96.2
Maryland	1995	5,075	26.5	0.3	3.6	3.4	66.1
	2025	6,343	32.7	0.3	6.4	6.9	53.7
Massachusetts	1995	6,154	6.1	0.2	3.1	5.8	84.9
	2025	7,098	9.2	0.3	7.5	13.2	69.8
Michigan	1995	9,577	14.4	0.6	1.4	2.4	81.2
	2025	10,126	16.8	0.7	2.9	4.3	75.3
Minnesota	1995	4,616	2.8	1.2	2.3	1.6	92.2
	2025	5,534	5.0	1.9	5.0	3.5	84.6
Mississippi	1995	2,698	35.9	0.3	0.6	0.7	62.5
	2025	3,145	36.9	0.3	1.0	1.2	60.5

STATE	YEAR	TOTAL*	AFRICAN AMERICAN	NATIVE AMERICAN	ASIAN AMERICAN	LATINO	WHITE
Missouri	1995	5,332	11.0	0.4	1.0	1.4	86.1
	2025	6,267	12.8	0.5	1.6	2.7	82.4
Montana	1995	873	0.3	6.1	0.6	1.8	91.2
	2025	1,122	0.5	8.2	1.2	3.5	86.5
Nebraska	1995	1,641	3.9	0.9	1.0	3.0	91.2
	2025	1,940	5.6	1.3	2.2	5.7	85.2
Nevada	1995	1,547	7.0	1.7	3.9	12.4	74.9
	2025	2,357	8.6	1.4	6.0	24.7	59.2
New Hampshire	1995	1,149	0.7	0.2	1.0	1.1	97.0
	2025	1,441	1.0	0.3	2.1	2.4	94.3
New Jersey	1995	8,076	14.3	0.2	4.6	11.1	69.8
	2025	9,804	17.4	0.3	10.1	18.8	53.4
New Mexico	1995	1,708	2.4	8.8	1.2	38.5	40.1
	2025	2,698	3.3	10.2	2.1	46.0	38.4
New York	1995	18,751	17.0	0.4	4.6	13.6	64.4
	2025	20,911	19.4	0.4	9.0	20.6	50.6
North Carolina	1995	7,211	22.2	1.2	1.0	1.4	74.2
	2025	9,376	23.9	1.2	1.8	2.2	70.8
North Dakota	1995	638	0.5	4.4	0.6	0.6	93.9
	2025	728	0.7	8.1	1.4	1.9	87.9
Ohio	1995	11,171	11.2	0.2	1.0	1.5	86.1
	2025	11,783	14.1	0.3	2.1	2.7	80.8
Oklahoma	1995	3,292	7.8	8.0	1.3	3.2	79.7
	2025	4,080	10.6	9.0	2.2	6.0	72.2
Oregon	1995	3,153	1.8	1.4	2.9	4.8	89.1
	2025	4,384	2.3	1.7	4.9	9.8	81.3
Pennsylvania	1995	12,115	9.6	0.1	1.5	2.3	86.5
	2025	12,787	12.0	0.2	3.2	5.0	79.6
Rhode Island	1995	1,002	4.8	0.4	2.2	6.0	86.6
	2025	1,178	7.7	0.8	5.3	14.9	71.1
South Carolina	1995	3,679	30.0	0.2	0.8	1.0	68.0
	2025	4,652	30.1	0.2	1.2	1.7	66.7
South Dakota	1995	730	0.4	7.4	0.5	1.0	90.7
	2025	864	0.8	10.3	1.0	1.6	86.2
Tennessee	1995	5,260	16.2	0.2	0.8	0.9	81.9
	2025	6,678	18.3	0.3	1.4	1.6	78.5
Texas	1995	18,892	12.1	0.4	2.4	27.4	57.6
	2025	27,826	13.9	0.6	3.8	36.8	44.9
Utah	1995	1,962	0.9	1.5	2.3	5.6	89.6
	2025	2,905	1.3	2.0	3.9	9.1	83.6
Vermont	1995	584	0.3	0.3	0.7	0.7	97.9
	2025	680	0.9	0.3	1.6	1.8	95.4
Virginia	1995	6,646	19.5	0.3	3.2	3.1	73.9
	2025	8,533	23.1	0.3	6.1	6.3	64.2
Washington	1995	5,468	3.3	1.8	5.3	5.2	84.4
	2025	7,881	3.5	1.9	9.1	10.1	75.4
West Virginia	1995	1,827	3.1	0.1	0.5	0.5	95.8
	2025	1,845	3.6	0.1	1.1	1.3	93.9
Wisconsin	1995	5,132	5.5	0.9	1.4	2.2	90.0
	2025	5,891	8.5	1.1	3.6	4.0	82.9
Wyoming	1995	480	0.6	2.3	0.6	5.6	90.8
	2025	706	1.6	3.8	1.7	10.5	82.4

Source: United States Bureau of the Census (1996, pp. 70–74).

In thousands.

that the United States has a history of excluding many groups from participation in our democracy based on their racial and ethnic backgrounds.

In the era between 1790 and the mid-1950s, Congress enacted a series of laws that excluded people of color from entering the United States and from realizing the benefits of American citizenship. The Naturalization Act of 1790 outlined a process by which new immigrants could become naturalized citizens of the United States, but this legislation restricted this privilege to white immigrants. The effect of the Naturalization Act was felt for over a century because of the foundational role it played in subsequent legislation to exclude people of color from becoming citizens of the United States.

In 1787, during the drafting of the Constitution of the United States and amid heated debates about representation and taxation, delegates from the North argued that slaves should not be counted as people, whereas delegates from the South argued that they should. Those from the South wanted slaves to be counted as "whole people" because of increased tax revenues and additional delegates they would gain by having blacks included in population counts for the southern states. At this point in time, there were approximately 654,000 slaves in the south. As a result, blacks accounted for about 35% of the population in the southern states (U.S. Bureau of the Census, 1970). The authors of the Constitution, in order to forge a compromise between the competing views held by the northern and southern delegates, decided that a slave would be counted as three-fifths of a man. Although Southerners argued that blacks should be fully counted for the purposes of tax revenues and representation, it is clear that they had no intention of granting slaves citizenship rights.

In 1857, a law was passed that excluded African Americans, slave or free, from any claim to citizenship. In its Dred Scott decision, the Supreme Court stated that no African American, free or slave, could become a United States citizen. Chief Justice Taney, in his 54-page majority opinion, wrote that blacks

> are not included, and were not intended to be included, under the word 'citizens' in the Constitution....On the contrary, they were at that time [1787] considered as a subordinate and inferior class of beings who had been subjugated by the dominant race, and...had no rights or privileges but such as those who held the power and Government might choose to grant them. (*Dred Scott v. John F. A. Sandford*, 1856).

Despite the Civil War and the passage of the 14th Amendment in the early 1900s, Congress enacted several other laws to limit the participation of people of color in the United States. The Alien Land Laws of 1913, 1920, and 1923 banned land ownership by those who were not citizens. This essentially prohibited people of color from owning land, because under the Naturalization Act, they were unable to become naturalized citizens. Moreover, the Immigration Act of 1924 stipulated that only those who were eligible to become naturalized citizens could enter the United States. Therefore, because people of color were not permitted to become naturalized citizens, the Immigration Act ultimately prohibited the entry of people of color to the United States.

Legislation targeting specific racial and ethnic groups was common in the late 1800s and early 1900s. For example, Congress enacted a series of laws called the Asian Exclusion Acts in 1882, 1917, 1924, and 1934 to prohibit immigrants from China, Japan, India, and the Philippines from entering the United States. The first piece of legislation that targeted a specific racial or ethnic group, the Chinese Exclusion Act of 1882, prohibited the immigration and citizenship of Chinese people for 10 years. Congress passed subsequent acts reinforcing the ban on Chinese immigration in 1884, 1886, and 1888.

Throughout much of our nation's history, legislation and immigration policy have been designed to exclude people of color from entering the United States and from being eligible to become citizens. It was not until 1952, with the passage of the Immigration and Nationality Act of 1952 (the McCarran-Walter Act), that the ban prohibiting people of color from becoming naturalized citizens was finally lifted. Beginning in 1965, Congress passed a series of immigration and nationality laws. These laws eliminated the provisions set forth by previous laws and expanded the ability of immigrants from all backgrounds to participate in the democratic activities afforded to citizens. In 1965, in his State of the Union Address, Lyndon Johnson said:

> Let a just nation throw open the city of promise to those in other lands seeking the promise of America, through an immigration law based on the work a man can do and not where he was born or how he spells his name. (Federal Register Division, 1966, p. 6)

President Johnson argued that our nation's history of exclusionary immigration policy was "incompatible with our basic American tradition" (Federal Register Division, 1966, p. 6). Other key leaders of his era shared Johnson's view. In 1963, Senator Hiram Fong of Hawaii argued before the United States Senate that "the racial restrictions inherent in our present immigration laws disparage our democratic heritage" and contradict "the spirit and principles of the Declaration of Independence, the Constitution of the United States, and our traditional standards of fairness and justice" (Fong, 1963).

Just as the 1965 Immigration Act allowed more individuals from Asia and Latin America to enter the United States, during the mid-1960s, Congress enacted legislation ensuring that the rights and privileges of citizenship were extended to all members of our democracy. The Civil Rights Act of 1964 (P.L. No. 88-352, 78 Stat. 241) prohibited employment discrimination based on race, sex, national origin, or religion, and prohibited public access discrimination, leading to school desegregation.

Although the United States is a nation of immigrants, only white immigrants were given the legal right to fully participate in its democracy until the mid-1960s. It was not until nearly 200 years after Washington made his remarks about how our nation would welcome immigrants that all the legal restrictions to participation in our democracy were finally lifted for all of our people. It has been only in the past 40 years that all people have been allowed by law to participate in our democracy, and we continue to face many challenges regarding our nation's diversity. These historical vestiges of discrimination highlight even greater challenges, as the United States becomes increasingly diverse. These challenges extend far beyond our homes and neighborhoods. Several pressing questions confront us as we enter this next phase of our nation's history. How do we finally overcome the vestiges of discrimination that are so apparent in the history of our nation? What responsibility do we have as participants in this increasingly diverse democracy? In particular, what role does higher education play in preparing students to participate in this democracy?

THE RESPONSIBILITY OF CITIZENS

As citizens of the United States, we have the unique opportunity and right to participate in shaping our nation's laws and policies. To participate successfully in these processes, we must be properly prepared. What are the skills that must be acquired to be effective citizens in our democracy that Barber (1992) discusses in the quote that opens this chapter? What must we do to be sure that all of our citizens develop these skills?

Clearly, the composition of our citizenry has changed dramatically since the founding of this country. The "We the People" of our founders is very different than that of today. No longer is citizenship restricted to those who are white and male, and no longer does our country seek to legally restrict the participation of people based on their race, gender, or religion. The growing diversity of our nation bestows us with our greatest challenges and opportunities as a democracy.

If we are to meet the challenges and maximize the opportunities that are before us, as citizens, we each must be willing and able to learn from the rich diversity in our country. Bernstein and Cock (1997) noted, "If democracies are to flourish, universities must prepare citizens who can look beyond their own borders" (p. B7). Clearly, one trait of the effective citizen is the ability to develop empathy and respect for those who differ from us. To do this, we must embrace pluralism and learn to connect with people across racial, religious, and economic differences. This can only happen if we learn to expand our capacities to think critically and complexly.

Specifically, this means that we must develop the ability to assess the strengths and weaknesses of our own positions on issues in relation to differing positions (Bernstein & Cock, 1997). Citizenship not only includes duties such as voting and obeying the law, but also includes "responsibility, mutual regard and understanding of differ- ence" (Boyte & Kari, 2000, p. 41). Greg Prince (2000), President of Hampshire College, argued that it is important for all citizens to engage in social criticism and activism. Similarly, Damon (1998) asserted that citizens must possess moral traits that include "dedication to honesty, justice, social responsibility, and the tolerance that makes democratic discourse possible" (p. B4).

THE ROLE OF HIGHER EDUCATION

Colleges and universities are uniquely situated to provide students the opportu- nity to engage with diversity in ways they never have before. They can be ideal laboratories in which students can engage, experiment with, and learn from the diverse people and ideas that they encounter. For many college students, college will be the first and only opportunity they have to interact with people who are different than they are, given that we live in a society that continues to be highly segregated regarding where we live, work, and go to school.

A THEORETICAL ARGUMENT FOR THE BENEFITS OF DIVERSITY

Gurin (1999) believes that undergraduates are at a critical stage in their human growth and development, in which diversity can facilitate greater awareness of the learning process, better critical thinking skills, and better preparation for the many challenges they will face as involved citizens in a democratic, multiracial society. Gurin (1999) noted that "universities are ideal institutions to foster such development" (p. 103).

In constructing her argument for the benefits of diversity in college, Gurin (1999) drew on Erikson's (1946, 1956) work regarding psychosocial develop- ment. Erikson argued that individuals' social and personal identities are formed during late adolescence and early adulthood—the time when many attend col- lege. Environments such as higher education can be structured in ways that fa- cilitate the development of identity. For example, college facilitates the develop- ment of identity through the opportunities it provides students to be exposed to people, experiences, and ideas that differ from their past environments (Gurin, 1999). Diversity and complexity in the college environment "encourage intellec- tual experimentation and recognition of varied future possibilities" (Gurin, 1999, p. 103). These conditions are critical to the successful development of identity.

Gurin (1999) used the work of Piaget (1971, 1975/1985) as a conceptual and theoretical rationale to explain how diversity facilitates students' cognitive development. Piaget (1971, 1975/1985) argued that cognitive growth is facilitated by disequilibrium, or periods of incongruity and dissonance. For adolescents to develop the ability to understand and appreciate the perspectives and feelings of others, they must interact with diverse individuals in equal status situations. This facilitates the process of "perspective taking" and allows students to progress in intellectual and moral development. For perspective taking to occur, both diversity and equality must be present (Gurin, 1999).

Although Piaget's (1971, 1975/1985) work was done with children and adolescents, Perry (1970) established the applicability of this work to the development of college students. Perry used the Piagetian model in his study of the intellectual and ethical development of college students at Harvard. His nine-stage model traces the development of students' thinking about the nature of knowledge, truth, and values, and the meaning of life and responsibilities (King, 1978). Specifically, Perry's theory examines students' intellect (their understanding of the world and the nature of knowledge) and identity (the meaning they develop regarding their place in the world; King, 1978). Key to the successful progression of students through the developmental stages in Perry's theory is the ability to recognize the existence of multiple viewpoints and "the indeterminacies" of "Truth" (Pascarella & Terenzini, 1991, p. 29). As students progress to the higher stages of development in the Perry schema, they develop commitments to beliefs, values, behaviors, and people. The process of developing these commitments is dynamic and changeable and is triggered by the exposure that students have to new experiences, new ideas, and new people. Perry (1981) argued that this process of development extends throughout our lifetimes.

A growing body of research in social psychology suggests that it is inappropriate to assume that active engagement in learning occurs as a matter of course during the college years (Gurin, 1999). In fact, what we had previously assumed to be active engagement in learning is actually a more automatic response, or "mindlessness" (Langer, 1978). This mindlessness results from learning that has occurred already and that has become so customary to us that thinking proves unnecessary. In the absence of what Coser (1975) described as complex social structures, people work off of scripts or schemas that do not require them to engage in active thinking processes. People who learn to interact with more complex social structures exhibit a heightened sense of individuality, while simultaneously showing a more complex attentiveness to the social world. Based on this body of theoretical work, Gurin (1999) argued that racially and ethnically diverse learning environments allow students to engage the complex social structures necessary for them to develop active thinking processes.

CONCEPTUALIZING CAMPUS DIVERSITY

Numerous other higher education scholars share Gurin's view about the unique opportunity that higher education has to prepare students for their roles as citizens in an increasingly diverse democracy (Alger, 1997; Bowen & Bok, 1998; Hurtado, Milem, Clayton-Pedersen, & Allen, 1997, 1999; Lawrence & Matsuda, 1997; Liu, 1998; Milem & Hakuta, 2000). What, then, does a campus look like that provides a positive diverse learning environment that fosters better citizenship and democratic outcomes in students?

Building on the work of Gurin (1999), Chang (1999b), Milem (2003) and Milem and Hakuta (2000), three primary types of diversity in colleges and universities can influence the learning and development of college students. The first, *structural diversity*, refers to the numerical and proportional representation of students from different racial or ethnic groups in the student body (Gurin, 1999; Hurtado et al., 1998, 1999). A second type of diversity involves *diversity-related initiatives*, such as core diversity requirements, ethnic studies courses, diversity-related "teach-ins," structured intergroup dialogues, racial and cultural awareness workshops, and so forth. Although demographic shifts or changes in the structural diversity of campuses frequently provide the stimulus for diversity-related initiatives (Chang, 1999a), some colleges and universities incorporate these types of initiatives although their campuses are racially and ethnically homogeneous. The final type of diversity, *diversity of interactions*, is characterized by the exchanges students have with racially and ethnically diverse people and with diverse ideas, information, and experiences. Simply put, students are influenced by the interactions they have with diverse ideas and information as well as the interactions they have with diverse people while in college.

These three types of diversity are not discrete. In fact, we are most frequently exposed to diverse information and ideas through the interactions we have with diverse people. Although diversity-related initiatives benefit students who are exposed to them—even on campuses that are almost ethnically homogenous—the effect of these initiatives on students tends to be much stronger on campuses that are structurally diverse (Chang, 1999a). Although each type of diversity confers significant positive educational benefits to students, the effect of each is enhanced measurably by the presence of the other types of diversity (Chang, 1999b; Gurin, 1999; Hurtado et al., 1998, 1999; Milem, 2003; Milem & Hakuta, 2000). On the other hand, the effect of each type of diversity on students is diminished on campuses where the other types of diversity are absent.

How Students Are Influenced by Diversity

Research on the effects of diversity on college students indicates that four primary types of outcomes are influenced by the interactions that students have with diversity while they are in college. Gurin (1999) described two types of outcomes influenced by campus diversity. *Democracy outcomes* refer to the ways higher education prepares students to become involved as active participants in a society that is increasingly diverse and complex. *Learning outcomes* refer to active learning processes students become involved in while in college, the engagement and motivation that students exhibit, the learning and refinement of intellectual and academic skills, and the value students place on these skills after they leave college.

Milem (2003) and Milem and Hakuta (2000) offer two other types of outcomes that can be enhanced by student interactions with diversity in college. *Process outcomes* reflect the ways students perceive that diversity has enriched their college experience. Measures of student satisfaction and perceptions of campus climate are examples of outcomes included in this category. *Material benefits* are those that students accrue when they attend diverse colleges. Examples of material benefits include increased salary and wages and the attainment of advanced graduate or professional degrees or better job placements for students educated at more diverse institutions.

The Democratic Outcomes of Diversity

Democracy outcomes refer to the ways higher education prepares students to become involved as active participants in an increasingly diverse and complex society. Gurin's (1999) research on the educational outcomes of diversity suggests that three major categories of democracy outcomes can be enhanced by the interaction students have with diversity while in college. *Citizenship engagement* refers to students' interest in and motivation to influence society and the political structure as well as to students' participation in community and volunteer service. *Racial and cultural engagement* refers to students' levels of cultural awareness and appreciation and their commitment to participating in activities that promote racial understanding. *Compatibility of differences* refers to an understanding by students that common values exist across racial and ethnic groups, that group conflict can be constructive when it is handled appropriately, and that differences do not have to be a divisive force in society.

Other research supports the findings of Gurin (1999) regarding the positive effect of interaction with diverse people and ideas while in college. The extent to which students interact cross-racially increased the degree of acceptance students report for people from other cultures, the rate at which they participate in community service programs, and the amount of growth they exhibit in other areas of civic responsibility (Bowen & Bok, 1998). Similarly, involvement in more racially diverse environments and activities helps students develop higher levels of cultural awareness and acceptance and increased commitment to promoting positive race relations in our country (Milem, 1992, 1994; Sax & Astin, 1997). Conversely, other scholars found that the absence of interracial contact adversely influenced student views toward others, their support for campus initiatives, and other important educational outcomes. White students who had the least social interaction with individuals of a different background were less likely to express positive attitudes about multiculturalism on campus (Globetti, Globetti, Brown, & Smith, 1993).

A recent study of law students at Harvard University and the University of Michigan (Orfield & Whitla, 2001) indicates that the opportunity these students had to interact with diverse people and diverse ideas while in law school enhanced their legal education in fundamental ways. Specifically, these students indicate that exposure to racial and ethnic diversity at law school enhanced their learning by giving them opportunities to engage in discussions with others they would not otherwise have had. These students report that diversity improved the quality of their in-class discussions and enhanced their ability to work and get along with others. Moreover, these students reported that their views of our criminal justice system, their thinking about civil rights, and their attitudes regarding various social and economic institutions in society were strongly influenced by their exposure to diversity while in law school.

As we mentioned earlier, because we live in a racially segregated society, the first, and often only, opportunity that most students will have to live and work closely with people who are racially and ethnically different will occur in college. Research indicates that interacting with people from diverse backgrounds while in college disrupts the cycle of segregation that prevails in our society. Studies have shown that students who attend institutions with higher levels of diversity and report high levels of interaction with diverse people and information are more likely to live and work in desegregated environments after leaving college. Interacting with diverse ideas and people while in college encourages students to continue these behaviors throughout their lifetimes. Gurin's (1999) findings suggest this is particularly true for whites:

> Diversity experiences during college had impressive effects on the extent to which graduates in the national study were living racially and ethnically integrated lives in the post-college world. Students who had taken the most diversity courses and interacted the most with diverse peers during college had the most cross-racial interactions five years after leaving college. This confirms that the long-term pattern of segregation noted by many social scientists can be broken by diversity experiences during college. (p. 133)

How Diversity Enhances Student Learning

Students' learning outcomes are enhanced in a number of ways by their interactions with diversity in college. Students who interact more with diversity in college show greater relative gains in critical thinking and active thinking. Pascarella, Whitt et al. (1996) reported that students who participated in racial and cultural awareness workshops showed measurable gains in their critical thinking skills at the end of their first year of college. In another study using these data, Pascarella, Edison, Nora, Hagedorn, and Terenzini (1996) studied changes in students' openness to diversity and challenge after their first year of college. After controlling for precollege characteristics (including levels of openness to diversity and challenge when students first entered college), they found that students were likely to report greater openness to diversity and challenge after their first year in college if they perceived that their college was nondiscriminatory, participated in racial and cultural awareness workshops, and interacted with diverse peers.

In an extension of this study, Whitt, Edison, Pascarella, Terenzini, and Nora (1998) examined factors that predicted openness to diversity and challenge after the second and third years of college. They found that after controlling for the effect of individual student characteristics, perceptions of a nondiscriminatory racial environment at the college, participation in racial or cultural awareness workshops, having diverse student acquaintances, and engaging in conversations with other students in which diverse ways of thinking and understanding were emphasized predicted openness to diversity and challenge after the second and third years of college.

Research on the effect of a curriculum diversification project in a sequence of human development courses adds to our understanding of the effect of exposure to diverse ideas and information. MacPhee, Kreutzer, and Fritz's (1994) findings indicated that exposure to information through a curriculum diversification project enhanced students' openness to diversity and their critical thinking skills. They used both quantitative and qualitative methods to examine the effect of the curriculum transformation that occurred in these courses. The findings from the quantitative analyses suggested that student attitudes toward outgroups (particularly the poor) were broadly influenced by the transformation of the curriculum. They also found small but statistically significant changes in students' racial attitudes. The qualitative analyses revealed three primary findings: First, students had developed a number of critical thinking skills. Second, levels of ethnocentrism among students declined. Finally, students who had enrolled in these classes were able to make an appropriate distinction between poverty and ethnicity as developmental risk factors (MacPhee et al., 1994).

Gurin (1999) provided additional evidence regarding how diversity enhances students' learning outcomes. Students who reported higher levels of contact with diverse ideas, information, and people were more likely to show growth in their active thinking processes, which were represented by increases in measures of complex thinking and social and historical thinking (Gurin, 1999). These students were also more likely to show higher levels of intellectual engagement and motivation. Furthermore, students who had greater exposure to diversity in college were likely to report that they had higher postgraduate degree aspirations.

Gurin's (1999) analyses also showed that exposure to various types of diversity had different relative, or conditional, effects, based on students' racial or ethnic background. Although white students were more likely to benefit from exposure to diverse ideas, information, *and* exposure to diverse peers, African American students were more likely to benefit from the interactions they had with diverse peers. In addition, African American students experienced positive learning outcomes when they were exposed to close friends of their own race. Gurin's analyses indicate that for African American students to fully benefit from their exposure to diverse peers in college, they must also have opportunities for meaningful contact with same-race peers.

Clearly, the learning outcomes that result from exposure to diversity in college are the types of outcomes that citizens in a diverse democracy must have, including increased openness to difference, greater awareness, increased critical thinking, and increases in complex thinking. Given the increasing racial segregation in our neighborhoods and schools, however, most people in our country do not have a chance to interact in a meaningful way with diverse others prior to college. As a result, the only opportunity that many students have to be exposed to diversity occurs when they are in college. Of course, this assumes that students actually enroll in diverse colleges.

THINGS STUDENTS CAN DO TO MAXIMIZE THEIR LEARNING FROM DIVERSITY

College students can do a number of things while they are in college to maximize their opportunities to be exposed to and learn from diversity. The key to becoming involved in any of these activities is willingness on the part of students to take risks and become involved in activities in which they have not been involved previously.

- Enroll in more courses that expose them to information about the experiences of diverse people, both domestic and international. Courses that provide increased exposure to the diverse experiences and perspectives of people of color in the United States can be found in the curricular offerings of most institutions of higher education. They are frequently offered in ethnic studies programs, such as Chicano/Latino or Native American studies programs. Courses with diverse content can also be found in different academic departments across the campus. Courses that expose students to international perspectives are found in various academic departments scattered across the institution. Talk to your academic advisor to identify what courses are most appropriate for your interests.

- Become involved in structured opportunities to engage diverse others in conversation. Examples of these activities include intergroup dialogue programs that exist on many campuses, participation in community-based study groups, and participation in conflict mediation programs and related activities. There are several programs across the country that have received recognition for the work that they do in this area. Information about a few of these programs can be found at the following websites:

  - The Intergroup Relations Center at Arizona State University, http://www.asu.edu/provost/intergroup/index.html;

  - The Intergroup Relations Center at the University of Michigan, http://www.umich.edu/~igrc/; and

  - The Student Intercultural Learning Center in the Office of Human Relations Programs at the University of Maryland, http://www.inform.umd.edu/ CampusInfo/Departments/OHRP.

- Learn to speak another language. Every language a student speaks increases the opportunities they will have to engage others from diverse backgrounds. Language ability eliminates a potential barrier to communication with people from different cultural and ethnic backgrounds. Also, through learning of other languages, we frequently have the opportunity to learn about the cultural context of the people who speak the language.

- Organize or participate in living and learning communities that focus on diversity-related issues or themes. A great deal of research on college effects indicates that living and learning communities provide students important opportunities for learning that cannot easily be found elsewhere. Through exposing students to diverse ideas and the experiences students have living with diverse others, diversity-focused living and learning communities can expose students to the three types of diversity discussed earlier in important and powerful ways.

- Become involved in research being done by faculty on your campus that focuses on diversity. There is no better way to learn about the complexities of diversity and the many benefits that can come from it than to study it with faculty members who have expertise in a diversity- related area. In addition, getting involved in faculty research enables you to develop important scholarly skills that you will rely on throughout your academic and professional career.

- Attend events and programs sponsored by various racial and ethnic student organizations on campus. A variety of events are offered during the celebration of Hispanic Heritage Month, African American History Month, and Asian/Pacific American Heritage Month. Events can include speakers, cultural performances, and art shows, among other things.

- Make sure students take advantage of every opportunity to participate in informal social activities with diverse peers at your institution. An abundance of research indicates that a student's most important teacher is another student. Hence, the more opportunities that a student has to engage diverse others, the more he or she will have the opportunity to learn about them and they will have to learn about the student. A few examples of activities that can facilitate learning with and from your peers include sharing meals, forming discussion or study groups, and attending religious or spiritual activities with peers from diverse backgrounds.

- Continue to read about different races, ethnicities, and cultures. Do not let the learning that you have begun stop when a class ends or when a particular experience ends. Build on the information that you learn from these experiences by continuing your reading and exploration of relevant topics, themes, and issues.

- Encourage campus administrators to continue their efforts to build a diverse student body, faculty, and staff on campus. Although many campuses have made progress in diversifying their student bodies, other campus constituencies remain rather homogeneous. This is particularly true among the faculty and upper-level administrative ranks on campuses. Students are more likely to be exposed to diverse curricular offerings and have opportunities to engage in diversity-related research on campuses that have diverse faculty members. Students can influence campus decisions and policies regarding diversity by demanding that campus administrators recruit and retain people of color at the institution.

REFERENCES

Alger, J. R. (1997). The educational value of diversity. *Academe*, 83, 20–23.

Barber, B. (1992). *An aristocracy of everyone*. New York: Ballantine Books.

Bernstein, A., & Cock, J. (1997, November 14). Educating citizens for democracies young and old. *Chronicle of Higher Education*, B6F.

Bowen, W. G., & Bok, D. (1998). *The shape of the river: Long-term consequences of considering race in college and university admissions*. Princeton, NJ: Princeton University Press.

Boyte, H. C., & Kari, N. N. (2000). Renewing the democratic spirit in American colleges and universities: Higher education as public work. In T. Ehrlich (Ed.), *Civic responsibility and higher education* (pp. 37–59). Oryx Press.

Chang, M. J. (1999a, January). *An examination of conceptual and empirical linkages between diversity initiatives and student learning in higher education*. Presented at the American Council on Education Working Conference and Research Symposium on Diversity and Affirmative Action, Washington, DC.

Chang, M. J. (1999b). Does diversity matter? The educational impact of a racially diverse undergraduate population. *Journal of College Student Development, 40*, 377–395.

Coser, R. (1975). The complexity of roses as a seedbed for individual autonomy. In L. A. Coser (Ed.), *The idea of social structure: Papers in honor of Robert Merton* (pp. 85–102). New York: Harcourt Brace Jovanovich.

Damon, W. (1998, October 16). The path to a civil society goes through the university. *Chronicle of Higher Education*, B4F.

Dred Scott v. John F. A. Sandford. 60 U.S. 393 (1856).

Erickson, E. (1946). Ego development and historical change. *Psychoanalytic Study of the Child, 2*, 359–396.

Erikson, E. (1956). The problem of ego identity. *Journal of American Psychoanalytical Association, 4*, 56–121.

Federal Register Division, National Archives and Records Service, General Services Administration. (1966). *Public papers of the presidents: Lyndon Johnson 1965*. Washington, DC: Government Printing Office.

Fong, H. L. (1963, August 8). American immigration policy. *Congressional Record, 109*, pt. 12. p. 15765.

George Washington Papers. (1783, December 2). *Address to the members of the volunteer association and other inhabitants of the kingdom of Ireland who have lately arrived in the city of New York* (Microfilm reels, Series 4, Reel 93). U.S. Library of Congress.

Globetti, E. C., Globetti, G., Brown, C. L., & Smith, R. E. (1993). Social Interaction and Multiculturalism. *NASPA Journal, 30*, 209–218.

Gurin, P. (1999). Expert report of Patricia Gurin. In *The compelling need for diversity in higher education*, presented in *Gratz, et al. v. Bollinger, et al.*, and *Grutter, et al. v. Bollinger, et al.*, (pp. 99–234). Ann Arbor, MI: University of Michigan.

Hurtado, S., Milem, J. F., Clayton-Pedersen, A. R., & Allen, W. R. (1998). Enhancing campus climates for racial/ethnic diversity through educational policy and practice. *Review of Higher Education, 21*(3), 279–302.

Hurtado, S., Milem, J. F., Clayton-Pedersen, A. R., & Allen, W. R. (1999). Enacting diverse learning environments: Improving the campus climate for racial/ethnic diversity. *ASHE/ERIC Higher Education Reports Series 26*(8).

King, P. (1978). William Perry's theory of intellectual and ethical development. In L. Knefelkamp, C. Widick, & C. Parker (Eds.), *Applying new developmental findings* (New Directions for Student Services No. 4, pp. 35–51). San Francisco: Jossey-Bass.

Langer, E. J. (1978). Rethinking the role of thought in social interaction. *New Directions in Attribution Research, 2,* 35–58.

Lawrence, C. R., III, & Matsuda, M. J. (1997). *We won't go back: Making the case for affirmative action.* Boston: Houghton Mifflin.

Liu, G. (1998). Affirmative action in higher education: The diversity rationale and the compelling interest test. *Harvard Civil Rights-Civil Liberties Law Review, 33,* 381–442.

MacPhee, D., Kreutzer, J. C., & Fritz, J. J. (1994). Infusing a diversity perspective into human development courses. *Child Development,65,* 699–715.

Milem, J. F. (1992). *The impact of college on students' racial attitudes and levels of racial awareness* (Order Number 9301968). Ann Arbor: University Microforms International.

Milem, J. F. (1994). College, students, and racial understanding. *Thought and Action, 9*(2), 51–91.

Milem, J. F. (2003). The educational benefits of diversity: Evidence from multiple sectors. In M. Chang, D. Witt, J. Jones, & K. Hakuta (Eds.), *Compelling interest: Examining the evidence on racial dynamics in higher education* (pp. 126–169). Palo Alto, CA: Stanford University Press.

Milem, J. F., & Hakuta, K. (2000). The benefits of racial and ethnic diversity in higher education, featured report. In *Minorities in higher education: Seventeenth annual status report* (pp. 39–67). Washington, DC: American Council on Education.

Orfield, G., & Whitla, D. (2001). Diversity and legal education: Student experiences in leading law schools. In G. Orfield (Ed.), *Diversity challenged: Legal crisis and new evidence* (pp. 143–174). Cambridge, MA: Harvard Education.

Pascarella, E. T., Edison, M., Nora, A., Hagedorn, L. S., & Terenzini, P. T. (1996). Influences on students' openness to diversity and challenge in the first year of college. *Journal of Higher Education, 67,* 174–195.

Pascarella, E. T. & Terenzini, P. T. (1991). *How college affects students: Findings and insights from twenty years of research.* San Francisco: Jossey-Bass.

Pascarella, E. T., Whitt, E. J., Nora, A., Edison, M., Hagedorn, L. S., & Terenzini, P. T. (1996). What have we learned from the first year of the national study of student learning? *Journal of College Student Development, 37,* 182–192.

Perry, W. G. (1970). *Forms of intellectual and ethical development in the college years: A scheme.* New York: Holt, Rinehart and Winston.

Perry, W. G. (1981). Cognitive and ethical growth. In A. Chickering & Association (Eds.), *The modern American college: Responding to the new realities of diverse students and a changing society* (pp. 76–116). San Francisco: Jossey-Bass.

Piaget, J. (1971). The theory of stages in cognitive development. In D. R. Green, M. P. Ford, & G. B. Flamer (Eds.), *Measurement and Piaget* (pp. 1–11). New York: McGraw Hill.

Piaget, J. (1985). *The equilibrium of cognitive structures: The central problem of intellectual development.* Chicago: University of Chicago Press. (Original work published 1975)

Prince, G. S. (2000). A liberal arts college perspective. In T. Ehrlich (Ed.), *Civic responsibility and higher education* (pp. 249–262).Oryx Press.

Sax, L. J., & Astin, A. W. (1997). The development of "civic virtue" among college students. In J. N. Gardner & G. Van der Veer (Eds.), *The senior year experience: Facilitating integration, reflection, closure, and transition* (pp. 131–151). San Francisco: Jossey-Bass.

U.S. Bureau of the Census. (1970). *Historical statistics of the United States.*

U.S. Bureau of the Census. (1996). *Population projections of the United States by age, sex, race and Hispanic origin: 1995 to 2050.* Washington, DC: U.S. Government Printing Office.

Whitt, E. J., Edison, M. I., Pascarella, E. T., Terenzini, P. T., & Nora, A. (1998, November). *Influences on students' openness to diversity and challenge in the second and third years of college.* Paper presented at the Annual Meeting of the Association for the Study of Higher Education.

CHAPTER 5

THE MEANING OF CULTURAL COMPETENCE
Voices of Reality, Voices of New Vision

MATTHEW R. MOCK

> *I have an earache…*
> *2000 BC…Here, eat this root.*
> *1000 AD…That root is heathen. Here, say this prayer.*
> *1850 AD…That prayer is superstition. Here, drink this potion.*
> *1940 AD…That potion is snake oil. Here, swallow this pill.*
> *1985 AD…That pill is ineffective. Here, take this antibiotic.*
> *2000 AD…That antibiotic is artificial. Here, eat this root.*
> —Anonymous

In recent years, I have been fortunate to give invited presentations to audiences on cultural competence, ethnicity, and multiculturalism in relation to understanding mental illness and treatment leading to wellness. Dressed in coat and tie and armed with prepared overhead materials, clinical vignettes, and a panoply of professional materials, I inevitably tend to start at the same place: I tell personal stories that ground and personalize my perspectives. For many of us, our stories of culture, cultural solutions when we are ill, and competence in cultural practices are our individual and collective family histories we live by, want others to know us by, or hand to others to write their own stories in the future. It is my passionate contention and conviction that practitioners have cultural stories, and to tap into these would move us further toward cultural competence and responsiveness (Mock, 2000, 2001).

A PERSONAL CULTURAL STORY OF ILLNESS, WELLNESS, AND CULTURAL COMPETENCE

As a child, I remember becoming instantly aware of cultural practices in maintaining maximum health in my Chinese American family. When I came down with the mumps at age 4, my mother toted me off to an apothecary in the heart of Chinatown. Barely tall enough to see above the glass counter filled with bins of precious ginseng root, dried seahorses, preserved plums, and finely pressed leaves, I observed the Chinese herbalist hand-placing select ingredients from ancient wooden bins on different sheets of paper. In emphatic Cantonese, I heard the expert herbalist tell my mother how to prepare the poultice and then wrap my face to bring down the swelling from the mumps.

Following his every detail, my mother prepared the salve and carefully applied it to my face and upper body. Having been born in America, and therefore being more acculturated than my parents, I remember thinking that if something were not actually curative in the black, paste-like mixture adorning my face for several days, surely the smell and itchy feel of the stuff would mentally will me to get better quickly! Vividly, I remember being embarrassed by ever telling my friends, most of who were non-Asian, that my parents had tried this traditional Chinese cure. Now, generations later, I have great curiosity about the medicinal elements that made the salve so soothing and able to cure my childhood ailment.

The Historical Definition of Cultural Competence

Cross, Bazron, Dennis, Isaacs, and Benjamin (1989) defined *cultural competence* as a set of congruent practice skills, behaviors, attitudes, and policies that come together in a system, agency, professional, or consumer provider in ways that enable that system, agency, or professional/consumer provider to work effectively in cross-cultural situations. In this way, a culturally competent system "acknowledges and incorporates at all levels the importance of culture, the assessment of cross-cultural relations, vigilance toward the dynamics that result from cultural differences, the expansion of cultural knowledge, and the adaptation of services to meet culturally unique needs" (Cross et al., 1989, p. 2). Through the lens of managed care and behavioral health care, cultural competence may be viewed as

> the integration and transformation of knowledge, information, and data about individuals and groups of people into specific clinical standards, skills, service approaches, techniques and marketing programs that match the individual's or family's culture and increase the quality and appropriateness of health care and outcomes. (Johnson & Mock, 2000, p. 4)

In its most basic ways, cultural competence must be viewed as an intrinsic function of effective client care. There must be a recognition, promotion, and integration of elements of culture at all levels of mental health and service organizations. Different than other processes, striving toward cultural competency is not a linear process, and its attainment is relative, that is it must be continuously approached and developed.

Cultural competence in mental health is not a new concept, and it has levels of complexity. It can be viewed along a continuum of cultural destructiveness, cultural blindness, cultural precompetence, basic cultural competence, and advanced cultural competence or proficiency (Cross et al., 1989).

Cultural competence is a relative concept. Unlike other attainments, such as licensure or certification, cultural competence is an ongoing process and a dynamic, constantly challenging one. In this way, it is possible that a professional or organization may seem culturally competent one minute, but with the entry of a new client or service request from someone from a different language or cultural world view, the professional may need to implement additional efforts to stay culturally responsive. In other words, cultural competence is not a linear concept, that once a system, is there it is always there. In fact, I would contend the opposite: Workers should always make constant efforts to reach and maintain what seems to be culturally effective service delivery (Mock, in press). Perhaps when workers think they are "there," they need to be careful that they are not seducing themselves into believing so, but instead continually questioning, pushing, and striving to provide culturally relevant interventions.

An Increased Interest in Cultural Competence

World events, such as the terrorism of September 11, 2001, force us to examine cultural and deeply spiritual issues in profound ways. We must examine the ways people make connections or are divided more often through everyday occurrences on personal, community, and global levels. Conflicts worldwide push us to the edges of understanding.

Recently, professionals have also shown increased specific interest in cultural competence in mental health and clinical practice. There are several reasons for this:

- In 2000, approximately one-third of the United States population was of color.

- Demographic projections show that within the next decade, there will be no majority group in this country.

- School-age children in California are already more than 50% nonwhite, that is Asian American, African American, Latino, and American Indian combined.

- The number of individuals in the United States who are foreign-born reached 19.8 million in 1990. They come from more than 100 different countries. There are more than 11 million immigrants working in America, with a steady increase anticipated (Hall, 1997; Johnson & Mock, 2000).

- Due to affirmative action policies, there is a larger representation of women and people of color at all levels in many service systems. This increased diversity creates work force and service challenges as well as opportunities.

- An estimated 49 million Americans—almost 20% of the total population— have some kind of disability. Experts estimate that there is an 80% chance that the average person will experience some kind of disability during the course of their lifetime (Johnson & Mock, 2000, p. 3).

With this as the backdrop, the inclusion of cultural issues in service delivery is inevitable. To illustrate, in June 1998, former President Clinton ordered sweeping protection for all Medicare beneficiaries. These Medicare rules, stricter than the standards governing commercial health insurance in many states, included this requirement: "Health plans must provide services in a culturally competent manner to all Medicare patients, including those with limited English proficiency or reading skills, diverse cultural and ethnic backgrounds and physical or mental disabilities" (Pear, 1998, pp. A1, A5).

The American Medical Association, the American Psychological Association (2000), and the National Association of Social Workers, to name just three professional organizations, have developed guidelines for cultural competence. Furthermore, most states have passed cultural competence standards for service providers. Compliance with these standards are an integral part of ongoing program audits.

These are concrete examples of how cultural competence is no longer just hypothetical, but is being implemented in actual practice.

CULTURAL COMPETENCE: IMPERATIVES IN MENTAL HEALTH

Although it is clear that population changes and trends for the future underline the significance of understanding culture in mental health service delivery, other facts related to those who provide services show how out-of-step current providers are in reality. For example, in contrast to the diversity of consumers, the field of psychology is 94% white and only 6% African American, American Indian, Asian American, Latino, or Hispanic. A disproportion exists between mental health professionals and communities being served, including diverse ethnic and linguistic groups, gays and lesbians, and clients who are very young and elderly (Hall, 1997). Acknowledging these inequities, professionals have been concerned as to how to appropriately address "pipeline" (i.e., increasing the flow and matriculation of diverse future professionals) issues in the future of psychology, social work, child and family therapy, and other guilds. The California Mental Health Planning Council (1999) tried to proactively address these issues in a series of position papers. Among some of the conclusions reached specific to cultural competence were:

- work readiness in the classroom;

- field-based curriculum and faculty;

- licensing boards and professional recruitment;

- multilingual and multicultural pipeline and antistigma strategies;

- rural outreach strategies;

- school-to-career strategies;

- job retraining;

- peer counseling and parent advocate development; and

- community redefinition, corporate partnerships, and collaboration.

Trends in service delivery to specific cultural and ethnic groups have repeatedly revealed specific problems and inequities. For example, disproportionate percentages of diagnostic categories for specific groups exist, as well as disproportionate lengths of hospitalization and use of psychotropic medications. Only the most recent version of the *Diagnostic and Statistical Manual of Mental Disorders* (4th ed., *DSM-IV*; American Psychiatric Association, 1994) has acknowledged the importance of culture in diagnosing, but only as additional provisos or appendix items for consideration. In summary, the profile of clinicians providing mental health services and assessment, diagnosis, and intervention are out of step with the realities of the individuals and families being served.

Cultural competence is not only a practice issue but an ethical one as well. As an example, a review of the ethics under which all psychologists must provide services underscores the challenge. Psychologists are to be aware of the relevant research and practices related to the client, and therefore their community. To understand the client or consumer and their problem presentation, psychologists' practices should incorporate clients' cultures and ethnic backgrounds. As in all situations, psychologists must recognize the limits of their competencies and expertise, and when necessary, seek consultation, sometimes on an ongoing basis. The reality is that these resources may not be readily available, or when available may not be used in a timely way. In making their initial clinical assessments, psychologists should determine whether the psychological problem being presented may be related to such societal forces as racism, discrimination, or other forms of oppression. That is, how does the effect of societal injustices affect the client's or family's lives? It is interesting to note that while discrimination is listed as an example of a possible stressor in making a diagnosis in *DSM-IV* on Axis 4, it is rare that racism is listed as a stressor. In fact, academicians have discussed whether racism should also be considered a clinical syndrome (Dobbins & Skillings, 2000; Mock, 1999). Why is this so? Does racism not exist? Is racism marginal to the problem presentation? Is it looked at as a norm or expected reality in certain communities and is therefore treated as an "assumed reality?"

Because clinical interventions occur between one person (the client) and another (the clinician), it is important that professionals understand the variables in this interaction. In relation to culture, psychologists must be aware of their own cultural background and socialization, and how these might affect not only on the therapeutic relationship, but also interventions (e.g., if they have a different world view than their client, based on spiritual beliefs and practices).

Finally, psychologists must understand the limitations and potential biases in diagnoses and treatment. In the history of diagnostic categorization, one must not forget that there was a diagnosis preferred by a general physician named Cartwright called *drapetomania*, or flight-from-home madness, for slaves who tried to run away from their slave masters (Carter, 1995, pg. 33). Slaves who tried to rise up against their oppressors through confrontational acts were similarly labeled as deviant or disturbed. Similarly, in the *DSM-III* (American Psychiatric Association, 1980), homosexuality and masochism were potentially applied to women who chose to stay in battering relationships. The latter provisional diagnosis failed to appreciate inequities in power and family influence (e.g., income, responsibility, and disparate views on parental responsibilities between father and mother) and their relation to why a woman might feel forced to remain in an abusive relationship. Yet another example is to acknowledge that among some diverse communities, there may be different understandings of the concept of self and therefore, the focus of treatment.

In the area of research, which may serve as the foundation for interventions, theories, and other practices, a focus on cultural competence appears sorely lacking. First, a relative paucity of publications and research on topics devoted to issues of race, ethnicity, class, and culture in the major psychology journals exists. Existing mental health literature on ethnic minority groups is at a relatively low level, in part, due to subtle and systemic problems. For example, there may be a history of different standards applied toward different groups being researched. Sue (1998) commented on a situation in which professionals critiqued a body of research that focused on an African American sample because the authors did not compare the results to a white sample. Similar problems might be encountered when trying to do core research on gay or lesbian communities. In this case, must there be a comparable heterosexual sample to give the research credibility or relative norming? If this is so, why is the opposite not true (i.e., white sample studies needing ethnic comparison sample groups)? Clearly, many questions have been raised about psychological science's bias against minority research.

Other issues in which psychological research falls short of addressing the needs of communities of color and cultural competence include ongoing disagreement about the merits of specific research or scientific writings, including generalization or sophistication of design and an acceptable significant sample size. Ongoing debate exists about the acceptability of the validity of what is considered by some to be more descriptive or qualitative research over quantitative research. Internal validity, to draw causal inferences, and external validity, to be able to generalize results to the populations and settings of interest, are often not equal partners in the dynamic, ongoing tension of research (Sue, 1998).

Certainly, if practitioners practice responsibly and ethically with diverse individuals, families, or communities using research to support their work outcomes, they should look at how they applied culturally appropriate, effective, and competent services. Often, researchers use linear paper-and-pencil processes to measure consumers or clients and their community's or family's attitudes regarding success or reduction of measurable problem behaviors. Significant questions may be raised about how well such assessment tools may be taking into account the relevance or significance of race, culture, or class in treatment outcomes. For example, because mental illness is a stigma in some Asian families, what would be the desirability of filling out a computerized outcome measure? On one occasion, a consumer questioned whether the results would determine whether her child and family would continue to receive critical mental health treatment. Might focus groups in the community be another way to answer questions of cultural relevance or efficacy? On another level, when language equivalency or relevance of instruments are taken into account, there seem to be potential weaknesses, flaws, and even outright dangers in using the results in policy making that will affect multicultural communities. Therefore, how results may be eventually used in a multicultural community may be different than in a mainstream community and, therefore, should be considered cautiously.

Additional questions about the use of outcomes include asking what is the appropriate level of input to be given by multiethnic consumers of services toward future service delivery, including modality, location, and type. Also, when cultural issues do have a less-than-positive effect on the treatment relationship and therefore potential feedback through outcomes, how often are changes actually made? In other words, when client satisfaction measures assess cultural or linguistic issues in treatment, are specific or larger programmatic changes made, or does the problem continue to reside in the client and be rationalized in such ways as, "individual (or community) is treatment resistant," rather than create understanding that he or she may be hesitant to seek services due to an unaddressed dynamic?

Cultural competency imperatives in clinical practices, ethics, research, and outcomes can be used to inform and drive mental health systems. Until they are fully understood and adopted, adequate services may be lacking for several cultural communities.

DYNAMICS OF CULTURAL MARGINALIZATION OR EXCLUSION

Systems that fail to fully address cultural competence include processes and dynamics that lead to marginalization or exclusion of consumers and families. Although some of these exclusionary processes may seem obvious, sometimes they operate on subtle levels, and they may not come with malicious intent. Defining and describing some of these processes, however, may lead to more effective and conscious confrontation of how they are exclusionary and fall short of the goal of cultural competence. It should be noted that the processes that follow may have some overlap or may operate simultaneously to different degrees.

At one time or another, we all engage in what might be referred to as "designs of omission" (Kunisawa, 1998). Acts of omission refer to values, items, or actions that are left out, kept separate, or put in a lower value category than others. One cited act of omission is although we have a world that consists of people who are right handed and left handed, right handedness is given preference. One can quickly be reminded of this by thinking how hard it still is to find left-handed desks or scissors. Even in the words we use, such as dexterous, which means "to the right," and sinister, which means "to the left," there seems to be a value base that underlies this omission. As psychotherapists, we collude with omissions in a major way related to psychiatric diagnosing through *DSM-IV*. Axis IV diagnoses reference psychosocial stressors, which contribute to the individual's current state. Although racism, heterosexism, oppression, and various forms of discrimination are certainly social stressors, they are grossly underused on Axis IV. One argument is that all minorities face discrimination, so there is no need to list the obvious (Mock, 1999).

Other acts that are not only culturally incompetent but lead to marginalization are processes in which we "take away voice." The vast majority of Americans are "strangers from a different shore" (Mock, 1998; Takaki, 1989). Processes of assimilation and acculturation lead to changes in who we are and what we value. As a child, my primarily Cantonese-speaking mother would refer to me as Matt. As an adolescent, I asked her to call me my full name, Matthew. In all her best efforts, she could not say Matthew correctly. When I asked my sister why this was, she said, "Don't you know that in Cantonese, there is no 'th' diphthong, so she struggles to pronounce what is foreign to her?" I then returned to directly ask my mother, "Then why did you name me a name you cannot say?" Her ready and assertive response was, "I give you a good American name because you are in America, not in China!" Although this example has a humorous side, there are other examples of people's names getting changed on immigration forms but remaining permanent. Taking away of voice can be seen as a metaphor of, when a large group is represented, what gets referenced or internalized as preferred, desired, or better. Often this entails a process of giving up something, of loss.

We all often engage in acts where there is a "pretending we are all the same." Although there are truisms in this (e.g., we are all human beings who bleed and can feel joy and pain), conditions or situations in which we are richly different exist. For example, early versions of *DSM* included general diagnostic categories, with no mention of culture. Now, *DSM-IV* gives provisions for different culturally based symptoms and even syndromes. For example, there is Chi Gong psychosis (Chinese), Fallen Awatick (American Indian), and Ataque de Nervios (Latino).

There are certainly situations in which we "perpetuate the legacy of inequality." Although there may be overall agreement that women have progressed in being treated more equal to men, certainly institutional inequities still exist in such obvious forms as jobs, pay, roles, and opportunities. In a major Bay Area newspaper, a major feature section focused on computer technology and advances. Reviewing the photos or pictorials accompanying these multipage articles, one reader noted that the vast majority were of men, and for that matter, were white men. In response, the editor of the section wrote that photos were taken randomly and seemed to want to convey that this process was out of his control. It might be argued, however, that he was not taking responsibility for what he could or might do, or was trying to explain the criticism away, or through his nonaction was perpetuating the legacy of inequality. It is interesting to note that in this example, even angrier letters followed his attempted explanation. The printing of these letters publicly indicated the need for increased awareness.

In competitive societies with finite resources, a dividing of the haves from the have-nots often exists. One example of this is college admissions and the debate about affirmative action, in which some argue that it is unfair to give added points to those previously underrepresented or disenfranchised, including people of color. What often gets lost in the argument of who is deserving of what and why, is why as a society, we do not focus more on working toward getting all people, especially young people who are forging their futures and who want a chance at higher education, into colleges and universities. In related arguments, a blaming the victim dynamic exists, that is, the attitude that people of color do not make the grade because they just do not try hard enough.

One other major act of exclusion and cultural incompetence is having a program or system that is designed for only a few, often the majority. Some local mental health programs in California serving children, families, and adults have been trying to work out more consolidated points of access. One program had all clients initially call a toll-free, 1-800 number. Although the area had a population that was nearly 10% African American, African Americans were seen in this mental health service. When clients calling on the toll-free line were asked if they were from a specific ethnic community or wished for a therapist from a particular background, along with other preferences, the response was, "We do not ask because African Americans do not seem to need services." I questioned this, suggesting reaching out to more community settings, such as churches, community-based organizations, and more direct face-to-face informing, rather than solely via phone. This is an example of a system designed for only a few, that is those who can verbally articulate their problems and can speak to an anonymous professional. If there are no calls, the problem apparently does not exist!

Although this list of exclusionary acts or processes contributing to falling short of cultural competence may seem daunting, alternative processes and stances can contribute to greater cultural awareness, sensitivity, and even commitment to competence.

VOICES OF NEW VISION: DYNAMICS OF INCLUSIVENESS, INTEGRATION, AND MORE ACCURATE REALITIES

One initial premise is to look at culture, which we all possess, although some people are more distant from or close to their cultural heritages, as a source of survival for many. Taking on this perspective, if our survival is threatened, we either take flight or fight. In working with others from different cultures than our own, even opening up a conversation about how one's culture has been a source of survival leads to many opportunities to talk about identity, family, and community. It can also open up difficult, yet often critical, dialogue about experiences of discrimination or oppression.

As service providers we might also struggle in trying to understand how legacies of oppression are still lived today. Consequences of historical injustices such as slavery, the Holocaust, internment, and antigay movements have not gone away. We have vivid, painful reminders of this in the dragging murder of James Byrd II, who was African American, and the brutal beating to death of Matthew Shepard, a gay man. Hardy (1994) discussed the continuing residuals of slavery in such processes as psychological homelessness and trying to deal with marginalization through violence or drug use.

Following governmental reparations for the internment of Japanese Americans, I treated several different Japanese American men who described their fathers as distant, closed, and unwilling to talk about the forging of their Japanese American identities. In these situations, it was uncovered that they had been interned during the war, and because of the resulting and continuing shame, did not want to talk about their own experiences, thereby leading to being emotionally cut off from their sons, who were struggling with their own issues about becoming family.

An important stance that a service provider might take in working with cultural "others" is understanding multiple oppressions as trauma. In her important work on trauma and recovery, Herman (1992) described some of the effect of trauma and potential interventions. Several years ago, violence was declared the number one health issue in America. Racist acts are certainly forms of violence along the continuum. Yet when they are not physical but are nonetheless repeated and degrading, they may not be treated as a trauma. Clinicians often try to explore potential roots or the original trauma leading to the current problem presentation. Are all clinicians willing to look at the trauma of racism, sexism, and homophobia? As they may become the therapeutic target in helping to work through these issues, are they adequately prepared, and have they worked out their own issues?

It is important to understand and perhaps even teach a process of "bicultural competence." We all are a part of the same earth, yet we exist in multiple contexts. That is, among my Asian American community, I might appear or even behave in certain ways, different from or even contrasting with my professional behavior. Because there are certain cues or values in the different contexts of society in which one interacts, it is important to teach these and understand their meaning and significance. Some youth of color with whom I have worked discussed how behaviors or manner of dress differ among their own inner circle of friends and in front of police or other authority figures. With evidence that certain police officers might stop certain teenagers who wear certain colors of clothing or frequent certain areas, youth who do not want police confrontation might be helped in understanding what attitudes or perspectives they might take on in such interactions to stay out of trouble.

As a contribution to community healing, we must look deep into our ability to share collective grief, shame, and loss. As has been said, "Racism: Getting sick wasn't our fault, but getting well is our responsibility." Although racism perhaps was not one of our creations, we must understand how we might perpetuate its continued existence. This means getting in touch with the ways we might feel privileged or be in power or influence. We have all been targets of mistreatment, or perhaps been the perpetrator of such injustices. We must own these circumstances and be able to share sadness and shame to move on. The terrorism of September 11, 2001, hurt us all and continues to force us to examine our grief and anger and the possibility of any reconciliation.

Last, we might also remember that sometimes solutions emanate from the community. Rather than assuming that trained professionals are always the most knowledgeable, workers must remember that community members know themselves best. Many marginalized communities have survived a series of challenges, but they have survived and even thrived. To tap into these sources of survival and be engaged in a process to empower these families and communities may be the most important source of culturally competent processes.

A New Vision: Cultural Competence as a Stance

One major perspective in moving practitioners and systems toward cultural competence is the stance in working with cultural others: the power of *not* knowing (Mock, in press). It is important to understand what it means to be in a power position in the therapeutic relationship and how to best use this in helping those who are often marginalized (Pinderhughes, 1988). Rather than going in with a fixed, set knowledge base of any cultural description, it is perhaps more informed for the practitioner to hold any knowledge base in a relative stance to the specific individual or family at hand. After all, "in some ways we are like some persons, like all persons and like no other persons" (Kluckhohn & Strodtbeck, 1961, p. 24). A practitioner striving toward cultural competence may be more effective in taking a respectful stance of naivete and curiosity (Dyche & Zayas, 1995). Finally, rather than getting caught up in solely acting out of political correctness, we should all be aware of what it means to be personally compassionate and personally connected (Mock, 1998). Rather that a simplistic, linear view of cultural competence, this author has formulated a multidimensional "Triple C-A-R-E" model (Mock, 2002a, 2002b, in press), which incorporates such concepts as compassion, accountability, responsiveness and effectiveness.*

Cultural Competence: The Telling of New Stories

To teach graduate students alternative perspectives of wellness and illness in families that are culturally different than their own, I often take them directly to cultural healers in the heart of the community. We might go to Chinatown to introduce them to a Chinese herbalist or traditional pharmacist. As I return with yet another ambitious group, the herbalist beams with pride, glad that someone as acculturated as myself, along with students of many cultures, are still interested in what wisdom he has to impart about the things that contribute to illness and wellness.

As one of the learning processes in understanding his perspectives on illness and wellness, I encourage my students to ask him how he would attempt to cure certain illnesses. "What do you consider to be the cause of depression?" inquires one student. "Problems related to the heart," says the pharmacist. "Perhaps it is too cold, or vital energy is out of balance." "How about schizophrenia or psychosis?" asks another one of these future clinicians. The pharmacist responds with quick authority, "I would look to something with the liver or kidney. Perhaps there is too much yin or yang. There would certainly be something out of balance." Reaching for one of many wooden drawers that line the walls behind him, he goes on to say "Do you see these dried cicada shells? These are very good for treating those forms of mental problems. These would be used in making a tea to help these symptoms."

---

* For a more complete explication of these concepts and this text see Mock (in press).

Inevitably, perhaps not being able to fully appreciate the ease with which he is able to prescribe natural cures for some common mental illnesses, someone asks about the procedure he uses to diagnose problems to make a prescription toward wellness. "I listen to the meridians and try to assess the *chi* or vital energy, our life force. I would want to know significant events in that person's life. I also learn a lot by looking at their tongue, focusing on its texture, coloring, smoothness, or bumpiness. I look for evenness in all of its many aspects," he responds with assuredness balanced with sensitivity. Among mostly Western-trained students, a response such as this is often met with amazement, mixed with some degree of silence, if not outspoken doubt. How would you know this? What do you actually see? And what scientific proof is there as a basis for how your prescriptions work in bringing one from illness to wellness? Time and time again, I can still hear him say gently yet affirmatively with an assuring smile,

> What I know and the way I practice has been handed down for generations, from my father's father, his father's father, and so on. My mother is also one of the most highly respected elder practitioners in this area. All of what we know and what works and what makes people well have been evidenced over generations. We have no simple explanation other than it works. What other evidence and support do we need than all of the generations, along with their testimonials that have challenged mental and physical illness and moved toward maintaining wellness?

With comments such as this, my students are often silenced with a humbleness of what they know through life experience and what they have been told is perhaps not the end all after all.

REFERENCES

American Psychiatric Association. (1980). *Diagnostic and statistical manual of mental disorders* (3rd ed.). Washington, DC: Author.

American Psychiatric Association. (1994). *Diagnostic and statistical manual of mental disorders* (4th ed.). Washington, DC: Author.

American Psychological Association, Public Interest Directorate. (2000). *Guidelines for psychotherapy with lesbian, gay, and bisexual clients.* Washington, DC: Author.

California Mental Health Planning Council. (1999, June). *The future of work force challenges.* Berkeley, CA: California State Department of Mental Health.

Carter, R. (1995). *The influence of race and racial identity in psychotherapy: Toward a racially inclusive model.* New York: John Wiley and Sons.

Cross, T. L., Bazron, B. K., Dennis, K. W., Isaacs, M. R., & Benjamin, M. P. (1989). *Towards a culturally competent system of care.* Washington, DC: CAASP Technical Assistance Center.

Dobbins, J., & Skillings, J. (2000) *Racism as a clinical syndrome.* American Journal of Ortho-psychiatry, 70*(1), 14–27.*

Dyche, L., & Zayas, L. (1995). The value of curiosity and naivete for the cross-cultural thera-pist. *Family Process, 34,* 389–399.

Hall, C. (1997). Cultural malpractice: The growing obsolescence of psychology with the chang-ing U.S. population. *American Psychologist, 52,* 642–651.

Hardy, K. (1994). *Psychological residuals of slavery.* Topeka, KS: Equal Partners.

Herman, J. (1992). *Trauma and recovery.* New York: Basic Books.

Johnson, J., & Mock, M. (2000, June). *The foundations of cultural competence in mental health.* Presented at the Adult Systems of Care conference, Santa Clara, CA.

Kluckhohn, F. R., & Strodtbeck, F. L. (1961). *Variations in value orientations.* Evanston, IL: Row, Peterson.

Kunisawa, B. (1998, November 4). *Addressing the third wave: The global challenge for the 21st century.* Presented at the Cultural Competence and Mental Health Summit VI, Bakersfield, CA.

Mock, M. R. (1998). Breaking barriers: A primary movement for social justice in psychology. In M. Mock, L. Hill, & D. Tucker. (Eds.). *Breaking barriers: Psychology in the public interest.* Sacramento, CA: American Psychological Association.

Mock, M. R. (1999). Cultural competency: Acts of justice in community mental health. *Commu-nity Psychologist, 32*(1), 38–40.

Mock, M. R. (2000). From illness to wellness: Appreciating our cultural perspectives. *Journal of NAMI California, 11*(4), 13–16.

Mock, M. R. (2001). Interactions with multicultural families: Working with Asian American Families. *Family Psychologist, 17*(3), 1–7.

Mock, M. R. (2002a, April 24–25). *Assessment and measurement of cultural competence.* Pre-sented at the County of Los Angeles Fourth Annual Multicultural Conference, Los Angeles, CA.

Mock, M. R. (2002b, April 24–25). *At the heart of the matter: Culture counts!* Presented at the County of Los Angeles Fourth Annual Multicultural Conference, Los Angeles, CA.

Mock, M. R. (2003). Cultural sensitivity, relevance, and competence in school mental health. In M. Weist, S. Evans, & N. Lever (Eds.), *Handbook of school mental health: Advancing practice and research* (pp. 349–362). Plenum Press.

Pear, R. (1998, June 23). Safeguards ordered for Medicare. *San Francisco Chronicle,* A1, A5.

Pinderhughes, E. (1988). *Understanding race, ethnicity, and power.* New York: Free Press.

Sue, S. (1998). In search of cultural competence in psychotherapy and counseling. *American Psychologist, 53,* 440448.

Takaki, R. (1989). *Strangers from a different shore.* Boston: Little, Brown.

CHAPTER 6

THE ROLE OF LEADERSHIP IN ADDRESSING ISSUES OF RACE AND ETHNICITY
Cultural Competence as a Framework and Leadership Strategy

MICHAEL L. BENJAMIN AND MARVA P. BENJAMIN

> *If we wish to inspire the peoples of the world…, if we wish to restore hope to those who have already lost their civil liberties, if we wish to fulfill the promise that is ours, we must correct the remaining imperfections in our practice of democracy. We know the way. We need only the will.*
> —President Harry S. Truman, Special Message to the United States Congress on Civil Rights, February 2, 1948

Throughout the history of the United States of America, a few courageous leaders acted on their beliefs that if social injustices, unequal access to services, and negative attitudes and beliefs about race, ethnicity, and civil rights were left unattended, the United States could spiral downward in a slippery slope toward economic strife, social turmoil, and cultural chaos, and lose its place as a world leader (West, 1994). These political, religious, and organizational leaders, whether at community, state, or national levels, have been effective in addressing issues of inequality, negative attitudes, beliefs, and behaviors involving issues of race and ethnicity. They believed that it was of paramount importance to correct the racial- and ethnic-related imperfections in the way our country practices democracy and in the way we deliver services to culturally diverse populations.

This chapter provides selected historical and current examples of the contributions of religious, organizational, and political leaders who have risen to champion the cause of eradicating the separate but equal doctrine in public accommodations, which are rooted in historic inequalities, economic considerations, and longstanding cultural stereotypes. For example, Martin Luther King Jr., a courageous religious leader of the civil rights movement, convinced large numbers of people that racism was not simply un-American in some provincial sense of being against our creed of fair play, but was in fact, a sin against God, and that it jeopardized America's special destiny as a world leader (Early, 2000).

Moreover, King and his supporters were convinced of the necessity for nonviolent protests in confronting issues of inequality. Indeed, King believed that social change did not result from "sitting around having nice conversations," but making "the country uncomfortable, embarrassed, downright guilty, explosively tense" (Early 2000, p. 194). As such, he was an activist who was arrested several times for his role in nonviolent campaigns directed at African American voter registration, desegregation, equal education, and fair housing opportunities. As a leader, King was certainly proactive, outcome oriented, and determined to realize his vision of a nation that did not judge people by the color of their skin. Because of King's leadership in the civil rights movement, he was honored with the Nobel Peace Prize in 1964.

At the organizational level, national organizations like the board of directors of the National Mental Health Association (NMHA) have taken a strong leadership role in ensuring that the mental health needs of Americans from culturally diverse backgrounds are met in a culturally competent manner. To accomplish its goals, NMHA employs a change strategy involving a cultural competence model of service delivery and advocacy discussed later in this chapter.

Critical to the successful implementation of any change strategy for improving services or for attempting to perfect our practice of democracy is the role of an effective leader. Without question, effective leadership, whether at the very highest levels of government or at the grassroots level, is key to success in any major system change strategy for addressing issues of race and ethnicity (Hernandez, Isaacs, Nesman, & Burns, 1998). To be effective, leaders must be systemic, outcome oriented, proactive, and determined to realize their vision for their organization or program. Furthermore, effective leaders have styles that are inclusive and goal oriented and that place strong emphasis on the accountability of key players (Bernard, 1998).

This chapter provides examples of how executive, legislative, and programmatic leadership have been successful in addressing issues of race and ethnicity as these issues relate to increasing accountability and access to services and resources for culturally diverse citizens. Certainly, numerous attempts have been made by the government, national organizations, and local community agencies to institutionalize broad-based approaches for addressing issues of race and ethnicity, including those human service organizations that are sensitive to cultural differences. The authors of this chapter have taken the position that positive leadership is a key ingredient in the successful outcome of reform movements, and as such, have chosen to highlight the culturally competent model of service delivery as one example of effective leadership (Mason, Benjamin, & Lewis, 1996). Certainly, it is known that culturally diverse populations are often unserved, underserved, or inappropriately served by the service delivery system.

This chapter focuses on the concept of cultural competence in mental health to meet the needs of underserved populations, however, it should be noted that in the late 1990s, many federal grants and initiatives required grantees to address and apply culturally competent strategies in their programmatic implementation efforts. The public systems with these requirements included mental health, substance abuse, child welfare, education, maternal and child health, and juvenile justice (Hernandez et al., 1998).

EXECUTIVE LEADERSHIP AND LEGISLATION ADDRESSING ISSUES OF RACE AND ETHNICITY

Executive leadership carries with it official sanction to establish and carry out policy implementation decisions. For example, approximately 50 years ago, President Harry S. Truman signed Executive Order No. 9981, which mandated equal treatment and opportunity in the U.S. Armed Forces and was designed to end racial discrimination in the military. Acting on findings of the President's Committee on Civil Rights' landmark report, "To Secure These Rights: The Report of the President's Committee on Civil Rights" (1947), President Truman set in motion the public policy mechanisms to condemn segregation throughout the United States and specifically in the armed forces. Executive Order No. 9981 held that "it is hereby declared to be the policy of the President that there shall be equality of treatment and opportunity for all persons in the armed services without regard to race, color, religion, or national origin" (p. 162).

In addition, the order established the President's Committee on Equality of Treatment and Opportunity in the Armed Services. He also created the President's Commission on Civil Rights and the Division of Civil Rights in the U.S. Department of Justice. These actions laid the framework and essentially provided the first major national wake-up call on issues of race and ethnicity since President Lincoln signed the Emancipation Proclamation of 1865 (McCullough, 1992).

Another national and political leader, President Lyndon B. Johnson provided effective leadership in working with Congress on legislation that addressed issues of race and ethnicity during his distinguished political career. Prior to serving as president of the United States from 1963 through 1969, Johnson served in the U.S. House of Representatives, in the U.S. Senate, as a minority and majority leader, and as vice president of the United States. Johnson's (1971) "perceptions of America persuaded me that three separate conditions were required before social change could take root and flourish—a recognition of need, a willingness to act, and someone to lead the effort" (p. 10).

Johnson's view of leadership was an activist one, and he saw himself as having opportunities to get things done. As president, he took the position that he could not ask Congress to take a risk that he would be unwilling to take himself in the area of making the civil rights for African Americans a legislative priority. Thus, he gave to the fight everything he had in prestige, power, and commitment. At the same time, he deliberately tried to tone down his personal involvement in the daily struggle so that his former colleagues in Congress could take tactical responsibility and credit for the enactment of a civil rights bill. Thus, under the leadership of the late Senator Everett Dirksen of Illinois, Congress passed the Civil Rights Act of 1964, and Johnson signed the bill into law in the East Room of the White House on July 2, 1964 (Johnson, 1971).

It is significant that Johnson was the first southern president in the 20th century. As a Southerner, Johnson did more to advance the civil rights of African Americans than prior presidents from the North and South combined. He passionately espoused equal rights for all. Johnson passed into law four major civil rights measures, including the Civil Rights Act of 1964; the Voting Rights Act of 1965; the Civil Rights Act of 1968, which bars discrimination in housing; and the Federal Jury Reform Act of 1968, which bars discrimination in the jury selection process. It is safe to say that without the leadership and vision of Lyndon Baynes Johnson, the opportunity for people from culturally diverse backgrounds to participate fully in American society would have been less available than it is today. By building on the leadership successes of Johnson and others, modern-day human service professionals who are leaders in their field can take advantage of opportunities for developing mechanisms such as culturally competent systems of care to benefit ethnically diverse populations in today's changing world.

Significantly, almost 50 years after President Truman established the Committee on Civil Rights, in June 1997, President William J. Clinton appointed his President's Advisory Board on Race. This board focused its attention on matters of race and racial reconciliation. Out of this effort came the President's Initiative on Race, for developing a coordinated strategy to close the opportunity gaps that existed for minorities and the underserved in this country. In fact, the President's fiscal year (FY) 2001 budget included a $5 million request for "One America" dialogues to promote and facilitate discussions on racial diversity and understanding (Office of the Press Secretary, 1999).

In the waning days of his presidency, Clinton again issued regulations, this time involving racial and other forms of segregation in public housing. Essentially, these regulations "deconcentrate poverty and promote integration" in public housing (Editorial Board, 2000). That is, families from different social and economic walks of life would have a chance to live in diverse communities that can lead to breaking down "destructive barriers of race and class" (Editorial Board, 2000). This action would permit public housing authority directors to create opportunities for people with different incomes to obtain housing in the same complex and not simply segregate people with the lowest income to particular projects (Office of the Press Secretary, 2000).

David Satcher, Surgeon General of the United States in the Clinton Administration, who completed his term of office one year into President George W. Bush's Administration, convened a planning board in 1998 that led to the generation of the first surgeon general's report on mental health to address issues of race and ethnicity. The report spoke to the remarkable advances in understanding mental disorders, and stated that "leaders in the mental health field...have been insistent that mental health flow in the mainstream of health" (Surgeon General, 1999, p. v). For the first time in such an official document, it was acknowledged that "many racial and ethnic minority group members find the organized mental health system to be uninformed about cultural context and, thus, unresponsive and/or irrelevant" (p. 456). In the report, the surgeon general called for all mental health practitioners to be culturally competent: to recognize and to respond to cultural concerns of ethnic and racial groups, including their histories, traditions, beliefs, and value systems.

In a supplement to the 1999 Report of the Surgeon General issued in August 2001 (U.S. Department of Health and Human Services, 2001), Satcher again exercised leadership by placing strong emphasis on the accountability of key players. He indicated that

> while mental disorders may touch all Americans either directly or indirectly, all do not have equal access to treatment and services and that the failure to address these inequities is being played out in human and economic terms across the nation, on our streets, in homeless shelters, public health institutions, prisons and jails. (U.S. Department of Health and Human Services, 2001, p. 1)

He went on to state that culture counts and that we need to enhance the nation's diversity in the conduct of research, in the education and training of our mental health service providers, and in the delivery of services. Furthermore, the supplement identified striking disparities in knowledge, access, utilization, and quality of mental health care for racial and ethnic minorities.

Reducing or eliminating these disparities requires a steadfast commitment by all sectors of American society. Changing systems of mental health care must bring together the public and private sectors, health and other service providers, universities and researchers, foundations, mental health advocates, consumers, families and communities. Overcoming mental health disparities and promoting mental health for all Americans underscores the nation's commitment to public health and to equality. (p. 2)

We continue to need leaders like King, Truman, Johnson, Clinton, and Satcher, neither saints nor sparkling television personalities, who can situate themselves within the larger historical narrative of this country and our world and who can grasp the complex dynamics of our peoplehood and imagine a future grounded in the best of our past, yet who are attuned to the frightening obstacles that now perplex us (West, 1994). Our leadership challenge today is to help Americans build a multiracial, multicultural democracy that can be sustained and that can ensure access to basic social needs of housing, food, health and mental health care, education, jobs, and so on. We must invigorate the common good with a mixture of effective leadership from our political, organizational, religious, human service professional, and grassroots community.

Programmatic Leadership Involving Cultural Competence in Mental Health Services

In addressing issues of race and ethnicity in the United States, it is clear that government has played an important role. In the case of mental health, it was the federal National Institute of Mental Health that assumed the leadership role that culminated in the surgeon general's 1999 report and its supplemental report in August 2001 (U.S. Department of Health and Human Services, 2001) on meeting the needs of people of color by providing culturally competent services. This report concluded that workers must account for cultural differences to ensure that all Americans, regardless of race or ethnicity, receive mental health services tailored to their needs.

The concept of cultural competence in the delivery of mental health services had its roots in the 1980s under the leadership of the Cultural Competence Resource Committee at Georgetown University in Washington, DC. (Cross, Bazron, Bennis, & Isaacs, 1989; Stroul & Friedman, 1986). The funding and support for this initiative came out of the National Institute of Mental Health's Child and Adolescent Service System Program under then-director Ira S. Lourie.

In the first of a three-volume monograph series on cultural competence (Cross, Bazron, Dennis, & Isaacs, 1989), *cultural competence* was defined as a set of congruent behaviors, attitudes, and policies that come together in a system or agency, or among professionals, and that enable the system, agency, or professionals to work effectively in cross-cultural situations. The word *culture* is used because it implies the integrated patterns of human behavior that include thoughts, communications, actions, customs, beliefs, values, and institutions of a racial, ethnic, religious, or social group. The word *competence* is used because it implies having the capacity to function effectively. A culturally competent system of care acknowledges and incorporates the importance of culture, the assessment of cross-cultural relations, vigilance toward the dynamics that result from cultural differences, the expansion of cultural knowledge, and the adaptation of services to meet culturally unique needs. Cultural competence occurs at all levels, including the policy-making, administrative, and direct service levels of an organization. Practice must be based on accurate perceptions of behavior, policies must be impartial, and attitudes should be unbiased (Cross et al., 1989).

Isaacs and Benjamin (1991) continued to test the validity of the methodology developed by the Cultural Competence Resource Committee. They provided a benchmark for identifying programs that exemplified principles of cultural competence that existed in 1990. These programs represented every region of the country. The whole notion of cultural competence, cultural diversity, multiculturalism, pluralism, and similar terms came to dominate discussions and debates in many aspects of national policy and in calls for reforms of core institutions in American society.

Isaacs and Benjamin (1991) articulated the major values and principles that were established by the Cultural Competence Resource Committee that should guide the development of culturally competent systems and services for children and families of color. These values and principles are:

- The family as defined by each culture is the primary system of support and preferred intervention.

- The system must recognize that minority populations have to be at least bicultural and that this status creates a unique set of mental health issues to which the system must be equipped to respond.

- Individuals and families make different choices based on cultural forces; these choices must be considered if services are to be helpful.

- Practice is driven in the system of care by culturally preferred choices, not by culturally blind or culturally free interventions.

- Inherent in cross-cultural interactions are dynamics that must be acknowledged, adjusted to, and accepted.

- The system must sanction and, in some cases, mandate the incorporation of cultural knowledge into practice and policy making.

- Cultural competence involves determining a client's cultural location to apply the helping principle of "starting where the client is" and includes understanding the client's level of acculturation and assimilation.

- Cultural competence involves working in conjunction with natural, informal support and helping networks within the minority community, such as neighborhoods, churches, spiritual leaders, and healers.

- Cultural competence extends the concept of self-determination to the community.

- Cultural competence seeks to match the needs and help-seeking behavior to the client population.

- An agency staffing pattern that reflects the makeup of the client population, adjusted for the degree of community need, helps ensure the delivery of effective services.

- Culturally competent services incorporate the concept of equal and nondiscriminatory services, but go beyond that to include the concept of responsive services matched to the client population.

To better understand the process of becoming culturally competent, it is useful to think of the possible ways of responding to cultural differences by examining a six-point cultural competence continuum. The continuum developed by the Cultural Competence Resource Committee at Georgetown University ranges from cultural destructiveness to cultural proficiency. The most negative end of the continuum is characterized by attitudes, policies, and practices that are destructive to cultures and subsequently to individuals within cultures, and the most positive end of the continuum is characterized by holding culture in high esteem.

Cultural Destructiveness

A system of care that practices cultural destructiveness assumes that one race or culture is superior and should eradicate or control lessor races because of their perceived inferior position. Bigotry coupled with power differentials allow the dominant groups to disenfranchise, control, exploit, or systematically destroy less-powerful populations. Examples are to deny people of color access to their natural helpers or to purposefully risk the well-being of these individuals in social or medical experiments without their knowledge or consent.

Cultural Incapacity

Cultural incapacity implies that an organization does not intentionally or consciously seek to be culturally destructive, but rather lacks the capacity to help individuals and communities of color. Characteristics include discriminatory hiring practices, subtle messages to people of color that they are not valued, and lower expectations of people of color.

Cultural Blindness

At the midpoint along the cultural competence continuum, culturally blind agencies are characterized by the belief that helping approaches traditionally used by the dominant culture are universally applicable. This view reflects a well-intended liberal philosophy, however, the consequences of such a belief are to make people so ethnocentric as to render them virtually useless to all but the most assimilated people of color. Culturally blind agencies suffer from a lack of information and often do not know where they can obtain needed information. Although these agencies often view themselves as unbiased and responsive to minority needs, their ethnocentrism is reflected in attitudes, policies, and practices.

Cultural Precompetence

The precompetent organization realizes it has weaknesses in serving people of color and attempts to improve some aspect of their services to a specific population. Such agencies hire people of color as staff, explore how to reach culturally diverse populations in their service area, initiate training for their employees on cultural issues, enter into needs assessments concerning people and communities of color, and recruit people of color for their boards of directors or advisory committees. Precompetent organizations are characterized by the desire to deliver quality services and a commitment to civil rights.

Basic Cultural Competence

Culturally competent organizations are characterized by acceptance and respect for difference, continuing self-assessment regarding culture, careful attention to the dynamics of difference, continuous expansion of cultural knowledge and resources, and a variety of adaptations to better meet the changing needs of people of color. The culturally competent organization works to hire unbiased employees, seeks advice and consultation from the community, and actively decides what it is and is not capable of providing to people of color. Often, ongoing dialogue with and input from culturally diverse communities at all levels of the organization and an external network with other formal and informal supports from the communities they serve are part of basic cultural competence.

Cultural Proficiency

Cultural proficiency is the most positive end of the scale. The culturally proficient organization seeks to add to the knowledge base of culturally competent programming and practice by conducting research, developing new service approaches based on culture, evaluating and disseminating the results of their projects, and experimenting with changes in organizational structures that support critical cultural values and beliefs. The culturally proficient organization hires staff who are specialists in culturally competent practice and advocates for improved relations between cultures throughout society (Hernandez et al., 1998).

One of the conclusions reached in the monograph series was that cultural competence requires the creation of an infrastructure for its development and implementation (Isaacs, 1998). There are at least 13 core components for building a solid infrastructure for cultural competence development and implementation:

- commitment from the top leadership of the organization to cultural competence and diversity;

- willingness to conduct an organizational cultural competence self-assessment;

- needs assessment and data collection, both quantitative and qualitative, to assist in knowledge development about culturally diverse groups and communities within the organization or program;

- identification and involvement of key people of color in a sustained, influential, and critical advisory capacity;

- development of mission statements, definitions, policies, and procedures that explicitly state the agency's cultural competence values and principles;

- development of a cultural competence strategic plan with clear and measurable goals and anticipated outcomes;

- commitment to recruitment and retention of staff or volunteers who are reflective of all communities served;

- commitment to ongoing cultural competence training and skill development for all staff or volunteers at all levels of the organization or program;

- development of certification, licensure, and contract standards that include cultural competence requirements and measures;

- targeted service delivery strategies that are culturally appropriate and centered on improved outcomes for the population served;

- development of an internal capacity, within the organization, to oversee and monitor the implementation process (specialized job descriptions, internal team, management information system capacity, performance standards, etc.);

- evaluation and research activities that provide ongoing feedback about progress, lead to needed modifications, and guide next steps; and

- commitment of agency resources, both human and financial. (Isaacs, 1998, pp. 87–88)

A decade after the publication of Volume 2 of the monograph series, it is clear that leadership in promoting culturally competent systems of care has continued (Isaacs & Benjamin, 1991). For example, in 2000, the Substance Abuse and Mental Health Services Administration (SAMHSA) and its Center for Mental Health Services (CMHS) targeted the "four underserved and underrepresented populations— notably, African Americans, Hispanic Americans/Latinos, Native Americans/Alaska Natives and Asian/Pacific Islander Americans" in developing standards for effective service delivery for these populations (CMHS, 2000, p. v). The focus this time was on behavioral health care issues in a managed care environment.

With assistance from the Western Interstate Commission on Higher Education (WICHE) Mental Health Program, in 2000, CMHS produced the *Cultural Competence Standards in Managed Mental Health Care Services: Four Underserved/ Underrepresented Racial/Ethnic Groups.* This represented "both a series of standards for culturally competent care in managed behavioral health care settings and an implementation plan" (CMHS, 2000, p. vi). It addressed issues such as personnel hiring and management, marketing plans for community partnership building, funding strategies, and quality assurance. As organizational leaders in the federal system, Nelba Chavez, former director of SAMHSA, and Bernard Arons of CMHS stated, "This volume is but a starting place for the creation of managed mental health services that are responsive to the changing face of America" (CMHS, 2000 p. vi).

The guiding principles on cultural competence in the WICHE document mirrored those in the earlier Georgetown University monograph series. The WICHE strategy created a cultural competence plan (CCP) that would move both the public and private sectors to develop and integrate a planning process within an agency's overall strategy to include manageable but concrete timelines. CCP included the following 14 elements:

1. the participation and representation of top and middle management administrators, consumers and their families, sovereign tribal nations, and community stakeholders in the development and implementation of the plan;

2. an executive with responsibility for and authority to monitor implementation of CCP;

3. individual managers accountable for the success of CCP based on their level within the organization;

4. a process for integrating CCP into the overall state or department plan and for including the principles of cultural competence in all aspects of organizational strategic planning and other planning activities;

5. a process for determining unique regionally based needs and ecological variables within the communities or populations served;

6. identification of service modalities and models that are appropriate and acceptable to the communities served (i.e., urban, frontier, and rural) and targeted population subgroups (e.g., children, adolescents, adults, families, elders, and sexual minorities);

7. identification and involvement of community resources (e.g., tribal and community councils, family members, clans, spiritual leaders, and civic clubs and community organizations) and cross-system alliances (e.g., corrections, juvenile justice, education, social services, substance abuse, developmental disability, primary care plans, public health, and tribal health agencies) for purposes of integrated consumer support and service delivery;

8. identification of natural supports or community resources for purposes of reintegrating the individual within his or her natural environment;

9. assurance of cultural competence at each level of care within the system;

10. stipulation of adequate, culturally diverse staffing and minimal skill levels for all staff, from clerical through executive management;

11. use of culturally competent indicators, adapted for specific minority cultural beliefs and values, in developing, implementing, and monitoring the plan;

12. development of rewards and incentives for cultural competence performance, as well as sanctions for culturally destructive practices. Cultural competence performance shall be an integral part of the employee/provider and provider/organization performance evaluation systems;

13. development of a plan to integrate ongoing training and staff development into the overall CCP; and

14. development and ongoing monitoring of indicators to assure equal access, comparability of benefits, and outcomes across each level of the system of care and for all services. (pp. 23–24)

Essentially, what emerged was agreement concerning the knowledge and principles of cultural competence and its applicability. A culturally competent system of care is not only disposed to provide services to people of color, but concepts of cultural competence can be a vehicle to purposefully address needs and concerns of people of color regardless of the service system that is providing services to these populations.

STATE LEADERSHIP INVOLVING RACE AND ETHNICITY

With regard to governmental initiatives, states such as Georgia, Minnesota, and California are assuming a leadership role in developing and implementing culturally competent systems of care. For example, in June 2000, the Georgia Department of Human Resources (DHR), Division of Mental Health, Mental Retardation and Substance Abuse issued a request for information (RFI) to complete a comprehensive training needs assessment in cultural competence involving mental health service providers.

Because the Georgia DHR has the responsibility to safeguard and promote the health and welfare of its citizens, who are becoming more diverse, Georgia needs to enhance cultural competence training among its public mental health providers. As indicated in its RFI, "shifts in ethnic diversity are not just about numbers, but are also about the impact of differences" (Georgia DHR, 2000, p. 4). The RFI stated that true cultural competence is not only adherence to core standards and principles, but is also the acquisition of knowledge, skills, and attitudes "to enable administrators and practitioners within systems of care to provide effective care for diverse populations."

Almost one thousand miles due north of Georgia, Minnesota and its Children's Mental Health Division has taken the leadership in the provision of culturally competent services to people of color within the public mental health system. The Children's Mental Health Division has made a strong commitment to systems change and the acceptance of the expanding ethnic and racial populations in Minnesota in the development of its strategic efforts to provide services to all its citizens. As the country is becoming more diverse, so, too, is Minnesota. From 1990 to 1998, Minnesota's ethnically and racially diverse populations increased about 46%, or 400,000 people (about 14% of the statewide population).

Minnesota's mental health services are provided by the counties, and as such, action in addressing these populations has come from the local government level as well as from state government. Since 1998, the Children's Mental Health Division has undergone a process of planning and developing a statewide cultural competence strategic agenda based on an integrated system's approach to service delivery. As reported in its statewide cultural competence strategic plan, "The Children's Mental Health Division has prioritized work on an extensive cultural competency agenda in an attempt to improve both access and quality of mental health services delivered to diverse children and families" (Minnesota Department of Human Services, 2000, p. 10).

In the West, where demographics have also changed significantly during the last decade, California's mental health system has focused its efforts on meeting the mental health needs of diverse communities through the establishment of a cultural competence task force (CCTF). Although the California Department of Mental Health (DMH), the California Mental Health Directors Association (county mental health directors), and CCTF support the importance of culture, assessment of cross-cultural relations, vigilance toward the dynamics that result from cultural differences, expansion of cultural knowledge, and adaptation of services to meet culturally specific needs, this group takes cultural competence issues a step further. These organizations acknowledge that "providing services in a manner that fails to achieve its intended result due to cultural and linguistic barriers is not cost effective" (California DMH, 1997, p. 1).

In fact, California's DMH has codified cultural competence planning language in state statute:

> Each plan shall provide for culturally competent and age-appropriate services, shall assess the cultural competence needs of the program, include a process to accommodate the significant needs with reasonable timelines,…[and] performance outcome measures shall include a reliable method of measuring and reporting the extent to which services are culturally competent and age-appropriate. (Welfare and Institutions Code, 14684 (h), 1997, p. 3)

Of course, the concept of cultural competence does not reside solely in the governmental sector. For example, in June 1998, under the direction of Michael Faenza, NMHA President and CEO, and the board of directors, NMHA (2000) established a task force on diversity. The purpose of this task force was to recommend an organizational plan to increase the cultural competence of NMHA's national staff and board, and 340 local affiliates. According to Jose A. Bernard (1998), "a basic strategy for making meaningful changes aimed at achieving cultural competence should include the requirement that all aspects of the organization be examined, modified, and changed accordingly" (p. 33). Clearly, NMHA is focusing attention on ways to develop such a strategy.

NMHA believes it must provide leadership, guidance, support, education, and good modeling to move forward. The desired outcomes of its cultural competence initiative include the following:

- More closely live out a vision of a just, humane, and healthy society, in which all people are accorded respect, dignity, and the opportunity to achieve their full potential free of stigma and prejudice.

- Have the composition of the national staff and board more accurately reflect the richness of the different cultures that exist nationally.

- Provide education and cultural competence training for national board and staff.

- Develop an implementation plan for national office staff and board.

- Have sufficient appreciation of cultural differences to be effective advocates for culturally competent treatment systems at the local, state, and
  national levels.

- Assure fairness in hiring and promotional practices for diverse groups.

- Have the composition of affiliate boards, staff, and volunteers more accurately reflect the communities they serve.

- Provide education and cultural competence training for the affiliate
  network.

- Incorporate cultural competence planning within the standards expected
  of affiliates when they apply for reaffiliation beginning in 2002.

- Provide consultation to assist affiliates with their diversity efforts (NMHA,
  2000).

Not all efforts to address diversity are focused on the human service systems of
mental health, health, child welfare, education and juvenile justice. For example,
the National Respite Coalition, comprised of 25 national organizations, was successful in getting the National Family Caregiver Support Act passed as part of the
2000 amendments to the Older Americans Act. This legislation provides comprehensive, multifaceted support, including respite to caregivers of the elderly, to elderly caregivers of adult children with disabilities, and to grandparents who are prin-
cipal guardians of their grandchildren. Following their congressional efforts, the
coalition continued to provide leadership by working with the states on implementation strategies. As part of its vision statement, the coalition believes in "flexibility to
meet culturally diverse needs" (Lifespan Coalition, 2001, p. 2). The draft report
states that 1 of the 10 principles of a quality respite care system is that

> families have an array of options and can choose respite services that meet
> their unique needs. A wide array of options, including in-home and out-of-
> home care, that meet family needs should be available. Caregivers should be
> free to choose their respite providers and *culturally competent* (emphasis
> added) providers should be available to all families.

Other examples targeting diversity issues include community-level initiatives
on addressing issues on diversity and race as well as issues involving diversity in
the media. For example, the League of Women Voters (2000) of Minnesota has
undertaken its Changing Faces, Changing Communities Initiative. The purpose of
this project, although not using the rubric of cultural competence, is to initiate

discussion of immigration and diversity and all the accompanying issues, such as jobs, housing, schools, and language differences. The project took place in 16 communities in Minnesota during 2000 and generated recommendations for future action at a local, regional, or state level.

A 1995 communications conference on mental health issues raised the question, Why should communication professionals be concerned with cultural competence in the media? The participants pointed out that the answer was in part contained in their conference literature: "We are a nation in which diversity is a legacy and that successful communicators need to be visionary and empower themselves to develop effective strategies for dealing with critical issues of the day" (National Mental Health Information Association, 1995, p. 3), including the demographic shifts that are taking place in the United States (National Mental Health Information Association, 1995).

Indeed, people of color are the fastest growing segments of the U.S. population. In 1990, these groups comprised 19.7% of the total population. According to the 2000 census, people of color make up 28% of the U.S. population (Grieco & Cassidy, 2001). Children and adolescents will show even greater diversity, because 53.7% of the total population younger than 18 are children of color.

Furthermore, we know through research that the media, particularly television, have had an effect on the beliefs and behaviors of viewers (Media Factsheet, 1997). For example, in a letter to the Federal Communications Commission on the proposed new federal rules that would define children's educational television, one mother wrote,

> Television influences my children's language patterns, the clothes they wear, how they behave, and their view of others. So there's no reason to underestimate how television might give children the tools they need "to grow up as full, complete and passionate human beings." ("Federal communication," 1995, B5)

Statements such as these underscore the importance of cultural competence in addressing issues of race and ethnicity in the media.

Summary

It is clear that effective leadership is a prerequisite for meaningful progress in advancing racial and ethnic equality in this country. Dynamic leaders such as Harry S. Truman; Martin Luther King, Jr.; Lyndon B. Johnson,; Bill Clinton; and David Satcher have been instrumental in setting the stage for ethnic and racial progress in the multicultural and multiracial society in today's world through executive, legislative, and civil rights mechanisms. Although the road to equality remains an uphill struggle, leading professionals in the field are making strides in developing and implementing a culturally competent system of care to meet the unmet service delivery needs of unserved, underserved, and inappropriately served populations in this country. The jury is still out. It may take another decade or more before we are able to state with any degree of certainty that organizational, religious, political, and human service professional leaders were successful in turning the corner on equal access to effective and appropriate human services for culturally diverse populations in the United States.

REFERENCES

Bernard, J. A. (1998). Cultural competence plans: A strategy for the creation of a culturally competent system of care. In M. Hernandez & M. R. Isaacs (Eds.), *Promoting cultural competence in children's mental health services* (pp. 29–45). Baltimore: Paul H. Brooks.

California Department of Mental Health. (1997, October). *Operationalizing cultural competency standards in a managed care environment.* Sacramento, CA: Author.

Center for Mental Health Services, Substance Abuse and Mental Health Services Administration. (2000). *Cultural competence standards in managed mental health care services: Four underserved/underrepresented racial/ethnic groups.* Washington, DC: U.S. Department of Health and Human Services.

Cross, T., Bazron, B., Dennis, K., & Isaacs, M. R. (1989). *Towards a cultural competent system of care: A monograph on effective services for minority children who are severely emotionally disturbed* (Vol. 1). Washington, DC: CASSP Technical Assistance Center, Georgetown University Child Development Center.

Early, G. (2000). The end of the civil rights coalition. In P. A. Winter (Ed.), *The civil rights movement* (pp. 191–199). San Diego, CA: Greenhaven Press.

Editorial Board. (2000, December 28). Deconcentrate poverty and promote integration in public housing. *Washington Post,* A22.

Federal communication draft rules. (1995, September 12). *Washington Post,* B5.

Georgia Department of Human Resources. (2000). *Request for information. Developing and implementing culturally competent systems of care.* Atlanta, GA: Georgia Department of Human Resources, Division of Mental Health, Mental Retardation and Substance Abuse.

Grieco, E. M., & Cassidy, R. C. (2001). *Overview of race and Hispanic origin: Census 2000 brief.* Washington, DC: U.S. Census Bureau.

Hernandez, M., Isaacs, M. R., Nesman, T., & Burns, D. B. (1998). Perspectives on culturally competent systems of care. In M. Hernandez & M. R. Isaacs, Mareasa R. (Eds.), *Promoting cultural competence in children's mental health services.* Baltimore: Paul H. Brooks.

Isaacs, M. R. (1998). *Towards a cultural competent system of care: The state of the states responses to cultural competence and diversity in child mental health* (Vol. 3). Washington, DC: National Technical Assistance Center for Children's Mental Health, Georgetown University Child Development Center.

Isaacs, M. R., & Benjamin, M. P. (1991). *Towards a cultural competent system of care: Programs which utilize culturally competent principles* (Vol. 2). Washington, DC: CASSP Technical Assistance Center, Georgetown University Child Development Center.

Johnson, L. B. (1971). *The vantage point: Perspectives of the presidency 1963–1969.* New York: Holt, Rineholt and Winston.

League of Women Voters. (2000). *"Changing Faces, Changing Communities" initiative.* Minneapolis, MN: League of Women Voters of Minnesota Education Fund.

Lifespan Coalition. (2001). *Lifespan Respite task force draft report.* Washington, DC: Lifespan Coalition.

Mason, J. L., Benjamin, M. P., & Lewis, S. A. (1996). The cultural competence model: Implications for child and family mental health services. In C. A. Heflinger & C. T. Nixon (Eds.), *Families and the mental health system for children and adolescents: Policy, services, and research* (pp. 165–190). Thousand Oaks, CA: Sage.

McCullough, D. (1992). *Truman.* New York: Simon & Schuster.

Media factsheet. (1997). Washington, DC: Institute for Mental Health Initiatives, George Washington University.

Minnesota Department of Human Services. (2000, March). *Minnesota's statewide cultural competency strategic plan for children's mental health services, overview and recommendations.* St. Paul, MN: Children's Mental Health Division.

National Mental Health Association. (2000). *Task force on diversity.* Alexandria, VA: Author.

National Mental Health Information Association. (1995). *National Mental Health Information Officers annual conference brochure.* Galveston, Texas: National Mental Health Information Officers Association.

Office of the Press Secretary. (1999, February 5). *One America.* Washington, DC: White House.

Office of the Press Secretary. (2000, December 23). *Mixed income public housing opportunities.* Washington, DC: White House.

Office of the U.S. Surgeon General. (2001, August 26). *Culture counts in mental health services and research finds new surgeon general report.* Rockvillle, MD: Office of the Surgeon General.

Stroul, B., & Friedman, R. (1986). *A system of care for severely emotionally disturbed children and youth.* Washington, DC: Georgetown University Child Development Center.

To secure these rights: The report of the President's Committee on Civil Rights. (1947). Washington, DC: U.S. Government Printing Office.

Truman, H. S. (1948). *Special message to the United States Congress on civil rights* (House Documents, 80th Congress, 2nd Session, No. 516). Washington, DC: U.S. Government Printing Office.

U.S. Department of Health and Human Services. (1999). *Mental health: A report of the surgeon general.* Rockville, MD: U.S. Department of Health and Human Services, Substance Abuse and Mental Health Services, Center for Mental Health Services, National Institutes of Health, National Institute of Mental Health.

U.S. Department of Health and Human Services. (2001). *Mental health: Culture, race, and ethnicity. A supplement to mental health: A report of the surgeon general.* Rockville, MD: U.S. Department of Health and Human Services, Public Health Services, Office of the Surgeon General.

West, C. (1994). *Race matters.* New York: Vintage Books.

CHAPTER 7

Developing Racial Understanding at the Grassroots Level
A Community Approach

Fannie L. Brown

> *The reason we came to Akron…in part is because of this Coming Together Project that you've done. I believe we can find constructive ways for people to work together, learn together, and be together. That's the best shot we've got to avoid some of the hard problems we see in the rest of the world, to avoid some of the difficult problems we've had in our history and to make progress on the problems we still have here today.*
>
> —President Bill Clinton (1997)

Following the verdict in the highly profiled Rodney King case, riots broke out in many major cities across the nation. Due to the racial tension caused by the King verdict, administrators at the *Akron Beacon Journal* wanted to assess the status of race relations in the Akron/Summit community. In 1993, the paper embarked on that quest by publishing a series of articles on race relations entitled "A Question of Color." Using interviews with members of the greater Akron community, the *Journal* explored race relations from several perspectives, which revealed the disparity of treatment and opportunity between African Americans and whites in housing, employment, the criminal justice system, and education.

The newspaper concluded that relations between African Americans and whites in the Akron/Summit community were not positive. Instead of simply reporting these findings, the newspaper (*Akron Beacon Journal,* 1994) issued a call to local citizens and organizations to come forward to work toward improving race relations. In addition, the newspaper series captured the Pulitzer Prize in 1994, journalism's most prestigious award, and catapulted Akron's attempt at racial reconciliation into the national spotlight.

The call from the newspaper received more than 22,000 responses from individuals and representatives of local organizations. John Dotson, publisher of the newspaper, was surprised by the quantity of responses received (*Akron Beacon Journal,* 1994). Initially, about three-dozen groups responded. That number grew to approximately 215 groups, representing business, civic, social, religious, and educational entities. The interest generated by the community was an indicator that citizens of Akron/Summit County wanted to address race relations.

HISTORY OF THE COMING TOGETHER PROJECT

Those who responded to the wake-up call formed the Coming Together Project in 1993. The Coming Together Project is a community-based organization committed to improving the status of race relations. Initially, the Coming Together Project focused on presenting community workshops, educational forums, and cultural events to participating individuals and organizations to give participants the tools to begin bridging the differences that existed between African Americans and whites.

The *Akron Beacon Journal* financed and housed the Coming Together Project. The *Journal* hired two part-time coordinators for the project in September 1993. The role of these coordinators was to advance the mission of the project, which included educating, leading, and advancing the community's positive response to improving race relations. The two coordinators were instrumental in planning major public events that heightened awareness of the project in Akron, including workshops such as "Christianity in the Workplace" and "Uncovering Racism in Our Community." The project workers presented these programs and facilitated dialogues on race and diversity. They offered strategies for creating an inclusive community. These forums increased community interest and fueled the desire for continuous program development, which resulted in a speakers bureau. Speakers made presentations to civic organizations, high school and college classes, church groups, and statewide leadership forums. Later, the project formed an advisory council with representatives from organizations responding to the newspaper's call. The 20-member council assisted the coordinators in planning and executing programs and served as a liaison between the community and the project.

Initially, the coordinators worked one-on-one with participating groups, realizing early on that no magic formula would help them build positive race relations. Project groups and individuals quickly determined what worked best for them, rather than accepting top-down imposition of ideas from others. The coordinators spent a great deal of time guiding and advising participating groups. Often, they worked to coordinate collaborations and partnerships between African American and white churches, including shared worship services and social gatherings.

Eventually, the coordinators established a teen advisory board to organize workshops for high school students. The teen board began planning and presenting workshops in January 1994. All Akron public schools participated and 75% of suburban schools participated in these teen workshops. These workshops shared ideas on how to create better race relations and reported positive outcomes in future sessions highlighting the reasons the programs had been successful. Principals, counselors, and teachers attested to the value and effectiveness of these workshops.

Later, the project created a newsletter to keep member groups updated on project happenings. Coordinators worked with the advisory council to continue program efforts, and the project flourished.

Now in its 10th year, in 2003, the Coming Together Project has greatly expanded its educational programs for young people (including middle- and high-school students), its member organizations, and the community at large. The project gained national attention in 1997, when then-President Bill Clinton visited Akron for the nation's inaugural town hall meeting on race. Clinton credited the efforts of the Coming Together Project as the primary reason for selecting Akron to inaugurate his yearlong series of forums.

NEEDS ASSESSMENT

Thirty years after the assassination of Dr. Martin Luther King, Jr., Americans are still debating how far we have come toward achieving his dream of racial equality. Every week, we are inundated with news reports of racial violence and hate crimes across the nation. Race relations, hate crimes, and violence continue to be issues in our nation's struggle toward justice and equality.

These national issues are borne out in Akron. Akron looks and feels like "Anytown," U.S.A. Nearly 75% of its 223,000 citizens are white, 23% are African American, and 2% are other nonwhite people. Like dozens of other blue-collar Midwestern cities, Akron is struggling with social ills such as unemployment, poverty, crime, poor schools, racism, and racial segregation. Unlike other cities, Akron is doing something about it through the Coming Together Project.

The articles printed in the *Akron Beacon Journal* acted as a community assessment tool. Clearly, a racial disparity existed in housing, employment, education, and the lack of fairness in the criminal justice system. The newspaper's results were indicative of the need to educate the entire community on issues of race.

THE COMING TOGETHER PROJECT'S MISSION AND GOALS

Mission Statement

The Coming Together Project is a diverse, community-based organization dedicated to the principles that every individual has equal worth, that an appreciation for diversity will build a strong sense of community, and that bringing people together through creative, innovative mechanisms will ensure racial harmony and cultural awareness.

The Coming Together Project believes that:

- People have equal worth.

- Citizens of goodwill are found in every racial, ethnic and religious group.

- Bringing people together will foster understanding.

- Diversity will be the key to society's survival.

- Racism is wrong.

The project believes people must act intentionally to develop friendships with those of other races, and offers guidance and sponsors events that promote such partnerships. The organization holds the belief that when people get to know those of other races who share the same values and goals, commonalities can be celebrated and differences appreciated.

The primary goals of the Coming Together Project are:

- Raise awareness of the project in the community and beyond.

- Educate community members on how to approach the issue of racism.

- Bring people together to foster awareness and appreciation of all cultures.

EDUCATIONAL, CULTURAL, AND SOCIAL PROGRAMS

Programs are the lifeblood of the project and can be categorized as educational, cultural, and social programs, as well as specialized programs. These programs are designed to meet project goals and objectives.

Workshops to Get Groups Started

The project holds workshops to get new groups started as the need arises. These workshops educate new groups on the process of progressive/effective dialogue sessions. Small group meetings of 10 to 12 representatives of new member groups meet to discuss ways to begin dialogue, and the representatives explore potential processes necessary to overcome the communication gap between races. Proven methods are shared with new group members by members of "senior" groups. A mentor is assigned to new groups for a period of one year, to help integrate the group.

Educational Programs

Educational programs target three audiences: youth, member group representatives, and the community at large. Youth programs include high-school workshops, high-school dialogues, and middle-school workshops, and two of each are presented during an academic term. An elementary-school program has been developed, however, it has not been implemented yet. These programs coincide with local academic terms, beginning in October and ending in April. All the educational programs have witnessed progressive attendance rates.

These programs are executed primarily with staff in conjunction with the project's high-school advisory board. The teen board is composed of students from 30 high schools in the area. A typical board is composed of 24 students from all four high-school grade levels, to ensure the council will never be void of experienced members.

Because students from the teen advisory board graduate annually, it is essential to fill open slots with students committed to the mission of the organization. Project coordinators recruit potential members at workshops, in addition to asking to school administrators for recommendations. The coordinators interview recruits each summer and select and orient them to the duties and responsibilities of teen advisory board members. The size of the teen board has more than tripled since its inception, and there has been an overwhelming response on the part of students to participate. That enthusiasm and commitment continue to carry individual high-school programs forward year after year.

The project's high-school advisory board plans and presents high-school workshops and dialogues. These students meet three times prior to each program, working with staff members to create an agenda for other students. Four or more students from each of 30 schools are invited to attend the seminars. These programs attract a growing number of participants—from 50 in 1994 to 115 in 2003.

Staff plan and execute middle-school workshops. These workshops include a discussion component, which is facilitated by teen advisory board members. This provides another opportunity for these students to share the message of inclusion with students who look to them for guidance.

Teen Advisory Board History

When the project began in 1993, many of the early members were public and private schools from elementary to high-school level (none were parochial or charter schools). Representatives of these groups became the core of the teen advisory board, and the project recruited additional high schoolers to expand the group's diversity. The student groups were varied in nature. One suburban middle school staged a peace day planned around the theme of multicultural awareness and racial harmony. A city high school let its name, PEACE, state its purpose— People Encouraging the Acceptance of Cultures Everywhere. From a suburban school came a commitment by the Key Club, which admittedly had not made race relations a priority and was not sure what to do. The club considered relations important and wanted to get involved in the effort.

During 1994, teen advisors met monthly with project coordinators and came together as a group, growing in their understanding of others' perspectives and learning and sharing what could be done in schools to bring about positive change. The next step for the teens was to put on a workshop. The first effort, presented in January 1995, became the model for subsequent workshops.

These workshops are planned by teens for teens. The centerpiece of each event focuses on elements of expanding understanding of race and diversity. For example, teens learn about prejudice through drama and videos. Students also listen to speakers, who talk about diversity in the workplace or what its like for a white mother and her teenage son to discover their family's African American heritage.

Workshops also include a cultural segment. Examples include music and dance from India, the steel drum music of Trinidad, or theatrical interpretations of African, Caribbean, and American folktales. Most of these performances by local artists have broadened the understanding and appreciation of student participants. At each event, students share what they are doing to promote race relations, and in turn, seek advice in overcoming obstacles to achieving that goal. Participation for these workshops has been tremendous. Figure 7-1 shows a typical agenda for a high-school workshop.

Since the workshops began, students have shared a wealth of ideas. Many were simple and easily replicated by other schools. Others were sophisticated efforts, revealing students' understanding and commitment. Projects included:

- assemblies presenting people and customs of other cultures;

- random acts of kindness;

- initiation of clubs organized to promote racial harmony in the student body;

- an exchange between students of one public and one private school to break down stereotypes and see each school's diversity;

- presentation of a play on racism, followed by audience interaction and discussion with cast members who remain in character;

- overnight lock-ins and international days held annually. Representatives of more than 20 high schools were invited to the overnighters, which focused on race relations and harmonious coexistence among all people. The international day included speakers from 15 nations who shared stories of the people and experiences of their homelands;

- presentation of a play written by high school students giving an African American perspective on all aspects of student life;

- cultural fairs and informal discussions with exchange students; and

- day-long visits between students of a predominately African American city school and a mostly white suburban school.

FIGURE 7-1

Typical High-School Workshop Agenda

COMING TOGETHER PROJECT FALL HIGH-SCHOOL WORKSHOP
TUESDAY, OCTOBER 21, 1997, 8 A.M.–NOON
FIRST CONGREGATIONAL CHURCH, AKRON

8: 00 A.M–8:30 A.M.	Registration and continental breakfast
8:30 A.M.–8:45 A.M.	**Welcome** Erika Green and Marco Blush, Coming Together Project High-School Advisory Council members Dr. Fannie L. Brown, Executive Director, Coming Together Project
8:45 A.M.–9:15 A.M.	**Introductory exercise: *Take a Stand*** Sharing viewpoints at your table
9:15 A.M.–10:00 A.M.	**Celebrating the culture of Native Americans through dance** North American Indian Cultural Center, Akron **The Cross of Changes** Your reflection and reaction Marco Blush, High School Advisory Council
10:00 A.M.–10:15 A.M	**What we are doing in our schools to improve race relations**
10:15 A.M.–10:30 A.M.	Break
10:30 A.M.–11:10 A.M.	**Video: The Lunch Date** Discussion at your table
11:10 A.M.–11:40 A.M.	**Point/Counterpoint** How would you respond to these statements, most of which are not true? Talking at your table and sharing with all
11:40 A.M.–11:50 A.M.	**Workshop evaluation**
11:50 A.M	**Adjournment**

As a result of the workshops, various high schools have instituted new programs to promote racial harmony among students. Workshops presenters encourage students to organize their own groups to serve their respective high schools. Students are also instructed on how to handle racially sensitive situations, language, and attitudes. In addition to increased participation, 66% of area schools can now measure success through the number of programs and organizations formed as a direct result of such workshops. Examples are:

- PEACE: People Encouraging Acceptance of Cultures Everywhere, a high-school group that has been meeting since 1990.

- STEP: Students Together to End Prejudice, formed at a Catholic high school. STEP has held yearly lock-ins for more than 20 area high schools, as well as International Day. Both events educate students and build racial understanding.

- SALAD: Salad is a program introduced at a suburban public high school to educate students and build racial understanding.

- CRAYOLA: A program created at a public high school to providing diversity programming for its students.

- KALEIDOSCOPE: A special program designed by a suburban high school to meet the needs of its students.

- Unity in Diversity: A program recently formed to serve students in a public high school.

- PUT: People United Together is a recently formed program from an inner-city school with a predominately African American population. The program promotes diversity and racial harmony in the school and also strives to expose students to diverse cultures outside the school environment.

- Harmony: Harmony is another program introduced at a public high school to promote acceptance among teenagers through talking and listening (see Figure 7-2).

Harmony has participated in or sponsored 21 programs for high-school students since its inception. This inner-city high school has a strong schedule and works to interact with students from urban and suburban schools. This successful program acts as an example for other high-school programs.

High-School Dialogues

After participating in several workshops with discussion components, students shared with staff a preference for additional discussion time. Given the structure of existing workshop agendas, no time existed. Workshops continually exceeded allotted time frames, so the answer was a program specifically for discussion. Thus, the project created high-school dialogues.

Dialogues are different from workshops in that they allow students the opportunity to discuss topics pertinent to their experiences. Typically, students assemble at a selected site. On arrival, teen council members greet them and give them a seat assignment and a package of materials. The council members assign students to tables using a diversity approach, never grouping students from the same school together. A typical table consists of pupils from different races, religions, genders, and school districts.

Tables are then led through an icebreaking exercise by council members who are assigned to facilitate that table. Next, all attendees file into an auditorium,

FIGURE 7-2

Portion of an Annual Program Agenda for Harmony Multicultural Organization

ACADEMIC SCHOOL TERM AGENDA

January 28

Right to Dream: Living Voice Presentation

"Right to Dream" is a living portrayal of the civil rights movement and an African American man's life growing up in the 1950s. The performance by J. B. Lunnon will provide a foundation for future discussions on racism and hatred in the United States and local community. Presentation for members of high school student body only.

March 6

Harmony Lock-In

This activity includes small-group discussions, guest speakers, and interactive activities. Students from high schools throughout the county are invited to attend. Students are locked into the host school from 8:00 P.M. to 8:00 A.M. Activities promote embracing ethnicity and building positive human relations.

September 24

National Council for Community and Justice Retreat for Harmony Students

This beginning-of-term retreat introduces students to others in northeastern Ohio who have a similar focus. The primary objective is to teach students how to build community within their respective schools through problem-solving activities. Other topics covered are tolerance and what it means, ridding ourselves of bias, and strategies for dealing with the prejudiced.

where they are entertained with a special skit performed by members of the council. Skits are based on dialogue themes. Often, themes include four to five discussion topics. Consequently, the skit is usually composed of several scenes, phases, or acts. Following the skit, students return to tables and discuss set topics. Later, conclusions are brought to the larger body. Students are allowed to share personal views on pertinent topics and consequently gain helpful strategies and benefit from advice and comments of others present. The majority of the event allows students the opportunity to share in large groups, which has become the participants' preference. The dialogues end with students completing evaluations, which are used to increase the effectiveness of the next program.

Middle-School Workshops

These programs are held twice a year to provide middle-school students with an opportunity to address how issues of diversity affect them and to learn more about people different from themselves. Using small-group discussions and simulations, participants gain the skills and resources needed to address issues such as peer pressure, cliques, stereotyping, exclusion, discrimination, and prejudice and the roles they play in their lives.

Students are welcomed and participate in two icebreaker activities at the beginning of each workshop. The first activity allows participants to engage with students from their home school; the second provides an opportunity to interact with students from other schools. Later, the leaders group students together for small-group discussion, where they are expected to discuss questions and issues and prepare a skit based on the workshop themes. After small-group discussions, students return to the larger group to validate their findings.

Finally, each group presents skits, and then the students regroup by school to prepare a piece of showcase art to commemorate the experience and for display at school. This is an effort to illustrate the workshop's theme to the rest of the student body.

These workshops also include a segment for administrators. Local organizations are requested to make presentations sharing new ideas, concepts, and current community issues. These sessions encourage administrators to develop programs for students at their respective schools. Teachers from urban schools are encouraged to partner with teachers from suburban schools.

While considering middle-school students, the project assists program developers in creating age-appropriate materials to aid participants in understanding how their everyday lives are affected by other cultures. Project leaders help developers focus on the programs' intent, targeted audience, mission, objectives, mode of delivery, and potential sites and outcomes.

Cultural Programs

Cultural programs attract participants from the entire community. The project leaders design them to offer new sources of enlightenment related to issues of diversity and target representatives from member groups for attendance.

Community Workshops

Project leaders invite nationally known speakers to Akron to conduct workshops on issues of racial harmony and racism. Although targeted primarily to representatives from member organizations, such events are open to the community at large.

Membership Commitment Mini-Workshops

Mini-workshops encourage an exchange of ideas and give hands-on guidance to representatives of member organizations. Member organizations of the project have encountered different challenges when attempting to execute programming to improve race relations in home agencies, which are local organizations with in-house programs. "Keeping the Commitment" mini-workshops teach member organizations how to overcome obstacles and advance bridge building across racial lines. The project holds these workshops three to four times annually to give all group representatives the opportunity to participate and contracts with various local consultants to facilitate the workshops. Each program is strategically placed throughout the project's year, allowing potential attendees flexibility with regard to work schedules. The project offers these educational workshops during evening hours, and diversity-training experts share information about discrimination and race and how they affect us in the workplace and in all facets of life.

Membership brown bag luncheons are held five times annually, at midday. One or two representatives of four member groups share what is being done to improve race relations organizationally. They share challenges and options offered by Project Coming Together to aid group efforts. The project plans to publish information gathered during sessions to share with similar organizations.

Social Programs

Social programs try to bring the entire community together using a basic message or theme. These activities are designed to attract large numbers of participants, and the entire community is invited to take part. The project evaluates all programs annually to determine effectiveness and profitability. Core programs continue to formulate overall project activity structure. Core programs are a series of annual educational, social, and cultural programs. The yearly series creates a basic structure for project programs.

Annual Race/Walk for Unity

This annual event, held in autumn, presents an opportunity for people of diverse backgrounds to meet, talk, and share in an informal setting, while publicly illustrating their support for Project Coming Together ideals. Participating runners compete in a 10-kilometer race with a tiered prize structure, while other participants converse with new acquaintances during a leisurely two-mile walk. The event offers local organizations the opportunity to expand awareness of their organization through displays and giveaways. Popular attractions include music, special activities for children, and door prizes.

Akron Aeros Annual Benefit Game

A local philanthropist and the owner of the city's minor league team, the Akron Aeros, created this event. The founder designed this special event to increase annual funding for and awareness of the project. This event attracts almost 9,000 participants and provides approximately 10% of the project's annual operating budget. The Coming Together Project profits from discount ticket sales and corporate contributions from program sponsors.

Community Cultural Collaborations

Since its inception, the Coming Together Project has worked with many organizations in cosponsoring events promoting improved race relations. Most notable among recent events are workshops cosponsored with the Summit County Alcohol, Drug and Mental Health Services Board; minority health month events, such as the appearance of Jackie Joyner Kersee, with Summa Health System; and work with the Tuesday Musical Club to present performers of color to multicultural audiences in Akron. The project collaborated with the mayor's office to present a youth town hall meeting in May 1998 as a follow up to President Clinton's visit to Akron. Collaborations continue with various departments at the University of Akron, including a community reception in March 1999 for the noted historian Dr. John Hope Franklin.

Specialized Programs

The Martin Luther King, Jr., Holiday Expansion Committee

The project led efforts to form the Martin Luther King, Jr., Holiday Expansion Committee to keep alive Dr. King's work for social justice. Organized in 1994, this volunteer committee serves to plan and coordinate approximately 21 days of activities commemorating the holiday. The Coming Together Project assumes the lead in publicizing holiday events by producing and distributing 2,000 posters and 10,000 fliers. The project's role has expanded in recent years to planning the holiday's Saturday-evening event at the city's largest performing arts hall.

SUSTAINED DIALOGUE

The Kettering Foundation selected Akron, Ohio, as one of five communities to participate in the sustained dialogue process developed by Hal Saunders (1999). Sustained dialogue is a five-step process that helps communities delve more deeply into underlying relationships and is designed to change the very nature of troublesome relationships. It is not designed to bring contending parties together to negotiate for an equal piece of the pie. Rather, participants examine the dynamics of contentious relationships, which may surface as a cause of the stated problem. Gradually, the discussion group works to develop a capacity for designing actions to change existing relationships for the better. The group then decides how to take steps to change the wider community.

STRUCTURE OF THE COMING TOGETHER PROJECT

The structure of the Coming Together Project is different from other organizations. Although it has the unified purpose of promoting better relations between the races, it acts as a clearinghouse or coordinator of various activities in the community that are aimed at accomplishing its goal.

Members of three boards work with the project staff in setting the organization's direction. The project has a 15-member board of trustees representing most segments of the community. Coming Together also has two volunteer advisory boards, one composed of 21 adults and one of 24 high-school students. They are used as sounding boards to test reactions to new programs, assist in determining community reception, and gather ideas and information. Both boards reflect the diversity of the organization.

The project staff consist of a full-time executive director, part-time coordinator, administrative assistant, development specialist, and project coordinator. It will be necessary to increase the staff, so they can execute increased activities and expand programs to allow the organization to grow and help the community foster acceptance and genuine understanding of Akron's diverse cultures.

The basic structure of the organization consists of 215 civic, social, religious, and educational groups, including corporations, as member organizations. It is through the member groups that the project realizes most of its goals. The project leaders invite these organizations to participate in all project activities and volunteer their varied expertise for most events. The project acts as a clearinghouse of information to the numerous groups, using newsletters and other formats to communicate project activities promoting racial harmony.

Evaluation Process

Most nonprofit organizations cite the ability to evaluate program effectiveness as top priority. Proposal requirements by contributors request measurable outcomes in addition to individualized programs. The designers decide on program categories (educational, social, and cultural), goals, and objectives based on the project's mission during the planning phase of program scheduling. Program objectives relate to the theme of each program as established by staff and selected presenters.

Most evaluations are administered following each event. Selected evaluators appraise these events, based on preset criterion. The evaluators then compile, record, and review the results to assist staff in enhancing program effectiveness. They evaluate social programs designed to bring large numbers of people together based on participant attendance, participant diversity, and program execution. Cultural programs, depending on event substance, may be evaluated using both methods: evaluations written by attendees and evaluations collected during a social or cultural event.

Evaluators created a special assessment tool to evaluate the effect of the project. They designed this instrument to determine the increase in community cultural awareness, changes in racial attitudes and behaviors, increase in participation in community-building programs, and increase in awareness of project ideals.

Due to the complexity of racism and discrimination, altering existing stereotypes and perceptions dictated a progressive approach. Therefore, planners set short-term, immediate, and long-term goals. The project must achieve short-term goals related to attitude before trying to attain immediate and, ultimately, long-term goals.

Short-Term (Attitudinal) Goals

- Change negative attitudes related to people of all cultures.

- Foster acceptance and appreciation of differences in people of all cultures.

- Increase awareness of people of all cultures.

Intermediate (Progressive) Goals

- Decrease number of discrimination complaints processed through the Ohio Civil Rights Commission regarding Akron/Summit County.

- Decrease number of discrimination complaints processed through the housing advocate agencies.

- Increase diversity of homeowners in segregated, affluent communities.

- Increase the number of high-profile employment positions held by people of color.

Long-Term (Behavioral) Goals

- Decrease number of hate crimes processed through associated agencies.

- Increase salaries and wages to members of minority groups.

- Decrease racist practices related to distribution of government contracts.

Thus, the evaluation process related to project programming has become and must continue as a vital component of the development, progress, and future of the organization.

CONCLUSION

> As we enter the 21st century, we know that one of the greatest challenges we still face is learning how we come together as One America. Over the coming decades, our country's ethnic and racial diversity will continue to expand dramatically. Will those differences divide us, or will they be our greatest strength? The answer depends upon what we are willing to do together. While we confront our differences in honest dialogue, we must also talk about common dreams and the values we share.
>
> —President Bill Clinton (1998)

President Clinton (1997) also described the United States as "two worlds, one white, one black, divided along a rift...that is tearing at the heart of America."

Similarly, Andrew Hacker (1992) stated, "A huge racial chasm remains, and there are few signs that the coming century will see it closed" (p. 219).

When and how can we close the racial divide? How can we realize the benefits of working together? How do we educate a nation to the fact that aptitude, competence, and erudition are colorless? What is the answer? Certainly, we do not have all the solutions, but we are convinced that relationships built through the Coming Together Project programming has been essential in the creation of lasting relationships.

America needs organizations like the Coming Together Project, with programs designed to bring people together who would not ordinarily do so. The time is long past for U.S. citizens to unite and work together for the common good. We have been divided, disjointed, disconnected, and virtually isolated from each other. We do not comfortably coexist unless forced to through employment or occasional social events, such as weddings or funerals. Often, during those times, an undeniable awkwardness is felt. As a diverse nation, we must put mechanisms in place to move people of all cultures together. The Coming Together Project is such a mechanism.

REFERENCES

Clinton, W. J. (1997, December 3). *One America—President Clinton's Initiative on Race: The Akron town meeting.* Presented at University of Akron, Ohio.

Clinton, W. J. (1998, March). *A nation transformed. One America. Expanding economic opportunity for all.* Available from http://www.loudvoice.com/homepage.html.

Hacker, A. (1992). *Two nations black and white, separate, hostile, unequal.* New York: Macmillan.

A question of color. (1994, January 6). *Akron Beacon Journal,* 1, 5.

Saunders, H. H. (1999). *A public peace process—Sustained dialogue to transform racial and ethnic conflicts.* New York: Palgrave.

CHAPTER 8

Can Society Afford Not to Promote Forgiveness and Reconciliation?*

EVERETT L. WORTHINGTON JR., AND JACK W. BERRY

Racial, ethnic, and religious understanding can be promoted through interventions with children and parents, college students and faculty, societal leaders and followers, media sources and consumers of information, mental health workers and mental health consumers, and policy makers and those who are affected by policies. These interventions can educate and train people for present and future actions. It is necessary, however, to deal with past injustices, offenses, and hurts across racial, ethnic, and religious divides if we are to ever have true understanding.

The past may be dealt with in many ways. Forgiveness is one way, but it is not the only way. In many cases, it might not be the best way. For some people, it might not even be an acceptable way. Yet forgiveness has become increasingly important in the United States and across the world—heightened in our consciousness because of significant world events. In the late 1980s, communism fell, and people began to ask, how do we live with former enemies? In the early 1990s, South Africa ended apartheid, and Nelson Mandela and Desmond Tutu became public symbols of forgiveness. On the other hand, negative examples, such as Rwanda, Bosnia, and Sierra Leone, have been wake-up calls that when forgiveness is not practiced, horrors can occur. In recent years, the increasing hostilities in Palestine, the terrorist attacks on the United States, and the response of bombing and invading Afghanistan, have certainly brought the importance of how people deal with transgressions into public scrutiny.

* Preparation of this chapter was partially supported under Grant 239 from the John Templeton Foundation and by *A Campaign for Forgiveness Research*.

Should the United States society value forgiveness and reconciliation? This is a crucial issue, especially to Muslim Americans and to people who lost loved ones in the attacks on the World Trade Center and Pentagon. The answer to that question depends on many factors. It depends on racial and ethnic differences, which are correlated with differences in socioeconomic status, whether people have or are aware of histories as slaveholders and slaves, whether people have been interned during wartimes, whether people have felt persecution for religious differences, or how long people have been in the United States. Whether people value forgiveness depends on religious differences in beliefs. For example, many Christians have emphasized forgiveness (Marty, 1998), but most (but not all) Jews see forgiveness as conditioned on repentance (which involves apology, restitution, and true remorse). Buddhists usually value compassion but might not eagerly forgive the way Christians or Jews do because Buddhists believe in karma, or immutable justice. Many Muslim governments and some Muslim people throughout the world see the attack on the United States as partly tied to its policies in the Middle East. Most Muslims throughout the world, however, differentiate between views of the United States government and the American people. Similarly, people in the United States are struggling to differentiate the actions of extremist Muslim terrorists from the beliefs and actions of moderate Muslim governments and individuals.

Whether societies invest time, energy, and resources in attempting to promote forgiveness and reconciliation depends on timing. People do not forgive in the midst of a fight. That probably would be counterproductive and would likely lead to injury if a fighter dropped his or her guard. Yet eventually, as hostilities cool, both sides of a conflict usually conclude that pursuit of justice or revenge will not balance the emotional books. The emotional pain of having been wronged and hurt by the other side must be dealt with is some way. This could involve reframing the events, psychologically defending oneself through denial or projection, simply accepting or forbearing the transgressions and their effects, or considering forgiveness. In the current world climate, that time will occur, both in the conflict between the United States and Afghanistan and the conflict between Palestinians and Israel.

Whether societies invest time, energy, and resources in attempting to promote forgiveness and reconciliation also depends on value judgments. Conversations are needed to determine societal values concerning forgiveness. Dialogue can be facilitated if some of the complex issues surrounding forgiveness could be reduced to a few subjects—moral, religious, historical, and economic discourses. In this chapter, the authors describe one of the many ways to discuss forgiveness and reconciliation.

This chapter attempts to aid dialogue and decision making by translating benefits and costs of forgiving into one common "language" to the extent possible—economics. This does not imply that the only, or even the most important benefits of an intervention are economic. We would like to believe, in fact, that when individuals actually decide to seek or to grant forgiveness or reconciliation, they do so with little or no thought about whether it is economically or politically beneficial to them. We would like to believe that people make personal decisions regarding forgiveness because they believes they are doing the right thing and are completely sincere. In this chapter, however, we are not as concerned with personal decisions to forgive as we are with societal dialogue about the costs and benefits of forgiveness. An economic analysis is simply one way to place as many benefits and costs as possible along a common yardstick to facilitate societal dialogue and understanding.

PROBLEMS IN CONDUCTING A COST-BENEFIT ANALYSIS

Conducting a rigorous cost-benefit analysis of forgiveness and related reconciliation in society is meaningless at this point in time. Frankly, we know too little about forgiveness and reconciliation to form sound judgments. A rigorous economic cost-benefit analysis of a societal or interpersonal intervention is only as good as the weakest assumption used to quantify the outcomes and costs (Yates, 1996). At present, such assumptions are so weak that any figures derived would be meaningless guesses.* Therefore, conducting a rigorous economic analysis of forgiveness is impossible for this young science. The authors thus consider a speculative, qualitative cost-benefit analysis and develop a structure that could eventually be used to make a quantitative analysis (see Figure 8-1).

Potential direct benefits from a forgiveness intervention might involve increases in (a) physical harmony, such as better health and less disease; (b) economic harmony, such as more productivity, fewer missed work days, more concentra-

---

* For example, let's take the relatively well-defined possibility that brief, 4- to 10-hour, psychoeducational groups aimed at promoting forgiveness in response to grudges can reduce people's cardiovascular risk. To estimate societal benefits, we would need to know (a) some quantification of the mean amount of forgiveness per person who attended the groups, (b) the number of people who could be induced to attend such groups, and (c) the benefit in dollars of saving in health care costs per unit of forgiveness.

We know fairly accurately the mean amount of forgiveness per person that will be brought about by a group intervention that lasts a given amount of time. A 0.75 correlation exists between the length of treatment and effect size (Worthington, Kurusu et al., 2000; Worthington, Sandage, & Berry, 2000). Effect size is the number of standard deviations a treatment group scores higher than a control group.

We do not know, however, how many people could potentially be affected. To illustrate how imprecise our knowledge is, at one extreme, suppose such groups were available in half of all high schools, college dormitories, family practice medical offices, selected HMOs, retirement homes, businesses with more than 25 employees, and prisons. In that case, perhaps as many as one-fifth of all U.S. residents might receive an intervention, or approximately 50 million people. At the other extreme, perhaps the estimate might be as low as several thousand if few people took advantage of the intervention even if it were widely available. At present, we have no way to estimate the potential usage throughout society.

We also do not know the dollars of benefit per unit of forgiveness. That calculation would require a chain of at least four ill-informed considerations. For illustration, consider the benefits to health from forgiving more often: (a) No longitudinal research

Figure 8-1

Pathways for Turning Potential Physical, Social, Political, and Economic Benefits into Direct (Solid Lines) and Secondary (Dashed Lines) Economic Benefit

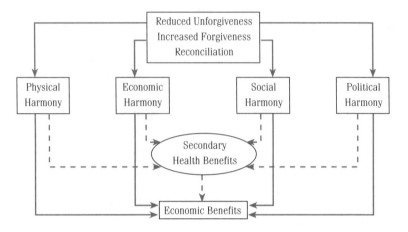

tion on work, and less interoffice conflict; (c) social harmony, such as less social dissent, better family harmony, better workplace environment, and less dissatisfaction in the workplace; and (d) political harmony, such as better racial or ethnic harmony, less political conflict, more lasting peace, and less war. Increased harmony could be translated directly into economic benefits (see solid lines in Figure 8-1).

Secondary economic benefits (dotted lines in Figure 8-1) could be realized because of improvements in health that accrued to people who experience better physical, economic, social, or political harmony. For example, if people forgive, and thus improve their marriages, that can result in a direct economic benefit (solid line). If because they have better marriages, they also have better health, that would constitute a secondary economic benefit (dotted line).

Purposes of this Analysis

Researchers have given little systematic attention to the overall potential societal effects that could come about through forgiveness. The purpose of this analy-

---

has established the long-term change in dispositional forgivingness that might occur through forgiving a particular transgression; (b) no empirical data relate the amount of change in forgivingness to the amount of reduction in cardiovascular risk; (c) some epidemiological medical data would permit an informed estimate of the savings in health costs from a given reduced cardiovascular risk; and (d) some epidemiological data might permit an estimate of other benefits of improved cardiovascular health, such as improved quality of life, higher work productivity, and savings from postponed medical care.

In addition, we have no accurate estimate of the costs of delivering forgiveness interventions. The same intervention would cost different amounts if it were conducted in (a) high schools, led by teachers or counselors; (b) universities, led by dorm counselors; (c) family practice offices, led by nurse-practitioners; (d) HMOs, led by staff counselors; (e) retirement communities, led by resident staff; (f) businesses, led by human resource personnel; and (g) prisons, led by trustees, chaplains, or prison psychologists.

sis is to provide an initial societal benefit analysis that might be subjectively weighed against an imprecise estimation of costs to affect such societal changes. A secondary purpose is to identify issues in the various areas of society to alert researchers and policy analysts to which data are needed to allow a more rigorous societal cost-benefit analysis.

First, the authors will define unforgiveness, forgiveness, and reconciliation and explore the implications of forgiveness (of an event) and dispositional forgivingness for society (McCullough, Hoyt, & Rachal, 2000). They will also discuss how society can promote forgiveness and describe alternatives to forgiveness and reconciliation that might, nonetheless, be socially beneficial. Second, they will qualitatively identify benefits to several social systems, according to the type of harmony to which each contributes most directly. Third, they will estimate some of the costs of interventions to promote forgiveness and reconciliation, including the costs of conducting research to establish whether interventions are effective. Fourth, they will examine the implications of the analysis for a variety of stakeholders in society.

DEFINITIONS AND DISTINCTIONS
What Are Unforgiveness, Forgiveness, and Reconciliation?

Transgressions are typically violations of boundaries, and transgressions are perceived as *offenses* if moral boundaries are transgressed. People typically respond to offenses with immediate anger. Transgressions that involve a violation of a person's psychological or physical boundaries are perceived as *hurts*. People typically respond to hurts with fear as well as anger. Many transgressions are both offensive and hurtful, resulting in an amalgam of anger and fear. Unforgiveness arises from transgressions in which people ruminate about the transgression and its effects. *Unforgiveness* is defined as a complex of emotions involving hatred, bitterness, resentment, anger, fear, and hostility that arise from rumination about perceived hurts and offenses; emotions of unforgiveness usually motivate the desire to reduce the unforgiveness as thoroughly and quickly as possible through any of several means (Worthington & Wade, 1999).

People may reduce unforgiveness in many ways involving social, acts such as exacting successful revenge, pursuing punitive justice, seeking restitution, turning over the judgment to God, and pursuing socially just conditions (Worthington, 2000). Unforgiveness may also be reduced through psychological acts such as unconsciously denying one's unforgiveness; projecting unforgiveness onto another person; cognitively reframing a transgression in a way that excuses, justifies, or denies the injustice; forbearing or accepting the transgression; or forgiving (Worthington, 2001). These categories are not necessarily independent. For example, a criminal might steal from a person, who becomes unforgiving toward the criminal. The person might reduce unforgiveness by accepting that crime happens. When the criminal is convicted and sentenced to jail, the person might reduce his or her unforgiveness further by seeing justice done. Later, the person might completely forgive, which further reduces unforgiveness.

Forgiveness is defined as the emotional replacement or juxtaposition of the negative emotions associated with a transgression with other emotions that motivate the person to seek reconciliation or conciliation with the transgressor, if that reconciliation or conciliation is safe, prudent, and possible (Worthington & Wade, 1999). The emotions that might replace the negative emotions are empathy, sympathy, unselfish love, compassion, and even romantic love. We have summarized the definitions above in Figure 8-2.

Importantly, when a transgression occurs, there are many prosocial ways that people can reduce their unforgiveness (Worthington, 2001). From a societal perspective, policy makers should not advocate a single method for reducing unforgiveness. Instead, they should provide a variety of options that can appeal to the largest cross-section of people as possible.

Reconciliation is the restoration of trust in a relationship in which trust has been damaged (Worthington & Drinkard, 2000). Reconciliation is interpersonal, whereas forgiveness is intrapersonal. Reconciliation might or might not involve forgiveness. Just as reducing unforgiveness might occur in many ways, reconciliation might occur in many socially acceptable pathways (de Waal, 1989b; Worthington & Drinkard, 2000).

Levels of Forgiveness

Forgiveness operates on at least four levels (see McCullough et al., 2000). At the most basic level, one can forgive a transgression. That transgression might be more or less severe. Transgressional unforgiveness can permeate a person's life or be relegated to infrequent recall.

At the most general level, one might develop a forgiving disposition, called *forgivingness* (Berry, Worthington, O'Connor, Parrott, & Wade, 2001; Berry, Worthington, Parrott, O'Connor, & Wade, 2001; Roberts, 1995). Forgivingness is cross-situational, enduring forgiveness. One might be dispositionally unforgiving and forgiving at the same time—reacting to many transgressions with unforgiveness, but also eventually forgiving them (Worthington, Berry, & Parrott, 2001).

At an intermediate level, one might be relationally forgiving or unforgiving. For example, a person might be dispositionally forgiving, yet have a poor relationship with his or her spouse. Unforgiveness for multiple transgressions might have generalized to the transgressor.

FIGURE 8-2

A Conceptual Model for Reducing Unforgiveness and Promoting Forgiveness Through
Emotional Juxtaposition

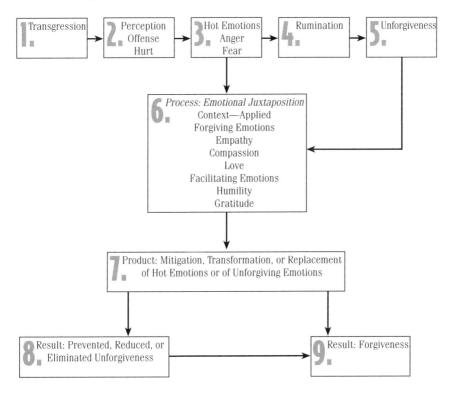

Source: Reprinted with permission from Worthington, 2001.

At another intermediate level, the person might be unforgiving about ethnic,
racial, or class transgressions. Ethnic, racial, or social class unforgiveness is
often confused with prejudice. Prejudice is an attitude of unfavorable discrimination toward a group or class of people. A prejudiced person holds negative attitudes and might engage in negative acts toward the target of prejudice. Racial,
ethnic, or social class unforgiveness, on the other hand, is a negative emotional
state that exists in response to transgressions. Transgressions might have harmed
the individual harboring unforgiveness directly or indirectly, or the person might
have experienced the transgression vicariously because it was perpetrated on a
forebear. Through identification with the forebear and rumination about historical transgressions, a person can become unforgiving. Prejudice does not require
transgression, though often prejudice comes about partly because of historical

transgressions. Unforgiveness requires transgressions. Therefore, the promotion of social forgiveness for ethnic, racial, social, or class transgressions can be dealt with specifically through recalling personal transgressions that (a) have been experienced personally, (b) have had an indirect effect, or (c) have become symbolic of one group's historical treatment of another group. Ethnic, racial, or social class forgiveness presumably would reduce a person's prejudice, if prejudice exists, and might help create a climate more conducive to reconciliation.

We hypothesize that these four levels of forgiveness or unforgiveness—transgressional unforgiveness, relational unforgiveness, ethnic unforgiveness, or dispositional unforgivingness—will be related to each other, but not necessarily correlated at a high level. Some data support such a contention (Berry, Worthington, O'Connor et al., 2001; Berry, Worthington, Parrott et al., 2001).

SOME BENEFITS OF FORGIVENESS

Figure 8-1 summarizes how reduced unforgiveness and increased forgiveness can lead to economic benefits to individuals, economic entities, social relationships, and political entities. In each case, secondary health benefits are likely. Thus, direct and indirect benefits can accrue to society, and researchers can estimate the economic effect of these benefits. This section considers how reducing unforgiveness, promoting forgiveness, and (perhaps) encouraging reconciliation can lead to increased physical, economic, social, and political harmony. Subsequently, each can lead to secondary health benefits and direct and indirect economic benefits.

Physical Harmony
Direct Benefits of Forgiveness to Individual Health
Although no one has conducted longitudinal, well-controlled research that definitively shows that reducing unforgiveness or forgiving will produce health benefits, a large amount of evidence suggests that reducing unforgiveness can reduce hostility and thereby lower cardiovascular risk (Thoresen, Harris, & Luskin, 2000; Worthington et al., 2001). Hostility is the core component of Type A behavior that has been related to cardiovascular risk (Thoresen et al., 2000). If people could become less dispositionally unforgiving and more dispositionally forgiving, such changes would translate into fewer myocardial infarctions, fewer strokes, less coronary artery disease, lower blood pressure, and fewer instances of hypertension. Because coronary artery disease is the largest health risk in the country (U. S. Department of Health and Human Services, 1993), reducing unforgiveness might contribute substantially to the health of many people throughout the country.

In addition, unforgiveness is stressful (Berry & Worthington, 2001; Witvliet, Ludwig, & Vander Laan, 2001). Researchers have shown that chronic stress is related to stress-related disorders (Sapolsky, 1999). These involve gastrointestinal difficulties, such as ulcers or colitis; cardiovascular problems; immune system disorders, such as myasthenia gravis, autoimmune disorders, and thyroid disorders; and others. Furthermore, stress can exacerbate other medical conditions. If people could reduce the stresses of unforgiveness and unreconciled relationships, this would improve their health, which could benefit society in many ways.

Let us consider the mere economics of improvements in physical health across society, ignoring benefits such as the reduction of suffering, improvements in quality of life, and increases in family happiness, or at least delayed family experiences of suffering due to early illness or death of a family member. Because of improvement in general health and delay of health problems, people would pay less in medical costs and insurance. Although this would negatively affect the medical industry, it would provide more usable income for the remainder of society. People would be productive at work more days per year for more years. They would earn more money, contributing to a stronger national economy. Quality of life would be improved, resulting in more commerce throughout the community. Financial burdens on families for health care would be reduced and postponed.

In each of these instances, health benefits accrue when unforgiveness is reduced. There are many ways to reduce unforgiveness, such as seeing justice done or forbearing (i.e., accepting) a hurt. Therefore, the economic benefits suggested previously are only partially attributable to forgiving. At the present, however, the contribution due to positive emotion is less well established than the contribution due to reducing unforgiveness.

Forgiveness not only reduces unforgiveness, but also increases positive emotional states, which might contribute to more robust immune system functioning and fewer mental health problems, providing more health benefits than alternative ways of reducing unforgiveness (Salovey, Rothman, Detweiler, & Steward, 2000; Worthington, Berry, & Parrott, 2001).

Benefits of Forgiveness in the Medical System

In 1986, the Lexington, Kentucky, Veterans Administration Medical Center (VAMC) was hit by two lawsuits for malpractice (Cohen, 2000; Kraman & Hamm, 1999; Wu, 1999). The lawsuits eventually resulted in settlements against VAMC for $1.5 million dollars. The VAMC management was appalled by the trauma to affected patients and their families, the extent of the damage done to the organization reputationally and financially, and the amount of time, energy, and money that the plaintiffs expended in resolving the suit. So the management made a radical decision—they adopted the policy that they would accept responsibility for any medical errors, apologize for any malpractice, seek forgiveness from the patients who were harmed, and offer fair restitution of damages incurred—all without resorting to legal wrangles to the extent it was up to VAMC.

The Lexington VAMC realized many intangible benefits, including high morale among VAMC personnel, a stellar reputation in the community, recognition in national media (Gerlin, 1999), and recognition as a model VAMC. What led to such benefits was the sincerity of VAMC in going beyond a hollow apology to back up their contrition with financial restitution for damages, willingness to take responsibility, and sincere efforts to make things right.

Let us consider the potential economic effect of the decision by the Lexington VAMC to make apology and seek forgiveness for wrongful, harmful errors. Since 1986, the amount of money paid out in reparations to patients was about $2 million—considerably less than they might otherwise have paid through lawsuits and out-of-court settlements, at least judging by the two lost suits in a single year.

Furthermore, additional costs might have been incurred had VAMC not adopted this policy. First, the amount of time lost by physicians, nurses, administrators, and other hospital personnel in safeguarding against possible extensive lawsuits and preparing legal documentation to avoid lawsuits would have been in the hundreds of hours. Second, for each major lawsuit that might have been launched against the hospital under its previous policy, the litigants undoubtedly would have spent hundreds of thousands of dollars in legal fees, lost hundreds of hours from work, and suffered enormous emotional turmoil with potential ill-health effects by dealing with each active lawsuit.

Third, during the time that the VAMC staff and plaintiffs would have been involved in lawsuits, opportunity costs for not doing other productive work would have accumulated. Those might have run in the hundreds of thousands of dollars. From an economic standpoint, the amount of money saved by VAMC that has resulted from its decision to apologize and seek forgiveness for errors has more than compensated any amount of potential future lawsuits. In addition, VAMC contributed to increased societal goodwill toward the medical community.

The potential economic effect of hospitals nationwide making similar decisions to offer preemptive apology, sincere contrition, and fair restitution, and to request forgiveness, are staggering. (This does not even consider that lawsuits against private hospitals result in twice the mean settlement as for VAMCs.) The enormity of economic effect can be seen by understanding the prevalence of medical errors.

The Institute of Medicine (1999) estimated that between 44,000 and 98,000 medical errors that lead to a patient's death are made in the United States each year. Some sources estimate that if doctors apologize for the medical mistakes that they make, 20% to 30% of the people who have brought suit against medical personnel for malpractice would not file such suits (Cohen, 1999; Hickson, Clayton,

Entman, & Miller, 1994; Minow, 2000; Vincent, Young, & Phillips, 1994). If physicians could reduce the amount of money paid in damages for medical malpractice by 10%, insurance companies could lower medical malpractice insurance by at least 5%. With medical malpractice insurance lower, many physician and hospital fees could be lowered. Every person in the United States who visits a physician would pay less out-of-pocket costs, allowing more money for disposable income among the population at large.

Such an economic analysis invites a Machiavellian attitude in behalf of corporate policy makers. "Let's apologize only because it is good business," they might reason. It also invites cynicism by some members of the public. "They don't care about my suffering; they are just saving money by 'cooling me out,'" a victim of a medical error might argue. These would be unfortunate, unintended, negative consequences of this economic analysis. That is certainly not its intent. Whether corporate apologies are perceived as positive depends on the sincerity of the apology, the willingness to accept responsibility, and the willingness to make fair negotiating settlements.

Nevertheless, what option does a physician have? Should the physician cover up a medical error, deny it, litigate it, or remain unapologetic for it? We would suggest that the answer to each question is no. Sincere apology accompanied by fair restitution is the right thing to do, and it also makes economic sense for victim and physician.

Benefits of Forgiveness in the Mental Health System

Within the mental health system, three targets for forgiveness offer promise for promoting forgiveness. Forgiveness could be promoted by providing (1) psychoeducational interventions for disgruntled family members of people with severe mental illness; (2) psychotherapeutic interventions in individual, couple, and family therapy; and (3) psychoeducational groups that can be used as adjuncts to therapy or as prevention or health-promotion interventions.

Family members. Serious mental illness in adults and serious emotional disturbance in children place enormous emotional and financial burdens on society. Despite increasing deinstitutionalization and treatment within communities and by families, much cost is still incurred publicly. Therefore, families involved in caring for the seriously mentally ill are often hostile to state organizations who administer and to providers who deliver psychological services. The level of unforgiveness within the mental health system is great.

If state departments of mental health or community service boards provide psychoeducational interventions to promote forgiveness in families, such a service is likely not to be well received by family members or advocates for mental health services. Such interventions might be perceived as efforts to quell dissatisfactions with the system. In the mental health system, promotion of forgiveness must be a grassroots effort initiated by families or advocates, because they see the physical and psychological costs incurred by families who hold onto bitterness and unforgiveness. Advocates can seek interventions to help family members forgive when advocates realize that forgiveness can be granted for injustices in the system without decreasing motivation to change unfair and unjust aspects of the system.

Psychotherapy. In individual, couple, and family therapy, many emotional and psychological problems are related to hurts, wounds, and injustices that people have experienced. Forgiveness interventions have been shown effective for incest survivors (Freedman & Enright, 1996) and men whose partners had abortions (Coyle & Enright, 1997). Currently, research is under way to promote forgiveness for other mental health and substance abuse problems. By providing interventions that address forgiveness directly or are adjuncts to other treatment modalities, practitioners might speed healing. Most counseling involves interpersonal relationships. In particular, couple and marital issues might be the largest single type of problem presented to counselors. Obviously, forgiveness and reconciliation looms large within relationships, making interventions to promote forgiveness particularly important to positive mental health throughout society (DiBlasio, 1998; Fincham, 2000; Gordon, 1997; Gordon, Baucom, & Snyder, 2000).

Adjuncts to therapy. Psychoeducational interventions can be used as adjuncts to therapy, as treatment for subclinical problems in anger or unforgiveness, as secondary prevention for high-risk clients, or as enrichment. Several researchers have shown such interventions to be effective for subclinical problems (McCullough & Worthington, 1995; McCullough, Worthington, & Rachal, 1997; Worthington, Kurusu et al., 2000). Other research has studied prevention and enrichment for couples (Burchard et al., 2003; Ripley & Worthington, 2002).

Overall Benefits of Forgiving in Individual Health and Health Care Systems

Individuals who are unforgiving are likely to be physically and mentally healthier if they forgive (for a review, see Worthington & Scherer, in press). Accurate estimates of savings due to applying forgiveness within physical and mental health systems are not available. Health and mental health difficulties are common. Frustration by patients and family caregivers with health care systems is frequent and often long lasting because of the long-lasting nature of health problems. Unforgiveness abounds. Together, these reasons suggest considerable economic potential deriving from improving health and reducing risks for illness. Such changes could come about from interventions to promote forgiveness.

Economic Harmony

Benefits of Forgiveness in the Business System

Why forgiveness is relevant in the workplace. Unforgiveness can have many tangible costs in the workplace, yet unforgiveness in the workplace has been seldom studied (see Bradfield & Aquino, 1999). In the workplace, many people interact daily. Workers, customers and customer-service personnel, and competitors interact, providing many opportunities to offend and hurt each other. It is not mere proximity that might make the workplace a breeding ground for unforgiveness, however. Rather, the environment is often characterized by competition between and within companies. Employees compete for attention, resources, and success. They are often rewarded with differential salaries. Employees invest their ego in their work, so pride in one's performance is likely to be high with regard to work-related behaviors (Exline & Baumeister, 2000). In addition, the importance people place on success is often a factor that enhances competition and might exacerbate the negative effects of hurts and offenses. Power differentials exist in the generally hierarchical corporate system. Finally, perceived discrimination due to race or gender can stimulate unforgiveness.

Many workplace behaviors and conditions can set the stage for unforgiveness. Negative evaluations by supervisors, or even the hint of negative evaluations, can stimulate employees to be unforgiving of supervisors. Supervisory decisions with which employees disagree can result in unforgiveness. Differential salaries among employees can result in bitterness within the ranks of employees and unforgiveness toward administrators. Disciplinary actions can result in unforgiveness. Supervisory decisions for assigning differential workloads, unpleasant duties, pay raises, and perks can stimulate resentment. Finally, hiring and firing provide many situations about which people experience transgressions. When downsizing occurs, one might be angry if one is terminated, but also might be unforgiving if one's friends are terminated.

To complicate matters, it often is not safe to talk about one's unforgiveness toward an employer, supervisor, or coworker. Power differentials result in real consequences for expressing dissatisfaction. Workers must deal with much unforgiveness alone. Conflict management skills could prevent a few transgressions, but many perceived transgressions are not likely to be addressed interpersonally, especially when they cross hierarchy boundaries.

Consequences of unforgiveness in the workplace. If workers harbor chronic workplace unforgiveness, they will likely have poor morale. Workers' attitudes might be characterized by resentment, bitterness, hostility, and hatred, as well as mistrust, suspicion, anger, and fear. When workers harbor chronic workplace unforgiveness, several effects on productivity are likely. Workers might stay home from work on days that they are ambivalent about whether to come to work. Also, they might be ill more often because of the health effects of chronic unforgiveness. Workers might change jobs to escape situations characterized by unforgiveness, which reduces company productivity by having more days in which no employee is available to do the work plus costing money and time to search for and retrain personnel. Workers might simply not cooperate with each other or management. Finally, by spending time ruminating about workplace conditions and past transgressions, workers might produce less.

Solutions to unforgiveness in the workplace. Companies have long recognized worker dissatisfaction, interpersonal conflict, and unforgiveness as being very costly to business. The costs are difficult to quantify. Many human relations departments try to prevent unforgiveness. Many businesses try to prevent transgressions through training in communication and conflict resolution. Leadership training has helped supervisors develop leadership styles that are less likely to provoke fear, anger, and unforgiveness in subordinates.

Human resources departments have devoted less attention to repairing relationships once a transgression has occurred (Worthington, Berry, Shivy, & Brownstein, in press). Efforts are usually limited to providing counseling by employee assistance programs or transferring disgruntled workers to different work units or locations. Usually, human resources departments simply ignore hurt feelings and emotional pain. Workers are expected to "deal with it" or seek employment elsewhere. In an environment as large and complex as many businesses, transgressions are inevitable, regardless of how much preventive training is available. So it is likely that productivity in companies could be substantially increased if companies offered workers and supervisors workplace-based training in forgiveness and reconciliation.

As with health issues, the cost of unforgivenesses to businesses cannot be estimated with current data. Thus, the economic benefit of strategies to reduce unforgiveness cannot be estimated. As with the medical system, the frequent opportunities that provoke unforgiveness suggest that substantial societal benefits in terms of increased worker productivity could be achieved by widespread, business-centered psychoeducational training to help workers deal with grudges and reconcile after squabbles.

Solutions to corporate mistakes. Forgiveness is relevant for businesses in dealing with public corporate blunders. When it was revealed that racism was occurring at Texaco, the company apologized publicly many times (Rosin, 1998). On the other hand, an explosion in India at a Union Carbide plant, which resulted in many deaths, was not promptly dealt with. In Texaco's case, many customers were probably saved. In Union Carbide's case, the human rights community likely cost the company much money.

To give a sense of the economic potential of seeking forgiveness, examine Toro Company, which manufactures lawn care products. Toro Company is sued often. Before 1991, company policy was to litigate all claims. From 1992 to 1996, Toro Company expressed sympathy for personal injuries and offered restitution. Cohen (2000) calculated that in five years, Toro Company saved $54,329,840.

We have argued repeatedly that although promoting the granting and seeking of forgiveness is good business, it is not merely good business. It is often the right thing to do, and it is an alternative that is vastly superior to denying wrongdoing, holding grudges, seeking revenge, and remaining emotionally negative toward either the victim or transgressor. Translating some of the benefits of seeking forgiveness by the Toro Company into savings of more than $54 billion in five years is simply one language of evaluating some of the effect of promoting forgiveness.

Social Harmony

The practice of forgiveness might increase social harmony in many social institutions. We will briefly consider four: the school, university, religious, and justice systems.

Benefits of Forgiveness in the Educational System

Within the middle and high school system, forgiveness interventions might reduce youth violence, promote less aversion to teachers, and result in better peer and dating relationships and ultimately better marriages and families. All three areas could result in more student productivity.

Reduction of youth violence. The potential for violence in the school system is great and has been dramatized by incidents such as the massacre at Littleton, Colorado. In that situation, two students were disgruntled, alienated, and unforgiving toward peers who had offended them. They took revenge through violence. Such incidents throughout the country have become almost commonplace, as youth have become disaffected and think they have no way of resolving their negative feelings other than through violent acting out.

Violence also can occur in the school setting by gangs. Youth violence can be acted out in the community. Schools may not necessarily be the site of the violence, but they provide an area to intervene to reduce school violence, because children are mandated to attend school.

Intervention in the school system has gained importance as welfare reform has changed the landscape of many lower socioeconomic status (SES) neighborhoods. This is due to two reasons. First, mothers who used to stay at home and monitor their children now work. Children in lower SES homes are now cared for by the mother's friends or relatives or by day care arrangements, or the children are simply left unattended. Coupled with the high rate of fatherlessness, especially in lower SES communities, some researchers expect youth crime to increase dramatically (Lykken, 2000; see Harris, 2000; Sampson, 2000; Scarr, 2000), making intervention more necessary. Second, community groups in lower SES neighborhoods are becoming more market savvy. Often, community groups are no longer as willing to participate in community-based interventions unless they are paid to do so. Such attitudes make interventions in the school system a desirable way to attempt to reduce youth violence.

Much youth violence is at least partly due to a backdrop of anger and unforgiveness among disenfranchised youth. Teaching youth how to forgive—if ways can be developed to make forgiveness palatable to potentially violent youth—can reduce this background of the number of unforgiven incidents that might occasion revenge or violence.

Reduced aversion to teachers. Many students hold unforgiveness toward teachers for acts as trivial as deservedly correcting a child for misbehavior or for assigning homework. Other students have more legitimate grounds for complaint, such as being discriminated against or being too harshly disciplined. Such unforgiveness, regardless of perceived transgression, can result in an aversion to school, which might occasion students to perform less well academically than they might in a more positive climate. Unforgiveness of teachers can result in missed days of school, which decreases academic achievement and ultimately economic productivity.

Improved peer relationships. Students from middle school on spend much of their waking time in relationships with their peers. These relationships are the basis for adolescents' concepts of self. When unforgiveness characterizes school interactions, a student can receive much negative feedback about himself or herself from peers, and thus might end up with a poor self-concept. Teaching students how to grant and seek forgiveness could have a direct effect on the number of suicide attempts, amount of childhood depression, and number of psychological disorders found in youth. It could have an indirect effect on the peer relationships developed in adulthood by students who have grown up in unforgiving school environments.

Interventions in schools can be effectively delivered at relatively low cost. Programs staffed by a few professionals can train high school students to deliver psychological services within groups of middle-school students. Developers expect the high-school student-teachers to benefit as much or more as the middle-school students they teach.

Benefits of Forgiveness in University Systems

Students in college learn how to deal with many differences by the interactions they have in dormitories. Dorms are practical laboratories where students learn how to resolve differences, deal with transgressions, and handle interpersonal conflict and transgressions that surround the conflict. In dorms, students also discuss dating relationships and the rejections and betrayals that attend college romantic life. Students also learn much about race relations in the college dorm. Most dorms encourage contact among people from a variety of ethnic backgrounds. They provide a place for conversation about how to deal with differences. Therefore, providing interventions to promote forgiveness within the dormitory might be a good way of preventing or ameliorating tensions.

The potential economic benefits of dormitory-based interventions are great. They might extend to (a) better mental health for many during adulthood, which could occur if students can reduce the number of betrayals and rejections that do occur; (b) better relational skills, which can result in less adult workplace disagreement and better marital and adult romantic relationships; and (c) better race relations, which could result in fewer adult hate crimes, less discrimination, and less prejudice.

Intervention within the dormitories can be relatively inexpensive. Dorm counselors or resident assistants can be trained to conduct psychoeducational interventions on the dorm floor.

Benefits of Forgiveness in Religious Systems

Religions differ. One of the most widespread social institutions in the country is the religious infrastructure. Not all religions value promoting forgiveness. For example, forgiveness is the central construct of Christianity (Marty, 1998). On the other hand, justice is more central to Islam (Rye et al., 2000) and Judaism (Dorff, 1998). Compassion, which often leads to forgiveness, is characteristic of Buddhism (Rye et al., 2000), which is highly relevant given the recent increase in Asian Americans living in the United States.

Worthington et al. (2001) suggested that religions seek to promote virtues in their adherents. Those virtues might be clustered into conscientiousness-based virtues, such as self-control and adherence to social standards, or warmth-based virtues, such as empathy, compassion, and forgiveness. Religions have a wide range of emphases across and within them. Worthington et al. (2001) have argued that religious individuals who emphasize conscientiousness-based virtues will in general be more interested in strategies to reduce unforgiveness through examples such as seeing justice done, appealing to divine judgment, and the like. Religious individuals who emphasize warmth-based virtues are more likely to try to promote compassion-based or empathy-based forgiveness among the members.

Unforgiveness across and within religions. For many, religion is at the core of life. It is not surprising that conflict, perceived transgressions, and unforgiveness can arise in religious contexts. Political activism has polarized both people within the same religion and religious people against nonreligious people on social and political issues. As a consequence of the political struggles between religious and secular society, people on both sides have experienced unforgiveness. It is likely that people of both sides experience negative health consequences.

People who value forgiveness are often able to rise above the differences that might have been caused by religious political conflict. They can mitigate their unforgiveness by forgiving their opponents. It is impossible to estimate accurately the amount of social impact that forgiveness associated with religion might produce for good or ill.

At the level of individual experience, the picture is less muddied. People who embrace an ethic of forgiveness tend to experience life more warmly. We hypothesize that warmth-based virtues are related to deeper levels of spirituality, but this has not been tested empirically. To the extent that religious people are more spiritually at peace and experience warmth-based emotions, we hypothesize that they derive health benefits.

Religious communities can effectively transmit values, beliefs, and practices to members of the community. They have less success (but still some success) in influencing people outside their communities. Nevertheless, almost half of the people in the United States are likely to be in religious services on their weekly day of worship. The potential for promoting forgiveness, if a religion took the task seriously, is enormous.

Religious communities could use top-down strategies, such as clergy or board initiatives, or bottom-up strategies, such as small groups or outreach programs. The economic effect, as in other cases, is hard to estimate. The sheer number of people affected suggests large economic benefits of improved health, mental health, productivity, and social relations.

The costs of promoting forgiveness in religious communities are small. Religious communities are volunteer organizations. Because potential benefits are high and costs are low, religious communities are ideal conduits for promoting forgiveness, when the religion values forgiveness.

Benefits of Forgiveness in the Justice System

The justice system is supposed to provide fair procedures and laws to guide the conduct of society and settle disputes, enforce laws, try alleged crimes, and carry out judicial decisions. In one respect, justice is independent of forgiveness. Justice is one way of balancing social, economic, and criminal injustices. Justice might prevent or reduce unforgiveness, although that is not the primary concern of justice.

In another respect, however, parties will inevitably feel that courts have made unfair decisions. Many will develop unforgiveness toward people in the justice system (e.g., police officers, judges, attorneys, criminals, plaintiffs, witnesses, or corrections officers) or procedures that aggravate or frustrate (e.g., court delays). There are at least six areas in which forgiveness can become an issue in the justice system: (1) law enforcement, (2) tort law and the redress of conflicting civil claims, (3) national law, (4) international law and the resolution of differences between and among countries, (5) criminal law and the punishment of civil offenses, and (6) the corrections system.

Law enforcement. Law enforcement officers often have been harmed by perpetrators of crimes or know other officers who have been harmed. Despite training, unforgiveness occasionally explodes in retaliation against perpetrators and suspected perpetrators and results in police violence and even torture (although we hope this occurs only in countries other than the United States). Even when unforgiveness does not result in violence, unforgiveness of crime can place police officers under stress and result in illness, marital strain, and workplace tension. If unforgiveness could be reduced in the law-enforcement community, the economic effect would be noticeable in (a) less police brutality, (b) less burnout of police officers, and (c) better job performance and stability of police officers.

Tort law and the redress of conflicting civil claims. Torts involve judicial disputes and lawsuits among parties. Usually, when a party has wronged another party, such as having an auto accident that is clearly the fault of one party, then the injured party sues the (presumed) at-fault party for restorative plus punitive damages. If acrimony is involved in the wrongdoing or subsequent communications, then the plaintiff may seek extremely large punitive damages.

Excessive claims could likely be reduced if wrongdoing parties would apologize to the injured parties (Cohen, 2000; Minow, 2000), similar to apologies for medical errors. Under current tort law, however, if a wrongdoer apologizes, they court takes this as an evidentiary admission of culpability and the wrongdoer is likely to lose any civil suit that follows. The general solution to this difficulty is to decouple apology from evidence. Minow (2000) suggested several ways this could be done. Passing apologies from evidence would stimulate forgiveness and provide savings to society in terms of reduced lawsuits, legal fees, and lost time from work by conflicting parties. It would also likely lower excessive punitive damages.

National law. When countries experience civil unrest, often the side that is victorious will exact harsh penalties on the losing side. In recent years, truth commissions have been set up in more than 20 countries to reduce punitive responses of victors to those with whom they had bloody conflicts. Truth commissions are separate and distinct from war crimes tribunals. The social benefits to the country (and world) of truth commissions can be large, although debate about their usefulness is often heated (Haynes, 1994). The prevention of death and persecution, as well as the prevention of incarceration of political personnel, save a large amount of productive work for society that would not be available if retributions were made.

International law. Hostilities often occur between sovereign nations. In most instances, those hostilities have historical roots in past transgressions—often from years before. International relations that are characterized by unforgiveness and mutual distrust between leaders can degenerate quickly if hot disputes occur. Treaties to promote cross-nation reconciliation, or proclamations such as those issued by Germany toward past injustices perpetrated toward Jews, might promote forgiveness and reduce the potential for international hostilities (Shriver, 1997).

The criminal justice system. In recent years, the United States has virtually abandoned a rehabilitative model of criminal justice and replaced it with a system that emphasizes punishment and protection of society from repeated offenders (colloquially called "trail 'em, nail 'em, and jail 'em"). Although this strategy is partly responsible for the reduction of violent crime (Dilulio, 1995), it has resulted in an overburdened court system and in more than 1.3 million people being incarcerated today (Lykken, 2000). The economic and moral costs of moving hundreds of thousands of people through adjudication procedures and then feeding, caring for, and providing security for so many people in prison is staggering.

Either in response to this societal trend or parallel with it, an approach to criminal justice called restorative justice has emerged (Zehr, 1995). In the restorative justice conceptualization, perpetrators (often youth and young adults) who have been charged with a crime or have already been sentenced are brought face to face with the injured parties, usually with the participation of community representatives, to attempt to mediate an agreement among the parties. The agreements seek to restore perpetrators to good standing with the community instead of merely incarcerating them. Restorative justice is more of an ideology than a methodology. It includes victim/offender reconciliation programs (VORPs), victim/offender mediation (VOM), therapeutic jurisprudence (Schma, 2000; Wexler & Winick, 1996), community justice committees, victim impact panels, and circle sentencing (Stuart, 1996).

Restorative justice, when it is successful, benefits the perpetrator, who receives less harsh punishments; provides the opportunity to apologize and make restitution; and helps reintegrate the offender into the community and into rehabilitative work. Restorative justice also benefits the victims, who might be the recipients of restitution. Restorative justice benefits society by allowing offenders to be restored to society and productive work, rather than to become a burden on society, which would fund incarceration and incur costs from the secondary problems that arise from exposing offenders to hardened criminals.

Restorative justice programs are often run relatively inexpensively using community volunteers. Participants might or not meet with attorneys present. Considerable savings to society are thus realized in terms of (a) positive benefits of restitution performed by the offender; (b) the quicker return to the productive workforce of offenders, resulting in a boost to the economy from extra work performed; (c) legal fees that are not expended due to appeals; and (d) cost savings of incarceration.

Yet restorative justice is justice, not forgiveness. True, it is a kinder and gentler justice than is punitive justice. Therein lies the connection to forgiveness. Because it provides an opportunity for offenders to apologize and make restitution, restorative justice putatively stimulates forgiveness in victims of crime as well as reduces their unforgiveness through seeing the operation of justice. Studies are needed to determine relative incidence of forgiveness and relative degrees of reduction of unforgiveness in victims when matched offenders do and do not participate in restorative justice.

In addition, to quantify the effects of restorative justice approaches, researchers must determine differential effectiveness between traditional punitive justice and programs such as VORPs and VOM regarding time spent, court costs, and outcomes such as recidivism and community morale. If researchers find that restorative justice programs are more effective than traditional justice, the effects of forgiveness should be partialed out.

Corrections system. Within the criminal justice system, the prisons and correctional facilities are hotbeds of unforgiveness. The amount of hostility, hatred, and unforgiveness prisoners have is likely related to the amount of additional crime they might commit when or if they are paroled or complete their sentence. If unforgiveness could be promoted among prisoners, millions of dollars might be saved by society due to reduced future crime, more contributions of previous offenders to work as a result of less recidivism, and fewer total hours consumed in law enforcement, future court proceedings, and additional correctional costs.

Corrections officers often are unforgiving toward prisoners and administrative personnel. That unforgiveness might result in retaliation toward prisoners or displaced aggression. Unforgiveness both in prisoners and corrections officers create a closed system of hostility and potential aggression that sometimes erupts in violence, harm, and pain.

Overall, the justice system is a hotbed of unforgiveness. It is thus a broad target for teaching and practicing forgiveness. Opportunities exist to institutionalize processes such as (a) programs to promote forgiveness among law enforcement officers, (b) laws making apologies nonadmissible in lawsuits, (c) truth and reconciliation commissions, (d) international proclamations of apology, (e) restorative justice mechanisms, (f) restorative justice programs, and (g) interventions in corrections. Such processes could stimulate substantial forgiveness without diminishing justice. As with other areas, however, the authors do not currently have data to evaluate the economic promise of forgiveness within the justice system.

Political Harmony

Benefits of Forgiveness in Public Policy

The political process is characterized by conflict. Conflict creates the potential for individual or corporate transgressions. Those transgressions frequently lead to unforgiveness, which can result in a social disaffection, hostility toward government, and armed conflict between and within nations.

Armed conflict is always costly in terms of loss of life, property, and productivity. It seems clear that society is best served by promoting nonviolent means of solving social problems. Obviously, not all governments are good. Governments can be unjust to some citizens. It would be socially disingenuous to recommend that forgiveness be the only stance promoted in a society toward transgressions. Governments must promote many nonviolent ways to solve social problems.

Ways of promoting forgiveness and reconciliation at the public policy level. Worthington (2001) suggested more than 20 ways to deal with unforgiveness. Forgiveness is only one way, and most of these ways are socially positive. These involve changes in the justice system, changes in law, or resolution of conflict. Others involve telling different stories about transgressions that do not promote violent responses, adopting different societal heroes who have worked for reconciliation of differences, employing a democratic system of government that allows social change without the necessity of armed rebellion, adopting governmental policies that do not squelch dissidence unless people and property are harmed, simply accepting minor transgressions, and forgiving. He outlined six suggestions that societies could use to promote forgiveness:

- Use multiple methods of dealing with unforgiveness.

- Tackle issues with a broad strategy of reconciling.

- Embrace heroes and stories to shape history.

- Be sensitive to serious consequences of advocating forgiveness.

- Use mass-media communication to focus on goals.

- Engage media cooperation to moderate the "hothead factor."

To the extent that societies can promote peaceful resolution of differences and, in particular, forgiveness among conflicting people, both nations and the world can experience social benefits and reduce the social costs of nonpeaceful conflict resolution.

At the public policy level, two primary ways to intervene exist. Thus far, this text has suggested policymaker initiatives. These top-down strategies promote forgiveness by establishing formal laws, policies, or structures that facilitate people's experience and practice of forgiveness and reconciliation. The second way to intervene is through grassroots initiatives. In grassroots initiatives, existing institutions, such as religious organizations and parent-teacher associations, and ad hoc groups, such as groups constituted to promote a particular issue or agenda and nongovernmental organizations (NGOs) seek to build consensus through dialogue and discussion. The consensus eventually pressures policy makers to change laws and policies. Both policymaker and grassroots initiatives can, of course, work together.

Types of public policy interventions. Forgiveness can be taught as a preventive or reparative strategy. At the societal and ethnic levels, forgiveness is taught as a reparative strategy. In Rwanda, Staub (in press) helps members of the Tutsi and Hutu tribes discuss differences and reduce tribal tensions. The hope is eventual reconciliation. In Northern Ireland, Cairns (2003) helps Protestants and Catholics reduce unforgiveness from many years of conflict. These public policy efforts are at the grassroots level.

As yet, no government has officially advocated the promotion of ethnic forgiveness as a preventive strategy, although the benefits of such a societal intervention might be great in terms of reduced conflicts in the future. To accomplish this, a government would have to conduct public information campaigns, modeled on successful public health campaigns, teach citizens how to forgive effectively, and urge, but not coerce them to forgive.

Policymaker-initiated interventions at the national, state, or local level are more likely to be successful than policymaker initiatives at the international level. The United Nations could proclaim a year or a decade of reconciliation, but it has no power to carry out programs within countries. It would depend on cooperative NGOs to stimulate change. At the national, state, or local level, however, legislators can pass legislation and resolutions and can appropriate funds to encourage interventions. Such resolutions could establish funds for interventions to increase the skills of individuals to forgive and reconcile.

The cost of such societal support of interventions would vary. Policymaker and grassroots initiatives could be combined if government programs fostered communities' or NGOs' involvement by integrating service-delivery professionals, community organizations, and government monitors. Governments could give block grants to states to set up community programs.

How society can promote forgiveness and reconciliation for past injustices. Besides the efforts of a society to foster reconciliation due to present injustices, society must also attend to the past. Most societies have a history of perceived injustices. Most governments have traditionally tried to suppress or ignore these historic injustices. Groups with a grievance understandably want not to forget historical injustice. They pass stories of injustice to generation after generation. Differing historical accounts can lead to unforgiveness that manifests itself in a present society, perpetuates unforgiveness in future generations who learn partisan histories, and can erupt suddenly in violence.

One alternative to forgetting injustice (which rarely has worked) is to redress historical injustices in the present. Redressing historical inequities is daunting. If a government makes economic restitution today for historical exploitation, the next generation will still have economic disparities across groups. They will desire additional restitution. This is especially true if the stories of injustice continue to be told without incorporating the stories of attempts to redress injustice. Failure to offer restitution for injustice perpetuates, if not intensifies, unforgiveness.

Each side's economic perceptions determine whether they perceive that the scales of justice are balanced. It is unlikely that all parties will be satisfied that justice has been accomplished through mandated or spontaneous redistribution of wealth. It is unlikely that all parties will transmit that belief to the generations to come, regardless of how fair a decision is on the day that historical inequities are redressed.

Justice that comes through redistribution, restitution, court judgments, and revision of social structures seem unlikely ever to eliminate class, race, or ethnic unforgiveness. At some point, the sides must grant forgiveness for past injustices. Granting forgiveness changes the emotional valence with which people view the issues and permits the transmission of new perceptions of history to future generations. Furthermore, granting forgiveness, along with making restitution, must be highly public and must change the stories about history.

Clearly, forgiveness alone should not bear the brunt of changing people's emotional reactions to history. Justice must be involved, and the efforts of both sides to arrive at reasonable restitution and understanding of each other are needed. Thus, efforts in behalf of both fair social justice and forgiveness are crucial to any country or ethnic group resolving historical injustices. We might estimate that the benefits of forgiveness for resolving historical injustices are great. Even with the best efforts to promote social justice, social change is unlikely to be enough without forgiveness.

This chapter has outlined several social strategies that could promote forgiveness within groups (e.g., making governmental restitution, public ceremony). Unforgiveness is like an airborne virus, however, in which one cough can spread the virus to many people. (Witness, for instance, the Rodney King beating or the O. J. Simpson criminal and civil verdicts.) Forgiveness is a treatment for the disease of unforgiveness that must be administered one dose at a time.

Social interventions are large-scale ways of getting individuals to consider the experiences of others empathically and to engage emotions of compassion and love for people on different sides of issues. Only after that can the emotion of forgiveness begin to overwhelm the negative emotions of unforgiveness. Of course, once individuals are inoculated with the antibodies of forgiveness, they can spread the good infection of forgiveness to other people.

ESTIMATING BENEFITS AND COSTS
Estimating Benefits
Scenarios in Making Cost-Benefit Estimates

Rigorous cost-benefit analyses often contrast the costs of conducting an intervention with the saving in costs of not conducting the interventions or with costs of conducting alternative interventions. Estimating cost-savings requires many value-laden judgments. Consider the following scenarios, and suppose each intervention costs the same amount of money. Different benefits would attend each.

- Scenario 1. A forgiveness intervention is conducted with all the senators and representatives. Some legislators' attitudes change toward forgiveness, leading to new laws. Changes in economic productivity might ripple throughout the country.

- Scenario 2. A forgiveness intervention is conducted with incarcerated criminals who are eligible for parole or are nearing the end of their sentence. The benefits to those people might be great, but other benefits might also ripple down—less crime, less property damage, less recidivism, and therefore less cost to society.

- Scenario 3. A forgiveness intervention is conducted with school-age children, teaching them to forgive and reconcile more effectively. Although the immediate payoff for school-age children changing their behavior might be small relative to the other two interventions, over their lifetimes, those children would make decisions that could very well be more sweeping than either Scenario 1 or 2.

- Scenario 4. A forgiveness intervention is conducted with clergy who are disaffected. They are helped to resolve their disaffections and continue to contribute positively to the lives of the parishioners with whom they interact weekly. That intervention might provide enormous cost-savings to society by preventing dropout of people who were genuine forces for forgiveness.

Five Issues in Estimating Costs and Benefits

These four scenarios raise at least five issues for policy analysts. First, people's contributions to society depend on their age. The societal cost of rearing children far outweighs the immediate benefits that children contribute to society. So the benefits of starting a school-based forgiveness program would have to be estimated into the future. Interventions with postadolescent adults will produce outcomes that are fairly immediate and perhaps even dramatic because those adults are already productive members of the workforce. In some cases, the future covers a long span. In other cases, such as with elderly, the future covers a shorter span.

Second, future benefits are not worth the same as present benefits. An analyst would need to calculate the present, discounted value of projected future contributions. Third, people differ in their relative power to contribute to society at different times in their lifespan. For children, virtually all of their contributions will be in the future; children have little power. People in the middle years are at the height of their power and make the most sweeping social changes. The effects of their acts are the most dramatic. People who are elderly have power of influence and wisdom, but they do not have the same amount of power to make decisions as those in the productive middle years.

Fourth, interventions that are aimed at prevention, enrichment, or remediation have different effects. Prevention stops deterioration before it occurs, or it retards the onset and rate of deterioration. Enrichment and remediation enhance people's functioning. Enrichment tends to benefit those who are already well functioning or at least who have no substantial problems. Remediation is apropos only for the troubled.

Fifth, from a social policy point of view, each segment of society—children, middle-aged adults, or elderly adults—must be targeted for some intervention. Using present value estimates of benefits, social policy makers must decide which interventions are most effective and where to apply them. Policy makers can strategically concentrate resources on those interventions and areas.

Estimating Costs

Estimates of Costs of Conducting Interventions

Conducting interventions requires money and time and includes the opportunity costs of not doing alternatives to interventions. Forgiveness-promoting programs will differ in the types of costs incurred. A public information campaign, preventive program in schools, and public remedial program for crime victims differ widely in resources needed to be successfully conducted. Those publicly financed programs might be very different from volunteer interventions by churches or privately funded interventions, such as counseling agencies that conduct fee-for-service interventions.

Estimates of Research Costs to Evaluate Interventions

Research is needed to estimate the potential benefits and costs of delivering interventions. Research is costly, and large-scale research is very costly. We assume that strategic high quality research is worth the cost. In the same way that advances in medical science have been brought about through basic and applied biological and medical research, advances in forgiveness and reconciliation will likely be brought about by large research studies of forgiveness and reconciliation.

Estimates of Some Personal Costs of Forgiving

When a person forgives, the person replaces bitterness, hostility, hatred, and anger with more positive emotions, such as compassion and empathy for the other person (Worthington & Wade, 1999). Giving up anger, however, can feel like giving up power. Anger is a person's best emotion for removing blocks to his or her pleasure. Letting anger go can result in less energy for righting injustices (Baumeister, Exline, & Sommer, 1998; Exline & Baumeister, 2000).

On the other hand, people have other motivations to right injustices, such as to do well for others. Anger motivates people to destroy blocks to justice. Altruism motivates people to construct just systems. Because many people are strongly motivated by anger, however, forgiveness does exact a cost on those people.

Forgiveness also can exact a personal cost if a person places himself or herself in a position of being taken advantage of after forgiving (Baumeister et al., 1998). A person who forgives does not have to place himself or herself at risk. Restoring trust in a relationship is reconciliation, which can occur apart from forgiveness (Worthington & Drinkard, 2000). Forgiveness does not demand reconciliation, but it motivates people to reconciliation only if it is safe, prudent, and possible to reconcile. If people misunderstand this difference, however, they may place themselves at risk of harm or of being taken advantage of.

IMPLICATIONS FOR SOME SOCIETAL STAKEHOLDERS

This chapter has detailed a qualitative summary of benefits of forgiveness in physical, economic, social, and political harmony. The authors have attempted, where possible, to place the consideration on an economic yardstick, while trying carefully to avoid reducing all decisions about forgiveness to economics. The analysis has considered costs due to conducting interventions, doing research on interventions, and making personal decisions to forgive. The authors tentatively conclude that the qualitative benefits to individuals and society seem to outweigh the qualitative costs. Until more data are gathered—much more data—the conclusion must remain tentative. Many implications of this analysis, although tentative, exist for society. The following includes some primary implications for a number of stakeholders.

Citizens

If convinced of the potential for overall betterment of society that is revealed in promoting forgiveness, citizens might practice personal forgiveness and seek interventions that help them forgive more easily and more thoroughly. At the societal level, citizens might contact legislators and encourage them to support revisions in laws and adoption of policies to promote widespread forgiveness.

Families

Families can benefit by having access to programs that teach family members how to prevent problems within the family, such as interventions that help new parents or parents-to-be learn how to forgive their children, newlyweds forgive each other, and elderly adults to resolve unforgiveness as they approach death. Such interventions might be available through physicians, private counseling agencies, or publicly supported psychoeducational interventions. Families with troubles can also seek family therapy to remediate problems.

Communities

Communities can cooperate with state and federal governments and service providers to create community-based programs to promote forgiveness and reconciliation. Community organizations, such as church-based and other volunteer organizations, are particularly good settings for delivering low-cost, high-benefit interventions. The authors urge counselors and psychotherapists to develop psychoeducational and psychotherapeutic interventions that target individuals, couples, families, and organizations. We also encouraged counselors and therapists to present cases to managed-care companies to be reimbursed by third parties for their services. Policy makers can consider whether to employ public resources to promote forgiveness and reconciliation as an integral part of violence-prevention efforts in communities and schools. University communities could sponsor low-cost dormitory interventions to teach forgiveness and reconciliation. Communities can also become involved in restorative justice programs.

Media

Media can attempt to promote forgiveness and reconciliation through television, radio, or print programs on the practicalities of forgiving and reconciling. When media report violence-related events, they can responsibly balance their coverage with stories about attempts to reconcile and forgive perpetrators of violence.

Philanthropists

The authors encourage philanthropists to support research on the fundamental understanding of forgiveness and reconciliation and the promotion of them. Such support of basic research is reminiscent of the beginning of the 20th century, when John D. Rockefeller was deciding where to make philanthropic donations. An advisor, Frederick T. Gates, suggested that he invest in medical research, rather than in funding then-current medical interventions. Through Rockefeller's and other investors' strategic philanthropic investing, modern advances in medical research were greatly enhanced.

At the beginning of the 21st century, philanthropists have the opportunity to concentrate their philanthropic gifts on understanding how to help people to forgive and reconcile, thus ushering in a scientifically founded age of reconciliation. The present cost-benefit analysis, although more qualitative than quantitative, suggests that strategic philanthropy aimed at understanding and promoting forgiveness is not only a good thing, it is a wise philanthropic investment.

Governmental Funding Agencies

The authors also encourage governmental funding agencies to invest in research on the promotion of forgiveness and reconciliation:

- The Centers for Disease Control and Prevention might supplement research on violence-prevention with forgiveness and reconciliation efforts.

- The U.S. Department of Health and Human Services could examine the effects of parents' learning to forgive on child health.

- The National Institute for Mental Health might fund research on the effects of learning to forgive on the mental health and mental disorders of family caregivers.

- The National Cancer Institute might fund research on the role of forgiveness in the treatment of cancer.

Private Businesses

The authors recommend that business organizations incorporate programs that help workers forgive into their human resource divisions. Such interventions would be helpful even if the company provides copious seminars and workshops on communication and conflict resolution. Furthermore, the authors suggest that more businesses follow the lead of Toro in deemphasizing litigation and emphasizing apology, contrition, and out-of-court restitution.

Policymakers

The authors recommend that policymakers advocate for programs that promote forgiveness and be willing to allocate resources of society toward that end. A number of targets seem especially promising for public policy revisions.

Perhaps the most immediate are revisions to civil, criminal, and international law in ways that make forgiveness more likely. Judicial system revisions permitting more restorative and therapeutic justice are possible. Executive-branch policymakers can also promote forgiveness in education (e.g., school programs to curb youth violence), public information campaigns, and family policy (e.g., teaching forgiveness and reconciliation to husbands and wives to reduce the likelihood of divorce). Executive decisions to publicly redress some historical inequities could complement efforts to include forgiveness in stories of historical injustices. Mental health policymakers could fund advocacy groups to teach forgiveness to families.

Conclusion

The authors tentatively conclude that society and individuals potentially benefit more by forgiving than it costs to help people forgive. We suggest that the implications of pursing forgiveness are largely positive within the society for most groups of individuals and the individuals themselves.

Forgiveness is not a panacea. Clearly, problems will continue, regardless of whether people know more about how to heal them. To date, few public expenditures have targeted forgiveness interventions.

We suggest that although teaching people how to forgive and reconcile better in a variety of settings can contribute to preventing problems and helping resolve serious disorders and problems, perhaps one of the major contributions to human health and welfare occurs at a midrange between these two extremes. That is, regardless of the effort expended, prevention cannot stop all negative interactions of individuals, families, communities, or societies. Remediation cannot heal all serious problems. Perhaps the best targets at which to aim forgiveness interventions are subclinical remediation and primary prevention. That is, society might best intervene before problems require psychotherapy or serious social interventions, such as an intervention by armed forces to quell social dissent. We recommend a social agenda that concentrates efforts on promoting forgiveness and reconciliation with normal, not-at-risk populations, while continuing to help prevent problems in at-risk populations.

In this chapter, we have sketched the results of a qualitative cost-benefit analysis of forgiveness and reconciliation. We hope that we have conveyed that many reasons to promote forgiveness are not reducible to the language of economics. We have used an economic language merely to stimulate additional debate. Despite the large amount of missing data and the lack of rigor in estimating economic effects of benefits and costs, we cannot help but pose the question, can society afford not to promote forgiveness and reconciliation?

REFERENCES

Baumeister, R. F., Exline, J. J., & Sommer, K. L. (1998). The victim role, grudge theory, and two dimensions of forgiveness. In E. L. Worthington, Jr. (Ed.), *Dimensions of forgiveness: Psychological research and theological perspectives* (pp. 79–104). Philadelphia: Templeton Foundation Press.

Berry, J. W., & Worthington, E. L., Jr. (2001). Forgiveness, relationship quality, stress while imagining relationship events, and physical and mental health. *Journal of Counseling Psychology, 49,* 287–310.

Berry, J. W., Worthington, E. L., Jr., O'Connor, L., Parrott, L., III, & Wade, N. G. (2001). *The measurement of trait forgivingness.* Unpublished manuscript, Virginia Commonwealth University, Richmond.

Berry, J. W., Worthington, E. L., Jr., Parrott, L., O'Connor, L. E., & Wade, N. G. (2001). Dispositional forgivingness: Development and construct validity of the Transgression Narrative Test of Forgivingness (TNTF). *Personality and Social Psychology Bulletin, 27,* 1277–1290.

Bradfield, M., & Aquino, K. (1999). The effects of blame attributions and offender likeableness on forgiveness and revenge in the workplace. *Journal of Management, 25,* 607–631.

Burchard, G. A., Yarhouse, M. A., Worthington, E. L., Jr., Berry, J. W., Killian, M., & Canter, D. E. (2003). A study of two marital enrichment programs and couples' quality of life. *Journal of Psychology and Theology, 31,* 240–252.

Cairns, E. (2003, October). *Intergroup forgiveness in Northern Ireland.* Paper presented at Scientific Findings About Forgiveness, Atlanta, GA.

Cohen, J. (1999). Advising clients to apologize. *Southern California Law Review, 72,* 1009–1069.

Cohen, J. (2000). Apology and organizations. *Fordham Urban Law Journal, 27,* 1447–1482.

Coyle, C. T., & Enright, R. D. (1997). Forgiveness intervention with post-abortion men. *Journal of Consulting and Clinical Psychology, 65,* 1042–1045.

deWaal, F. (1989). *Peacemaking among primates.* Cambridge, MA: Harvard University Press.

DiBlasio, F. (1998). The use of a decision-based forgiveness intervention within intergenerational family therapy. *Journal of Family Therapy, 20,* 77–94.

Dilulio, J. J., Jr. (1995, September 6). Why violent crime rates have dropped. *Wall Street Journal,* A10.

Dorff, E. N. (1998). The elements of forgiveness: A Jewish approach. In E. L. Worthington, Jr. (Ed.), *Dimensions of forgiveness: Psychological research and theological perspectives* (pp. 29–55). Philadelphia, PA: Templeton Foundation Press.

Exline, J. J., & Baumeister, R. F. (2000). Expressing forgiveness and repentance: Benefits and barriers. In M. E. McCullough, K. I. Pargament, and C. E. Thoresen (Eds.), *Forgiveness: Theory, research, and practice* (pp. 133–155). New York, NY: Guilford Press.

Fincham, F. D. (2000). The kiss of the porcupines: From attributing responsibility to forgiving. *Personal Relationships, 7,* 1–23.

Freedman, S. R., & Enright, R. D. (1996). Forgiveness as an intervention with incest survivors. *Journal of Consulting and Clinical Psychology, 64,* 983–992.

Gerlin, A. (1999, September 14). Accepting responsibility, by policy. *Philadelphia Inquirer,* A18.

Gordon, K. C. (1997). *Demystifying forgiveness. A cognitive-behavioral stage model.* Unpublished doctoral dissertation, University of North Carolina–Chapel Hill.

Gordon, K. C., Baucom, D. H., & Snyder, D. K. (2000). The use of forgiveness in marital therapy. In M. E. McCullough, K. I. Pargament, & C. E. Thoresen (Eds.), *Forgiveness: Theory, research and practice* (pp. 203–227). New York: Guilford Press.

Harris, J. R. (2000). The outcome of parenting: What do we really know? *Journal of Personality, 68,* 625–637.

Haynes, P. B. (1994). Fifteen truth commissions—1974 to 1994: A comparative study. *Human Rights Quarterly, 16,* 597–655.

Hickson, G. B, Clayton, E. E., Entman, S. S., & Miller, C. S. (1994). Obstetricians' prior malpractice experience and patients' satisfaction with care. *Journal of the American Medical Association, 272,* 1583–1587.

Institute of Medicine. (1999). *To err is human.* Washington, DC: Author.

Kraman, S. S., & Hamm, G. (1999). Risk management: Honesty may be the best policy. *Annals of Internal Medicine, 131,* 963–967.

Lykken, D. T. (2000). The causes and costs of crime and a controversial cure. *Journal of Personality, 68,* 559–605.

Marty, M. E. (1998). The ethos of Christian forgiveness. In E. L. Worthington, Jr. (Ed.), *Dimensions of forgiveness: Psychological research and theological perspectives* (pp. 193–317). Philadelphia: Templeton Foundation Press.

McCullough, M. E., Hoyt, W. T., & Rachal, K. C. (2000). What we know (and need to know) about assessing forgiveness constructs. In M. E. McCullough, K. I. Pargament, & C. E. Thoresen (Eds.), *Forgiveness: Theory, research, and practice* (pp. 65–90). New York: Guilford Press.

McCullough, M. E., & Worthington, E. L., Jr. (1995). Promoting forgiveness: The comparison of two brief psychoeducational interventions with a waiting-list control. *Counseling and Values, 40,* 55–68.

McCullough, M. E., Worthington, E. L., Jr., & Rachal, K. C. (1997). Interpersonal forgiveness in close relationships. *Journal of Personality and Social Psychology, 75,* 321–326.

Minow, M. (2000). Forgiveness in the law. *Fordham Urban Law Journal, 27,* 1394–1419.

Ripley, J. S., & Worthington, E. L., Jr. (2002). Hope-focused and forgiveness group interventions to promote marital enrichment. *Journal of Counseling and Development, 80,* 452–463.

Roberts, R. C. (1995). Forgivingness. *American Philosophical Quarterly, 32,* 289–306.

Rosin, H. (1998, February 2). Cultural revolution at Texaco. *New Republic,* 18.

Rye, M. S., Pargament, K. I., Ali, M. A., Beck, G. L., Dorff, E. N., Hallisey, C., et al. (2000). Religious perspectives on forgiveness. In M. E. McCullough, K. I. Pargament, & C. E. Thoresen (Eds.), *Forgiveness: Theory, research, and practice* (pp. 17–40). New York: Guilford Press.

Salovey, P., Rothman, A. J., Detweiler, J. B., & Steward, W. T. (2000). Emotional states and physical health. *American Psychologist, 55*, 110–121.

Sampson, R. J. (2000). Crime, criminals and cures: Medical model revisited. *Journal of Personality, 68*, 607–613.

Sapolsky, R. M. (1999). Hormonal correlates of personality and social contexts: From nonhuman to human primates. In C. Panter-Brick & C. M. Worthman (Eds.), *Hormones, health, and behavior: A socio-ecological and lifespan perspective* (pp. 18–46). Cambridge, MA: Cambridge University Press.

Scarr, S. (2000). Toward voluntary parenthood. *Journal of Personality, 68*, 615–623.

Schma, W. (2000). Judging for the new millenium. *Court Review: The Journal of the American Judges Association, 37*, 4–7.

Shriver, D. W. (1997). *An ethic for enemies: Forgiveness in politics.* Oxford, UK: Oxford University Press.

Staub, E., (in press). Undestanding and responding to violence: Genocide, mass killing, and terrorism. In F. M. Moghaddam & A. J. Marsella (Eds.), *Understanding terrorism: Psychosocial roots, consequences, and interventions* (pp. 151–168). Washington, DC: American Psychological Association.

Stuart, B. (1996). Circle sentencing in Canada: A partnership of the community and the criminal justice system. *International Journal of Comparative and Applied Criminal Justice, 20*, 291–309.

Thoresen, C. E., Harris, A. H. S., & Luskin, F. (2000). Forgiveness and health: An unanswered question. In M. E. McCullough, K. I. Pargament, & C. E. Thoresen (Eds.), *Forgiveness: Theory, research, and practice* (pp. 254–280). New York: Guilford Press.

U.S. Department of Health and Human Services, Public Health Service, National Institutes of Health, National Heart, Lung, and Blood Institute. (1993, July). *Facts about coronary heart disease* (NIH Publication No. 93-2265). Washington, DC: National Institutes of Health.

Vincent, C., Young, M., & Phillips, A. (1994). Why do people sue doctors? A study of patients and relatives taking legal action. *Lancet, 343*, 1609–1613.

Wexler, D. B., & Winick, B. J. (Eds). (1996). *Law in a therapeutic key: Developments in therapeutic jurisprudence.* Durham, NC: Carolina Academic Press.

Witvliet, C. V. O., Ludwig, T. E., & Vander Laan, K. L. (2001). Granting forgiveness or harboring grudges: Implications for emotion, physiology, and health. *Psychological Science, 21*, 117–123.

Worthington, E. L., Jr. (2000). Is there a place for forgiveness in the justice system? *Fordham Urban Law Journal, 27*, 1401–1414.

Worthington, E. L., Jr. (2001). Unforgiveness, forgiveness, and reconciliation and their implications for societal interventions. In R. G. Helmick & R. L. Petersen (Eds.), *Forgiveness and reconciliation: Religion, public policy, and conflict transformation* (pp. 161–182). Philadelphia: Templeton Foundation Press.

Worthington, E. L., Jr., Berry, J. W., & Parrott, L., III. (2001). Unforgiveness, forgiveness, religion, and health. In T. Plante & A. Sherman (Eds.), *Faith and health: Psychological perspectives* (pp. 107–138). New York: Guilford Press.

Worthington, E. L., Jr., Berry, J. W., Shivy, V. A., & Brownstein, E. (in press). Forgiveness and positive psychology in business ethics and corporate social responsibility. In R. A. Giacalone, C. Dunn, & C. L. Jurkiewicz (Eds.), *Positive psychology in business ethics and corporate social reponsibility.* Greenwich, CT: Information Age.

Worthington, E. L., Jr., & Drinkard, D. T. (2000). Promoting reconciliation through psychoeducational and therapeutic interventions. *Journal of Marital and Family Therapy, 26,* 93–101.

Worthington, E. L., Jr., Kurusu, T. A., Collins, W., Berry, J. W., Ripley, J. S., & Baier, S. N. (2000). Forgiving usually takes time: A lesson learned by studying interventions to promote forgiveness. *Journal of Psychology and Theology, 28,* 3–20.

Worthington, E. L., Jr., Sandage, S. J., & Berry, J. W. (2000). Group interventions to promote forgiveness: What researchers and clinicians ought to know. In M. E. McCullough, K. I. Pargament, & C. E. Thoresen (Eds.), *Forgiveness: Theory, research, and practice* (pp. 228–254). New York: Guilford.

Worthington, E. L., Jr., & Scherer, M. (in press). Forgiveness as an emotion-focused coping strategy that can reduce health risks and promote health resilience: Theory, review, and hypotheses. *Psychology and Health.*

Worthington, E. L., Jr., & Wade, N. G. (1999). The social psychology of unforgiveness and forgiveness and implications for clinical practice. *Journal of Social and Clinical Psychology, 18,* 385–418.

Wu, A. W. (1999). Handling hospital errors: Is disclosure the best defense? *Annals of Internal Medicine, 131,* 970–972.

Yates, B. T. (1996). *Analyzing costs, procedures, processes, and outcomes in human services.* Thousand Oaks, CA: Sage.

Zehr, H. (1995). *Changing lenses: A new focus on crime and justice.* Scottsdale, PA: Herald Press.

About the Editors and Contributors

ABOUT THE EDITORS

Thomas P. Gullotta, MA, MSW, is CEO of the Child and Family Agency, New London, CT. He holds editorial appointments on the *Journal of Early Adolescence, Adolescence,* and the *Journal of Educational and Psychological Consultation.* He serves on the Board of the National Mental Health Association and is an Adjunct Faculty Member in the psychology department at Eastern Connecticut State University, Windham. Gullotta is the founding editor of the *Journal of Primary Prevention.* He is also the editor of three series of books: *Advances in Adolescent Development* (Sage), *Issues in Children's and Families' Lives* (Kluwer), *and Prevention and Practice* (Kluwer). He has published extensively on adolescents and primary prevention.

Robert L. Hampton, PhD, is President of York College of the City University of New York. He has served as Dean for Undergraduate Studies, Professor of family studies, and Professor of sociology at the University of Maryland, College Park. He also served as Research Associate at Children's Hospital in Boston and the Harvard Medical School. He is a Gimbel Mentoring Scholar. He has published extensively in the field of family violence, including five edited books: *Violence in the Black Family: Correlates and Consequences, Black Family Violence: Current Research and Theory, Family Violence: Prevention and Treatment,* and *Preventing Violence in America.*

ABOUT THE CONTRIBUTORS

Patricia Aleman, PhD, is a doctoral student in educational psychology at the University of Wisconsin–Madison. She received her BA in psychology and BS in applied learning and development from the University of Texas at Austin. Patricia is a Spencer Fellow participating in the doctoral training program for the School of Education at the University of Wisconsin–Madison.

Marva P. Benjamin, PhD, is a pioneer in the field of cultural competence; served as the director of the Cultural Competence Initiatives for the National Technical Assistance Center for Children's Mental Health, Center for Child Health and Mental Health Policy, Washington, DC; and was Assistant Professor, Department of Pediatrics, at the Georgetown University Medical Center, Washington, DC, from 1988 through 2001. While at Georgetown University, Benjamin also served as director of the Maternal and Child Health National Center for Cultural Competence. She has authored or coauthored numerous articles, book chapters, and monographs on cultural competence, and her special interest is in the area of improving the service delivery system for culturally diverse children, families, and communities. Prior to her faculty appointment at Georgetown University, she was executive director of the community mental health center in Clark County, Washington. She is currently a child and program specialist and trainer for the Children's Bureau, Administration for Children and Families, U.S. Department of Health and Human Services, Washington, DC.

Michael L. Benjamin, PhD, is the Executive Director of the National Council of Family Relations. He has focused his career on public policy development and community mental health delivery. He is an expert on ethnic minority issues.

Jack W. Berry received his PhD in psychology from the Wright Institute, Berkeley, CA. He serves as a Research Faculty member at Virginia Commonwealth University. He is Director of Research for the Marriage Assessment, Treatment, and Enrichment Center at Virginia Commonwealth University (VCU), Richmond. Prior to VCU, he was an Associate Institute Faculty member of the Wright Institute, where he taught graduate courses in research methods, statistics, and psychometrics. Berry has also been a Research Associate at the Haight Ashbury Free Medical Clinics, Detoxification and Aftercare Project in San Francisco and at Walden House Drug Treatment Facility, San Francisco. For more than seven years, he has been a statistician and research methodologist for the San Francisco Psychotherapy Research Group.

Fannie L. Brown, PhD, is a community activist. She is the Executive Director of the Coming Together Project, which is committed to fostering better racial harmony in the Akron/Sommit County, Ohio, area.

Christine Clark, EdD, is the Executive Director of the Office of Human Relations Programs, an equity compliance and diversity research and education arm of the Office of the President at the University of Maryland. She is also Affiliate Faculty in the departments of Education Policy and Leadership and Curriculum and Instruction, and in the Maryland Institute for Minority Achievement and Urban Education in the College of Education at Maryland. Previously, Clark was an Associate Professor and the Coordinator of the Urban Educational Leadership Doctoral Program at the University of Cincinnati. Clark received a BA in economics with a minor in geology from Franklin & Marshall College in Lancaster, PA. She also received an MEd with areas of specialization in cross-cultural counseling and multicultural curriculum development and an EdD with areas of specialization in multicultural/bilingual education, multicultural organizational/community development, and urban educational leadership, both from the University of Massachusetts at Amherst.

Lucia A. Magarian, MFA, is an advanced graduate student in marriage and family therapy at the University of Maryland, College Park. She also holds an MFA in creative writing from the American University in Washington, DC, and has had several plays produced exploring ethnicity, family, and contemporary life. As a first-generation American, she is particularly interested in issues surrounding ethnicity, genocide, and intergenerational cultural transmission.

Jennifer C. Messina is a senior at Villanova University in Pennslyvania majoring in human services. Interested in afterschool activities that promote the well-being of youth, she intends to work with young people after graduation prior to attending graduate school.

Jeffrey F. Milem, PhD, is an Associate Professor and Graduate Program Director for the higher education program in the Department of Education Policy and Leadership in the College of Education at the University of Maryland, College Park. Milem's research focuses on racial dynamics in higher education, the educational outcomes of diversity, the effect of college on students, and the condition and status of the professorate, including the ways faculty view and use diversity in their classrooms. As a widely recognized expert in racial dynamics in higher education, Milem has been commissioned to do research by the Harvard Civil Rights Project, the American Council on Education, and the American Educational Research Association's Panel on Racial Dynamics in Higher Education.

Matthew R. Mock, PhD, is the Director of Family, Youth, Children's and Multicultural Services for Berkeley Mental Health, Berkeley, CA. He is also Director and Associate Professor of cross-cultural counseling at John F. Kennedy University, Orinda, CA. As a third-generation Chinese American, he is committed to issues of social justice, equity, and community efforts.

Stephen M. Quintana, PhD, is an Associate Professor with a joint appointment in the Department of Counseling Psychology and Department of Educational Psychology at the University of Wisconsin–Madison. He is the Director of Training for the counseling psychology program and has received support for his research from the Ford Foundation and UNICEF.

Jessica M. Ramos, BA, psychology, is a Research Assistant at Child and Family Agency of Southeastern Connecticut. She has served as Research Assistant editing, undertaking library research, and supporting the work of the editors, Thomas Gullotta and Martin Bloom on the *Encyclopedia of Primary Prevention and Health Promotion.* She has also assisted in the editorial process in *Asperger Syndrome: A Handbook for Professionals and Families,* and is involved in child observations and research for the Bingham *Early Childhood Prosocial Behavior Curriculum.*

Marie P. Ting is a doctoral candidate in the Higher Education Policy and Leadership program at the University of Maryland, College Park. She received an undergraduate degree in psychology and a master's degree in higher education from the University of Michigan, Ann Arbor. Her dissertation focuses on senior administrators, decisionmaking, and the campus racial climate.

Paul D. Umbach, PhD, is a doctoral candidate in the higher education program at the University of Maryland, College Park. Umbach's research focuses on equity and diversity as they relate to college administrators, faculty, and students. He is conducting a national study of senior college administrators that explores the relationship among race, gender, and forms of capital and their effects on career aspirations.

Everett L. Worthington Jr., PhD, is a licensed Clinical Psychologist and the Chair of psychology at Virginia Commonwealth University, Richmond. He has published 16 books and more than 100 articles. He also edits *Marriage and Family: A Christian Journal.* He is an advocate of forgiveness and directs "A Campaign for Forgiveness Research" (www.forgiving.org). This 501c(3) corporation, officed in Richmond, VA, has a mission of promoting scientific research on forgiveness and disseminating research findings about forgiveness. Worthington serves as Executive Director. The campaign sponsored two conferences on forgiveness in Atlanta, GA, October 24–25, 2003, which drew more than 80 scientists and 28 clinicians to present. The conference was featured in *USA Today* and numerous other news major outlets.